Aerospace Facts and Figures

Compiled by:
Aerospace Research Center
Aerospace Industries Association of America, Inc.

Director, Aerospace Research Center
David H. Napier

Manager, Electronic Data
Terry Ruby

Designed by:
Satterfield Graphic Design

Published by:
Aerospace Industries Association of America, Inc.
1000 Wilson Boulevard #1700
Arlington, VA   22209-3901
703-358-1015
703-358-1115 Fax
AIA@AIA-aerospace.org

1

Acknowledgments

Air BP Lubricants

Air Transport Association of America

The Boyd Company

Council of Economic Advisers

Export-Import Bank of the United States

Futron Corporation

General Aviation Manufacturers Association

Helicopter Association International

International Civil Aviation Organization

National Aeronautics and Space Administration

National Science Foundation

Office of Management and Budget

Office of Personnel Management

U.S. Department of Commerce (Bureau of Economic Analysis; Bureau of the Census; International Trade Administration)

U.S. Department of Defense (Air Force; Army; Comptroller; Directorate for Information, Operations, and Reports; Missile Defense Agency; Navy)

U.S. Department of Labor (Bureau of Labor Statistics)

U.S. Department of Transportation (Federal Aviation Administration, Office of Airline Information)

CONTENTS

FOREWORD

The economic downturn that began in 2001 bore down on the aerospace industry with far greater effect in 2002. Airline losses continued at near record levels as passenger traffic remained depressed. Faced with the deepest crisis in commercial aviation history, airlines canceled flights, grounded aircraft, postponed deliveries, canceled orders, and postponed new orders to match supply with demand. Likewise, commercial aircraft manufacturers and their suppliers continued their adjustment to the immediate decline in demand that followed 2001's terrorist attacks. On one hand, our nation's response to the 9/11 attacks resulted in a drop in new orders, a decline in production, and a reduction in employment for civil aircraft and parts manufacturers. On the other, Defense Department spending—both for operations and maintenance and for modernization—increased substantially. Increased defense activity lessened the blow to the overall industry from declining civil sales and perhaps sets the stage for a period when both sectors are economically robust.

It has been more than one year since the Commission on the Future of the U.S. Aerospace Industry issued recommendations on ways to maintain U.S. leadership in the global aerospace marketplace. As one of the commissioners, I have been a strong advocate of implementation of those recommendations by Congress and the administration. One of the findings of the commission—that the aerospace workforce is in crisis—has become a key issue for our association. The aerospace workforce is aging and declining in numbers; and, when the civil recovery arrives, there will be a shortage of skilled workers, if we do not act now. AIA is asking the presidential candidates to support the creation of a White House coordinating council to establish an integrated national aerospace policy, to support funding for scholarships for college and graduate studies in aerospace fields, and to establish a national policy to prepare our workforce for the future. To fire interest in young people's minds for careers in aerospace, AIA also co-hosted a national rocket contest as part of the celebration of the 100th anniversary of powered flight. It was such a success—with 873 teams and over 9,000 students—that we have decided to make it an annual event.

The industry's products led to the success of our armed forces on the battlefields of Afghanistan and Iraq in 2002 and 2003. From satellites to aircraft to precision guided munitions, the U.S. owned the high ground. The terrible events of 9-11 have opened a new chapter in American history—the war on terror—they also united us in this fight. America's aerospace systems allow our nation to take the war on terror to foreign shores and, if needed, to fortify our homeland. It is the association's members that are providing the equipment and services for Homeland Security—whether it is bomb detection equipment at the nation's airports or system integration as the federal government runs background checks. It is that unity that makes our nation and our association strong.

As we celebrate the 100th anniversary of the Wright Brother's flight, we have many accomplishments to look back on and be proud of: a dynamic global air transportation system, radar, supersonic flight, jumbo jets, unmanned aircraft, satellite navigation, satellite communication, space telescopes, and, of course, man landing on the moon. Similarly, as we begin the second century of flight, we have much to look forward to and much to do.

John W. Douglass
President and Chief Executive Officer
Aerospace Industries Association

AEROSPACE SUMMARY

U.S. aerospace industry sales decreased slightly in 2002 from record current dollar levels. However, declining orders, profits, and R&D funding as well as airlines posting near record losses, low capital equipment investment, and record-low total employment and employment of R&D-performing scientists and engineers indicate serious challenges ahead for the U.S. aerospace industry.

Highlights of the year in aerospace include:

Sales

Total aerospace industry sales declined—falling less than one percent or $0.8 billion—to $153 billion. DoD sales increased 14%, or $6.9 billion, to $57 billion, while sales to NASA and other civil agencies jumped 13%, or $1.9 billion, to $16.4 billion. Accounting for the entirety of the overall decline, sales to other customers fell $9.5 billion, or 15%, to $54 billion.

Similarly, DoD-dominated product group sales (i.e., military aircraft, missiles, and space) grew in 2002. Substantial missile defense funding helped push up missile sector sales to $12.7 billion despite a modest decline in procurement. Both the space sector and the military aircraft sector saw sales increases of more than $2.6 billion.

Aircraft sales—both military and civil combined—fell by $6.3 billion last year. Despite the above-mentioned military growth, the civil aircraft sector's 17% sales decline pulled overall sales down to $80 billion. Civil sales fell $9.0 billion to $42 billion.

For 2002, aerospace industry output accounted for 1.5% of the Gross Domestic Product and 3.9% of manufacturing sales.

Earnings

The aerospace industry generated $6.5 billion in net income after taxes on

$160 billion of corporate sales last year. 2002's net, while higher than profits posted before 1996, represented a decline of 36% from 1999's record-setting level. Net profit as a percentage of sales rose to 4.1%—the second lowest level since 1995—down from 6.5% in 1999 and 4.7% in 2000. The corresponding profit margin for all manufacturing corporations in 2002 was 3.3%, up sharply from 2001's 0.8%. Similarly, the aerospace industry's net profit as a percentage of assets and shareholders' equity rose marginally to 3.7% and 11.7%. For comparison, prior year aerospace returns were 3.6% and 11.6%; and the averages for all manufacturing corporations in 2002 were 2.9% and 7.7%, respectively.

Orders and Backlog

New orders fell $7.6 billion, or 6.3%, to $115 billion in 2002. While military orders rose nicely from $64 billion to $69 billion, civil orders dropped—down 21%, or $13 billion, to $46 billion. Orders for aircraft, engines, and parts fell. Combined aircraft sector orders fell $4.6 billion, or 7.4%, to $58 billion with military orders rising $6.9 billion, or 32%, to $29 billion and civil orders falling $12 billion, or 28%, to $29 billion.

The industry's year-end backlog, on the other hand, grew $2.6 billion to $223 billion. Growth in the military backlog continued for its third straight year after ending a three-year slide; and the civil backlog dropped $12 billion. After reaching record levels in 2000, unfilled orders for missiles, space, and rocket propulsion rebounded to a record $40 billion in 2002. Whereas, the aircraft sector declined for a second year from an eight-year-high backlog of $156 billion for year-end 2000 to $133 billion. Lastly, unfilled orders for "Other Aerospace" rose slightly to a strong $31 billion.

Civil Aircraft

The civil aircraft manufacturing industry produced and delivered 659 fewer aircraft than in 2001—2,900 in all. The majority of the decline came from general aviation aircraft, whose shipments dropped by 415 to 2,203, and from civil helicopters, whose production dropped from 415 to 318. Until 2001, general aviation aircraft production and billings had been steadily increasing since 1994 when Congress enacted the General Aviation Revitalization Act.

Transport aircraft production also fell in 2002 by 147 from 2001's 526. U.S. customers accounted for the entirety of this decline as exports grew to 262 while domestic shipment fell 57% to 117. According to Air BP's annual "Turbine-Engined Fleets of the World's Airlines," the world's airline fleet grew to 26,112 aircraft. International Civil Aviation Organization statistics show that the world's airlines carried fewer passengers, but flew slightly more passenger-miles in 2002. Load factors returned to historic high levels as airlines quickly adjusted to lower traffic by grounding aircraft.

Military Aircraft Production

Military aircraft production, as measured by acceptances, increased to its highest level in three years. Manufacturers delivered 355 aircraft of which 37% were destined to customers other than the U.S. government. The number of military aircraft exported declined for the fifth straight year—down 19 to 130—and those exported through the Foreign Military Sales program rebounded somewhat from their lowest level on record (29). Encouragingly, aircraft acceptances by the services for their own use increased for the third straight year.

U.S. military agencies accepted, for their own use, 225 aircraft in 2002—29 more than in 2001. The total flyaway cost increased—following three straight years of decline—to $9.5 billion.

Three programs dominated new aircraft procurement in FY 2002: the Air Force's C-17 Globemaster III cargo aircraft remained the largest with 15 planes worth $3.7 billion; followed by the Navy's 48 F/A-18E/F Super Hornet fighters costing $3.1 billion; and the Air Force's 13 F-22 Raptor fighters costing $3.0 billion. Eleven V-22 Osprey tiltrotor aircraft for $840 million logged a distant fourth. Scheduled for significant procurement funding increases in FY 2003 are the Air Force's C-17, F-22, and C-130J variants and the Navy's V-22.

Foreign Trade

Aerospace exports decreased by $2 billion to $57 billion. Civil exports accounted for the entirety of the export decline since military exports increased. In particular, aircraft and engine parts and complete engine exports dropped by a combined $3 billion.

The aerospace industry continued to enjoy a trade surplus even as the manufacturing sector, as a whole, saw its trade deficit balloon to a record $470 billion. The aerospace trade surplus reversed a three year slide—rising $3.5 billion to $30 billion. The all-important factor was a sharp $5.2 billion decline in imports. Imports of civil transport aircraft dropped by $2 billion to $4.6 billion. Imports of parts and complete engines also tumbled in 2002.

Space Programs

According to data compiled by the Bureau of the Census, sales of space vehicle systems fell $2 billion in 2002 to $7.1 billion. Military space sales fell 26% to $3.3 billion, while non-military sales fell 17% to $3.8 billion.

NASA, on the other hand, estimated total federal spending for space activities increased in FY 2002 to $29 billion. DoD's space-related outlays, at $14.9 billion, topped NASA's $13.4 billion. Space spending at all other agencies increased $110 million to a total of $1.1 billion.

Within the NASA budget, Science, Aeronautics, and Technology received $8.0 billion. Station and Shuttle budget items together accounted for 34% of NASA's $14.9 billion in total budget authority for 2002. NASA's FY 2003 budget should total $15.0 billion with the Shuttle receiving $3.8 billion; Space Science, $3.5 billion; and the ISS, $1.9 billion.

Missile Programs

Total DoD outlays for missile procurement fell $211 million to $5.2 billion in FY 2002. Major programs include: Air Force's JDAM with $1.0 billion in USAF/USN funding; BMDO's Patriot, $754 million; Navy's Trident II, $535 million; and Army's Javelin, $409 million.

Ballistic Missile Defense continues to dominate missile RDT&E. Funding totaled $6.9 billion in FY 2002 and is scheduled to increase to $7.7 billion in 2004.

Also, net new orders jumped 75% to $9.1 billion in 2002. The year-end 2002 backlog of unfilled orders stood at $11 billion.

Research and Development

R&D spending by the federal government increased $7.8 billion—the second year of real growth—after languishing for six years at the same real spending level. The DoD, with its $45 billion in outlays, continued to be the government's largest single spender on R&D, accounting for half of all federal funding. NASA's R&D totaled $6.8 billion; and the Department of Energy invested a slightly higher $6.8 billion. Other agencies also saw healthy growth. Organizations such as the National Science Foundation, the National Institutes of Health, and the Transportation and Agriculture Departments collectively saw their R&D outlays rise 14% to $29 billion. Federally-funded R&D is scheduled to increase $14 billion to $102 billion in FY 2003.

In addition to the previously-mentioned Ballistic Missile Defense, other major RDT&E programs in FY 2002 include: the Joint Strike Fighter received $1.4 billion; F-22 Raptor, $877 million; RAH-66 Comanche, $754 million; V-22 Osprey, $653 million; and SBIRS-High, $525 million.

Employment

Industry employment fell to its lowest level in at least 43 years to stand at 714,000. On an annual average basis, total employment declined by 76,000 in 2002. Production workers lost work at a higher rate than other categories of employees. Most of the jobs losses were in the aircraft, engines, and parts manufacturing sector.

Aerospace constituted 4.7% of all manufacturing employment and 7.5% of durable goods manufacturing employment. The aerospace share of manufacturing and durable goods employment has fallen from 7.4% and 12.1% in 1990, respectively.

STANDARD INDUSTRIAL CLASSIFICATIONS
APPLICABLE TO THE AEROSPACE INDUSTRY

3721 AIRCRAFT
37211 Military aircraft
37215 Civilian aircraft
37217 Modification, conversion, and overhaul of previously accepted aircraft
37218 Aeronautical services on complete aircraft, nec

3724 AIRCRAFT ENGINES AND ENGINE PARTS
37241 Aircraft engines for military aircraft
37242 Aircraft engines for civilian aircraft
37243 Aeronautical services on aircraft engines
37244 Aircraft engine parts and accessories

3728 AIRCRAFT PARTS AND AUXILIARY EQUIPMENT, NEC
37281 Aircraft parts and auxiliary equipment, nec
37282 Aircraft propellers and helicopter rotors
37283 Research and development on aircraft parts

3761 GUIDED MISSILES AND SPACE VEHICLES
37611 Complete guided missiles (excluding propulsion systems)
37612 Complete space vehicles (excluding propulsion systems)
37613 Research and development on complete guided missiles
37614 Research and development on complete space vehicles
37615 All other services on complete guided missiles and space vehicles

3663 RADIO AND TELEVISION COMMUNICATIONS EQUIPMENT
36631 Communication systems and equipment, except broadcast

3764 SPACE PROPULSION UNITS AND PARTS
37645 Complete missile or space vehicle engines and/or propulsion units
37646 Research and development on complete missile or space vehicle engines and/or propulsion units
37647 Services on complete guided missile or space vehicle engines and/or propulsion units, nec
37648 Missile and space vehicle engine and/or propulsion unit parts and accessories

3769 SPACE VEHICLE EQUIPMENT, NEC
37692 Missile and space vehicle components, parts and subassemblies, nec
37694 Research and development on missile and space vehicle parts and components, nec

3669 COMMUNICATIONS EQUIPMENT, NEC
36691 Alarm systems
36692 Traffic control equipment
36693 Intercommunication equipment

3812 SEARCH, DETECTION, NAVIGATION, GUIDANCE, AERONAUTICAL AND NAUTICAL SYSTEMS, INSTRUMENTS, AND EQUIPMENT
38121 Aeronautical, nautical, and navigational instruments, not sending or receiving radio signals
38122 Search, detection, navigation, and guidance systems and equipment

3829 MEASURING AND CONTROLLING DEVICES, NEC
38291 Aircraft engine instruments except flight

Source: Office of Management and Budget, "Standard Industrial Classification Manual, 1987."
NOTE: The Standard Industrial Classification (SIC) is a system developed by the U.S. Government to define the industrial composition of the economy, facilitating comparability of statistics. It is revised periodically to reflect the changing industrial composition of the economy.
NEC: Not elsewhere classified.

NORTH AMERICAN INDUSTRY CLASSIFICATION SYSTEM CODES APPLICABLE TO THE AEROSPACE INDUSTRY

33641   **Aerospace product & parts mfg**

336411   **Aircraft mfg**
3364111   Military aircraft
3364113   Civilian aircraft
3364115   Modification, conversion, and overhaul of previously accepted aircraft
3364117   Other aeronautical services on complete aircraft, nec
336411W   Aircraft manufacturing, nsk

336412   **Aircraft engine & engine parts mfg**
3364121   Military aircraft engines
3364123   Civilian aircraft engines
3364125   Aeronautical services on aircraft engines
3364127   Aircraft engine parts and accessories
336412W   Aircraft engines and engine parts manufacturing, nsk

336413   **Aircraft parts and auxiliary equipment mfg, nec**
3364131   Aircraft propellers and helicopter rotors
3364133   Research and development on aircraft parts (except engines)
3364135   Aircraft parts and auxiliary equipment, excluding hydraulic and pneumatic subassemblies and engines
336413W   Aircraft parts and auxiliary equipment, nec, nsk

336414   **Guided missile & space vehicle mfg**
3364141   Complete guided missiles
3364143   Research and development on complete guided missiles
3364145   Other services on complete guided missiles
3364147   Complete space vehicles (excluding propulsion systems)
3364149   Research and development on complete space vehicles
336414A   All other services on complete space vehicles
336414W   Guided missile and space vehicle manufacturing, nsk

336415   **Guided missile & space vehicle propulsion unit & parts mfg**
3364151   Complete missile or space vehicle engines and/or propulsion units
3364153   Research and development on complete missile or space vehicle engines and/or propulsion units
3364155   Other services on complete missile or space vehicle engines and/or propulsion units

3364157   Missile and space vehicle engine and/or propulsion parts and accessories
336415W   Space propulsion units and parts, nsk

336419   **Other guided missile & space vehicle parts & auxiliary equip mfg**

3327221   **Aircraft (including aerospace) fasteners other than plastics (meet specifications for flying vehicles)**

3345191   **Aircraft engine instruments mfg, except flight**

332912   **Fluid power valve and hose fitting mfg**
3329121   Aerospace type hydraulic fluid power valves
3329123   Aerospace type pneumatic fluid power valves
332912F   Aerospace type hydraulic and pneumatic fluid power hose or tube end fittings and assemblies

33399   **All other general purpose machinery mfg**
3339957   Aerospace type fluid power cylinders and actuators, hydraulic and pneumatic
3339967   Aerospace type fluid power pumps and motors
3339996   Filters for hydraulic and pneumatic fluid power systems, aerospace

3342201   **Communication systems and equipment, except broadcast, but including microwave equipment, and space satellites**

334290   **Alarm systems, traffic control equipment, and intercommunication and paging systems mfg**

334511   **Search, detection, navigation, guidance, aeronautical, and nautical systems and instruments mfg**
3345111   Aeronautical, nautical, and navigational instruments, not sending or receiving radio signals, except engine instruments
3345113   Search, detection, navigation, and guidance systems and equipment
334511W   Search, detection, navigation, guidance, aeronautical, and nautical systems and instruments, nsk

AEROSPACE INDUSTRY SALES BY PRODUCT GROUP
Calendar Years 1988-2002
(Millions of Dollars)

Year	TOTAL	Aircraft			Missiles	Space	Related Products & Services
		TOTAL	Civil	Military			
CURRENT DOLLARS							
1988	$114,562	$60,886	$19,019	$41,867	$10,270	$24,312	$19,094
1989	120,534	61,550	21,903	39,646	13,622	25,274	20,089
1990	134,375	71,353	31,262	40,091	14,180	26,446	22,396
1991	139,248	75,918	37,443	38,475	10,970	29,152	23,208
1992	138,591	73,905	39,897	34,008	11,757	29,831	23,099
1993	123,183	65,829	33,116	32,713	8,451	28,372	20,531
1994	110,558	57,648	25,596	32,052	7,563	26,921	18,426
1995	107,782	55,048	23,965	31,082	7,386	27,385	17,964
1996	116,812	60,296	26,869	33,427	8,008	29,040	19,469
1997	131,582	70,804	37,428	33,376	8,037	30,811	21,930
1998	147,991	83,951	49,676	34,275	7,730	31,646	24,665
1999	153,707	88,731	52,931	35,800	8,825	30,533	25,618
2000	144,741	81,612	47,580	34,032	9,298	29,708	24,123
2001[r]	154,188	86,448	51,256	35,193	10,391	31,651	25,698
2002	153,366	80,175	42,291	37,885	12,669	34,961	25,561
CONSTANT DOLLARS[a]							
1988	$112,869	$59,986	$18,738	$41,248	$10,118	$23,953	$18,812
1989	114,250	58,341	20,761	37,579	12,912	23,956	19,042
1990	123,734	65,703	28,786	36,916	13,057	24,352	20,622
1991	124,998	68,149	33,611	34,538	9,847	26,169	20,833
1992	118,555	63,221	34,129	29,092	10,057	25,518	19,760
1993	102,482	54,766	27,551	27,215	7,031	23,604	17,081
1994	90,104	46,983	20,861	26,122	6,164	21,941	15,017
1995	86,572	44,215	19,249	24,965	5,933	21,996	14,429
1996	92,196	47,590	21,207	26,383	6,320	22,920	15,366
1997	102,959	55,402	29,286	26,116	6,289	24,109	17,160
1998	115,168	65,332	38,658	26,673	6,016	24,627	19,195
1999	118,784	68,571	40,905	27,666	6,820	23,596	19,798
2000	108,583	61,224	35,694	25,530	6,975	22,287	18,097
2001[r]	112,628	63,147	37,440	25,707	7,590	23,120	18,771
2002	110,654	57,846	30,513	27,334	9,141	25,224	18,442

Source: Aerospace Industries Association.

NOTE: See Glossary for explanation of "Aerospace Industry", "Aerospace Sales", "Other Customers", and "Related Products and Services".

a   Based on AIA's aerospace composite deflator 1987=100.

AEROSPACE INDUSTRY SALES BY CUSTOMER
Calendar Years 1988-2002
(Millions of Dollars)

Year	TOTAL	Aerospace Products and Services				Related Products and Services
		TOTAL	U.S. Government		Other Customers	
			Dept. of Defense	NASA and Other Agencies		
CURRENT DOLLARS						
1988	$114,562	$ 95,468	$61,327	$ 7,899	$26,242	$19,094
1989	120,534	100,445	61,199	9,601	29,645	20,089
1990	134,375	111,979	60,502	11,097	40,379	22,396
1991	139,248	116,040	55,922	11,739	48,379	23,208
1992	138,591	115,493	52,202	12,408	50,882	23,099
1993	123,183	102,653	47,017	12,255	43,380	20,531
1994	110,558	92,132	43,795	11,932	36,405	18,426
1995	107,782	89,818	42,401	11,413	36,004	17,964
1996	116,812	97,344	42,535	12,391	42,418	19,469
1997	131,582	109,651	43,702	12,753	53,196	21,930
1998	147,991	123,326	42,937	13,343	67,047	24,665
1999	153,707	128,089	45,703	13,400	68,986	25,618
2000	144,741	120,617	47,505	13,382	59,730	24,123
2001[r]	154,188	128,490	50,096	14,477	63,917	25,698
2002	153,366	127,805	56,975	16,375	54,454	25,561
CONSTANT DOLLARS[a]						
1988	$112,869	$ 94,057	$60,421	$ 7,782	$25,854	$18,812
1989	114,250	95,209	58,009	9,100	28,100	19,042
1990	123,734	103,111	55,711	10,218	37,181	20,622
1991	124,998	104,165	50,199	10,538	43,428	20,833
1992	118,555	98,796	44,655	10,614	43,526	19,760
1993	102,482	85,402	39,116	10,196	36,090	17,081
1994	90,104	75,087	35,693	9,725	29,670	15,017
1995	86,572	72,143	34,057	9,167	28,919	14,429
1996	92,196	76,830	33,571	9,780	33,479	15,366
1997	102,959	85,799	34,196	9,979	41,624	17,160
1998	115,168	95,974	33,414	10,384	52,177	19,195
1999	118,784	98,987	35,319	10,355	53,312	19,798
2000	108,583	90,485	35,638	10,039	44,809	18,097
2001[r]	112,628	93,857	36,593	10,575	46,689	18,771
2002	110,654	92,211	41,108	11,815	39,289	18,442

Source: Aerospace Industries Association.
NOTE: See Glossary for explanation of "Aerospace Industry", "Aerospace Sales", "Other Customers", and "Related Products and Services".
a   Based on AIA's aerospace composite deflator 1987=100.

SALES OF MAJOR AEROSPACE COMPANIES
AS REPORTED BY THE BUREAU OF THE CENSUS
Calendar Years 1988-2002
(Millions of Dollars)

Year	GRAND TOTAL	TOTAL		Aircraft, Engines, & Parts		Missiles, Space, & Rocket Propulsion	Other Aerospace		Non-Aerospace
		Military	Non-Mil.	Military	Non-Mil.		Military	Non-Mil.	
CURRENT DOLLARS									
1988	$113,548	$69,448	$44,100	$25,068	$25,674	$21,514	$16,382	$2,946	$21,964
1989	122,148	71,647	50,501	24,287	29,538	22,643	16,908	3,605	25,167
1990	136,646	73,616	63,030	27,667	38,622	22,040	15,773	4,342	28,202
1991	123,862	67,089	56,773	25,385	43,155	23,311	13,472	4,281	14,258
1992	118,736	61,410	57,326	23,509	44,160	21,349	12,153	3,377	14,188
1993	109,926	56,102	53,824	20,099	40,987	18,134	11,936	3,592	15,178
1994	104,296	58,012	46,284	23,652	30,901	18,406	11,981	4,417	14,939
1995	102,797	52,476	50,321	22,944	32,085	18,366	11,921	4,462	13,019
1996	103,115	53,153	49,962	24,804	32,722	18,506	12,171	4,624	10,287
1997	114,946	50,648	64,298	23,944	42,614	21,354	12,320	3,922	10,792
1998	119,258	45,110	74,148	23,795	52,708	16,109	7,818	5,035	13,796
1999	124,181	49,690	74,491	26,043	56,406	15,661	9,062	4,472	12,535
2000	109,311	43,256	66,055	23,196	46,477	15,603	6,035	4,785	13,215
2001 [r]	117,088	47,232	69,856	22,133	52,504	15,512	8,187	5,732	13,020
2002	111,317	54,403	56,914	25,498	41,193	15,011	10,152	5,242	14,221
CONSTANT DOLLARS[a]									
1988	$111,870	$68,422	$43,448	$24,698	$25,295	$21,196	$16,140	$2,902	$21,639
1989	115,780	67,912	47,868	23,021	27,998	21,463	16,027	3,417	23,855
1990	125,825	67,786	58,039	25,476	35,564	20,295	14,524	3,998	25,969
1991	111,187	60,224	50,963	22,787	38,739	20,925	12,093	3,843	12,799
1992	101,571	52,532	49,038	20,110	37,776	18,263	10,396	2,889	12,137
1993	91,453	46,674	44,779	16,721	34,099	15,087	9,930	2,988	12,627
1994	85,001	47,280	37,721	19,276	25,184	15,001	9,764	3,600	12,175
1995	82,568	42,149	40,418	18,429	25,771	14,752	9,575	3,584	10,457
1996	81,385	41,952	39,433	19,577	25,826	14,606	9,606	3,650	8,119
1997	89,942	39,631	50,311	18,736	33,344	16,709	9,640	3,069	8,444
1998	92,808	35,105	57,703	18,518	41,018	12,536	6,084	3,918	10,736
1999	95,967	38,400	57,566	20,126	43,590	12,103	7,003	3,456	9,687
2000	82,004	32,450	49,554	17,401	34,866	11,705	4,527	3,590	9,914
2001 [r]	85,528	34,501	51,027	16,167	38,352	11,331	5,980	4,187	9,511
2002	80,315	39,252	41,063	18,397	29,721	10,830	7,325	3,782	10,260

Source: Bureau of the Census, "Aerospace Industry (Orders, Sales, and Backlog)" (Annually).
a Based on AIA's aerospace composite price deflator, 1987=100.

ORDERS AND BACKLOG OF MAJOR AEROSPACE COMPANIES
AS REPORTED BY THE BUREAU OF THE CENSUS
Calendar Years 1988-2002
(Millions of Dollars)

Year	GRAND TOTAL	TOTAL		Aircraft, En-gines, & Parts		Missiles, Space, & Rocket Propulsion	Other Aerospace		Non-Aero-space
		Mili-tary	Non-Mil.	Mili-tary	Non-Mil.		Mili-tary	Non-Mil.	

NET NEW ORDERS

Year	GRAND TOTAL	Military	Non-Mil.	Military	Non-Mil.	Missiles	Military	Non-Mil.	Non-Aerospace
1988	$147,128	$ 69,209	$ 77,919	$24,242	$ 57,906	$20,240	$18,423	$3,044	$23,273
1989	173,635	79,992	93,643	28,818	67,773	26,820	17,814	3,945	28,465
1990	145,965	56,405	89,560	17,735	64,651	20,207	12,945	3,556	26,871
1991	122,485	63,017	59,468	26,675	40,815	24,955	11,329	4,360	14,351
1992	100,306	57,383	42,923	19,631	30,110	22,849	11,201	3,256	13,259
1993	79,770	49,541	30,229	19,518	16,090	14,919	11,121	4,629	13,493
1994	88,706	53,268	35,438	23,352	20,166	13,705	12,924	5,395	13,164
1995	109,109	49,350	59,759	19,854	36,467	19,181	13,716	5,261	14,630
1996	126,267	62,127	64,140	25,343	45,281	27,067	12,136	5,070	11,370
1997	118,993	47,802	71,192	21,424	49,676	21,326	12,348	4,125	10,096
1998	109,993	38,678	71,314	16,870	47,613	19,699	7,628	4,468	13,715
1999	115,257	49,696	65,561	25,009	48,018	18,824	10,261	4,152	8,992
2000	140,086	54,525	85,165	31,396	65,459	18,368	7,046	3,900	13,917
2001ʳ	122,206	63,619	58,587	21,762	40,731	12,727	25,659	5,876	15,451
2002	114,567	68,547	46,020	28,653	29,210	20,260	10,610	5,432	20,402

BACKLOG AS OF DECEMBER 31

Year	GRAND TOTAL	Military	Non-Mil.	Military	Non-Mil.	Missiles	Military	Non-Mil.	Non-Aerospace
1988	$191,518	$ 99,117	$ 92,401	$35,515	$ 75,765	$29,078	$20,584	$4,734	$25,842
1989	252,401	114,070	138,331	44,026	115,124	33,771	24,186	7,652	27,642
1990	250,079	88,471	161,608	33,788	139,152	31,648	18,501	4,999	21,991
1991	245,241	89,517	155,724	39,149	134,527	32,657	17,213	4,907	16,788
1992	236,076	92,139	143,937	44,255	124,322	32,933	14,886	4,859	14,821
1993	211,814	91,751	120,063	46,177	96,228	29,511	16,668	7,958	15,272
1994	192,561	84,445	108,116	44,624	85,305	24,746	15,599	8,043	14,244
1995	202,638	82,309	120,329	44,642	92,239	27,113	17,534	8,214	12,906
1996	229,871	89,500	140,371	47,635	106,341	35,440	16,176	9,339	14,940
1997	218,951	78,870	140,082	43,615	111,931	34,585	12,125	4,754	11,942
1998	200,288	69,962	130,326	37,530	106,166	31,174	9,665	3,488	12,264
1999	188,409	68,379	120,029	36,565	96,596	33,880	9,904	3,051	8,413
2000	214,966	73,741	141,225	41,250	115,241	36,283	10,028	4,081	8,083
2001ʳ	220,148	90,968	129,180	39,623	102,880	34,449	27,625	3,699	11,872
2002	222,773	105,339	117,434	42,791	90,300	39,576	28,065	3,373	18,668

Source: Bureau of the Census, "Aerospace Industry (Orders, Sales, and Backlog)" (Annually).

AEROSPACE SALES AND THE NATIONAL ECONOMY
Calendar Years 1988-2002
(Billions of Dollars)

Year	Gross Domestic Product	Industry Sales			Aerospace Sales as Percent of		
		Manufac-turing[r]	Durable Goods[r]	Aero-space	GDP	Manufac-turing[r]	Durable Goods[r]

CURRENT DOLLARS

Year	GDP	Mfg	Durable	Aero	GDP%	Mfg%	Dur%
1988	$ 5,108.3	$2,694.0	$1,420.5	$114.6	2.2%	4.3%	8.1%
1989	5,489.1	2,837.8	1,475.9	120.5	2.2	4.2	8.2
1990	5,803.2	2,909.0	1,483.1	134.4	2.3	4.6	9.1
1991	5,986.2	2,878.8	1,453.2	139.2	2.3	4.8	9.6
1992	6,318.9	2,904.0	1,518.9	138.6	2.2	4.8	9.1
1993	6,642.3	3,020.5	1,604.5	123.2	1.9	4.1	7.7
1994	7,054.3	3,238.1	1,764.1	110.6	1.6	3.4	6.3
1995	7,400.5	3,479.7	1,902.8	107.8	1.5	3.1	5.7
1996	7,813.2	3,597.2	1,978.6	116.8	1.5	3.2	5.9
1997	8,318.4	3,834.7	2,147.4	131.6	1.6	3.4	6.1
1998	8,781.5	3,899.8	2,231.6	148.0	1.7	3.8	6.6
1999	9,274.3	4,031.9	2,326.7	153.7	1.7	3.8	6.6
2000	9,824.6	4,208.6	2,373.7	144.7	1.5	3.4	6.1
2001[r]	10,082.2	3,970.5	2,174.4	154.2	1.5	3.9	7.1
2002	10,446.2	3,891.8	2,131.4	153.4	1.5	3.9	7.2

CONSTANT DOLLARS[a]

Real Annual Growth[b]

Year	GDP	Mfg	Durable	Aero	GDP	Mfg.[r]	Durs.[r]	Aero.
1988	$ 6,369.5	$3,359.1	$1,771.1	$112.9	4.2%	5.4%	6.0%	2.6%
1989	6,589.6	3,406.7	1,771.8	114.3	3.5	1.4	0.0	1.2
1990	6,708.9	3,363.0	1,714.5	123.7	1.8	(1.3)	(3.2)	8.3
1991	6,673.6	3,209.3	1,620.1	125.0	(0.5)	(4.6)	(5.5)	1.0
1992	6,883.3	3,163.4	1,654.6	118.6	3.1	(1.4)	2.1	(5.2)
1993	7,058.8	3,209.9	1,705.1	102.5	2.5	1.5	3.1	(13.6)
1994	7,348.2	3,373.0	1,837.6	90.1	4.1	5.1	7.8	(12.1)
1995	7,543.8	3,547.1	1,939.7	86.6	2.7	5.2	5.6	(3.9)
1996	7,813.2	3,597.2	1,978.6	92.2	3.6	1.4	2.0	6.5
1997	8,163.3	3,763.2	2,107.4	103.0	4.5	4.6	6.5	11.7
1998	8,509.2	3,778.9	2,162.4	115.2	4.2	0.4	2.6	11.9
1999	8,858.0	3,850.9	2,222.3	118.8	4.1	1.9	2.8	3.1
2000	9,181.9	3,933.3	2,218.4	108.6	3.7	2.1	(0.2)	(8.6)
2001[r]	9,215.9	3,629.3	1,987.6	112.6	0.4	(7.7)	(10.4)	3.7
2002	9,352.0	3,484.2	1,908.1	110.7	1.5	(4.0)	(4.0)	(1.8)

Source: Council of Economic Advisers, "Economic Indicators" (Monthly); Bureau of Census; and Aerospace Industries Association.
  a Aerospace industry constant dollar sales based on AIA's aerospace composite price deflator, 1987=100. Others based on GDP deflator, 1996=100.
  b Parentheses indicate negative real annual growth.

GROSS DOMESTIC PRODUCT, FEDERAL BUDGET, AND DEFENSE BUDGET
Fiscal Years 1971-2004
(Billions of Dollars)

| Year | Fiscal Year GDP | Federal Budget Outlays | | Defense Outlays as Percent of | |
		Net Total[a]	National Defense[b]	GDP	Federal Budget
1971	$ 1,081.4	$ 210.2	$ 78.9	7.3%	37.5%
1972	1,181.5	230.7	79.2	6.7	34.3
1973	1,308.1	245.7	76.7	5.9	31.2
1974	1,442.1	269.4	79.3	5.5	29.5
1975	1,559.8	332.3	86.5	5.5	26.0
1976	1,736.7	371.8	89.6	5.2	24.1
Tr.Qtr.	454.8	96.0	22.3	4.9	23.2
1977	1,971.3	409.2	97.2	4.9	23.8
1978	2,218.6	458.7	104.5	4.7	22.8
1979	2,503.8	504.0	116.3	4.6	23.1
1980	2,732.1	590.9	134.0	4.9	22.7
1981	3,061.6	678.2	157.5	5.1	23.2
1982	3,228.6	745.8	185.3	5.7	24.8
1983	3,440.5	808.4	209.9	6.1	26.0
1984	3,839.4	851.9	227.4	5.9	26.7
1985	4,136.6	946.4	252.7 [b]	6.1	26.7
1986	4,401.4	990.5	273.4	6.2	27.6
1987	4,647.0	1,004.1	282.0	6.1	28.1
1988	5,014.7	1,064.5	290.4	5.8	27.3
1989	5,405.5	1,143.7	303.6	5.6	26.5
1990	5,735.6	1,253.2	299.3	5.2	23.9
1991	5,930.4	1,324.4	273.3 [c]	4.6	20.6
1992	6,218.6	1,381.7	298.4 [c]	4.8	21.6
1993	6,558.4	1,409.5	291.1 [c]	4.4	20.7
1994	6,944.6	1,461.9	281.6	4.1	19.3
1995	7,324.0	1,515.8	272.1	3.7	17.9
1996	7,694.6	1,560.5 [r]	265.8	3.5	17.0
1997	8,185.2	1,601.3	270.5	3.3	16.9
1998	8,663.9	1,652.6	268.5	3.1	16.2
1999	9,137.7 [r]	1,701.9	274.9	3.0	16.2
2000	9,718.8 [r]	1,788.8	294.5	3.0	16.5
2001 [r]	10,021.5	1,863.9	305.5	3.0	16.4
2002	10,336.6	2,011.0	348.6	3.4	17.3
2003 [E]	10,756.8	2,140.4	376.3	3.5	17.6
2004 [E]	11,303.1	2,229.4	390.4	3.5	17.5

Source: Office of Management and Budget, "The Budget of the United States Government" (Annually).

a   "Net Total" is government-wide total less intragovenmental transactions.

b   "National Defense" includes the military budget of DoD and other defense-related activities. Beginning in 1985, the Federal Budget reflects establishment of a military retirement trust fund. Data for prior years adjusted for comparable treatment of the military retired pay.

c   1991-1993 reflects transfers from the Defense Cooperation Account funded by foreign government and private cash contributions reducing total U.S.-funded military outlays.

FEDERAL OUTLAYS FOR DEFENSE, NASA, AND AEROSPACE
PRODUCTS AND SERVICES
Fiscal Years 1976-2004
(Millions of Dollars)

Year	Total National Defense	Total NASA	Federal Outlays for Aerospace Products and Services			Aero-space as Percent of Total National Defense and NASA
			TOTAL	DoD[a]	NASA	
1976	$ 89,619	$ 3,669	$12,364	$ 8,816	$ 3,548	13.3%
Tr.Qtr.	22,269	951	2,855	1,959	926	12.3
1977	97,241	3,945	13,229	9,389	3,840	13.1
1978	104,495	3,983	13,926	10,067	3,859	12.8
1979	116,342	4,197	16,686	12,622	4,064	13.8
1980	133,995	4,852	20,269	15,558	4,711	14.6
1981	157,513	5,421	24,276	19,002	5,274	14.9
1982	185,309	6,035	29,501	23,575	5,926	15.4
1983	209,903	6,664	35,364	28,808	6,556	16.3
1984	227,413	7,048	39,663	32,723	6,940	16.9
1985	252,748	7,318	44,483	37,335	7,148	17.1
1986	273,375	7,404	49,773	42,558	7,215	17.7
1987	281,999	7,591	51,871	44,429	7,442	17.9
1988	290,361	9,092	48,848	39,922	8,926	16.3
1989	303,559	11,036	52,933	42,072	10,861	16.8
1990	299,331	12,429	53,194	40,992	12,202	17.1
1991[b]	273,292	13,878	53,630	40,089	13,541	18.7
1992[b]	298,350	13,961	50,569	37,085	13,484	16.2
1993[b]	291,086	14,305	45,496	31,763	13,733	14.9
1994	281,642	13,695	41,082	27,774	13,308	13.9
1995	272,066	13,378	36,696	23,638	13,058	12.9
1996	265,753	13,881	32,947	20,530	12,417	11.8
1997	270,505	14,360	32,808	19,888	12,920	11.5
1998	268,456	14,206	33,184	20,380	12,804	11.7
1999	274,873	13,664	32,968	20,564	12,404	11.4
2000	294,495	13,442	34,617	22,222	12,395	11.2
2001[r]	305,500	14,095	36,721	23,420	13,301	11.5
2002	348,555	14,430	39,223	25,776	13,447	10.8
2003[E]	376,286	14,599	39,068	25,484	13,584	10.0
2004[E]	390,419	15,255	42,257	28,007	14,250	13.0

Source: Office of Management and Budget, "The Budget of the United States Government" (Annually).

NOTE: "National Defense" includes the military budget of the Department of Defense and other defense-related activities. "Total NASA" includes all categories of the NASA budget; NASA construction is not included in "Aerospace Products and Services." See additional explanation with following table.

a Outlays for aircraft and missile procurement. Does not include RDT&E, which DoD has not reported by product group since 1977, and which, for comparability, has been subtracted from data previously reported in this table for earlier years. Also included are revisions to missile procurement data.

b 1991–1993 reflects transfers from the Defense Cooperation Account funded by foreign government and private cash contributions reducing total U.S.-funded military outlays.

FEDERAL OUTLAYS FOR AEROSPACE PRODUCTS AND SERVICES
Fiscal Years 1971-2004
(Millions of Dollars)

Year	TOTAL	Department of Defense[a]			NASA[b]
		TOTAL	Aircraft	Missiles	
1971	$12,918	$ 9,580	$ 6,549	$ 3,031	$ 3,338
1972	12,309	8,936	5,927	3,009	3,373
1973	11,360	8,089	5,066	3,023	3,271
1974	11,168	7,987	5,006	2,981	3,181
1975	11,554	8,373	5,484	2,889	3,181
1976	12,364	8,816	6,520	2,296	3,548
Tr.Qtr.	2,885	1,959	1,557	402	926
1977	13,229	9,389	6,608	2,781	3,840
1978	13,926	10,067	6,971	3,096	3,859
1979	16,686	12,622	8,836	3,786	4,064
1980	20,269	15,558	11,124	4,434	4,711
1981	24,276	19,002	13,193	5,809	5,274
1982	29,501	23,575	16,793	6,782	5,926
1983	35,364	28,808	21,013	7,795	6,556
1984	39,663	32,723	23,196	9,527	6,940
1985	44,483	37,335	26,586	10,749	7,148
1986	49,773	42,558	30,828	11,730	7,215
1987	51,871	44,429	32,956	11,473[c]	7,442
1988	48,848	39,922	28,246	11,676	8,926
1989	52,933	42,072	27,569	14,503	10,861
1990	53,194	40,992	26,142	14,851	12,202
1991	53,630	40,089	25,689	14,400	13,541
1992	50,569	37,085	23,581	13,504	13,484
1993	45,496	31,763	20,359	11,404	13,733
1994	41,082	27,774	18,840	8,934	13,308
1995	36,696	23,638	16,125	7,513	13,058
1996	32,947	20,530	14,331	6,199	12,417
1997	32,808	19,888	14,663	5,225	12,920
1998	33,184	20,380	15,473	4,907	12,804
1999	32,968	20,564	16,484	4,080	12,404
2000	34,617	22,222	17,991	4,231	12,395
2001	36,721	23,420	17,979	5,441	13,301
2002	39,223	25,776	20,546	5,230	13,447
2003[E]	39,068	25,484	20,284	5,200	13,584
2004[E]	42,257	28,007	22,118	5,889	14,250

Source: Office of Management and Budget, "The Budget of the United States Government" (Annually).
  a Outlays for aircraft and missile procurement. Does not include RDT&E, which DoD has not reported by product group since 1977, and which for comparability, has been subtracted from data previously reported in this table for earlier years.
  b Excludes Construction of Facilities, Office of Inspector General, and Air Transportation.
  c Beginning in 1978, DoD combined Navy Missile Procurement with torpedoes and other related products into Navy Weapons Procurement, of which missiles comprise approximately 80 percent.

DEPARTMENT OF DEFENSE
MILITARY OUTLAYS BY FUNCTIONAL TITLE[a]
Fiscal Years 1995-2004
(Millions of Dollars)

	1995	1996	1997	1998
TOTAL	$259,442	$253,187	$258,311	$256,122
Procurement—TOTAL..............	$ 54,982	$ 48,913	$ 47,690	$ 48,206
Aircraft......................................	16,125	14,331	14,663	15,473
Missiles[b]	7,513	6,199	5,225	4,907
Ships..	8,780	7,346	7,085	6,784
Weapons[b]................................	1,783	1,788	1,918	1,824
Ammunition	1,339	1,232	1,615	1,761
Other[c]	19,441	18,017	17,184	17,457
Military Personnel—TOTAL	70,809	66,669	69,724	68,976
Active Forces...........................	61,606	57,843	60,371	59,793
Reserve Forces	9,203	8,826	9,353	9,183
RDT&E	34,594	36,494	37,015	37,420
Operations & Maintenance	91,078	88,759	92,461	93,473
Military Construction	6,823	6,683	6,187	6,044
Family Housing..........................	3,571	3,828	4,003	3,871
Other..	(2,415)	1,841	1,231	(1,868)

(Continued on next page)

DEPARTMENT OF DEFENSE
MILITARY OUTLAYS BY FUNCTIONAL TITLE[a]
Fiscal Years 1995-2004, continued
(Millions of Dollars)

1999	2000	2001[r]	2002	2003[E]	2004[E]
$261,380	$281,223	$291,015	$331,951	$358,155	$370,707
$ 48,826	$ 51,696	$ 54,986	$ 62,515	$ 63,220	$ 67,903
16,484	17,991	17,979	20,546	20,284	22,118
4,080	4,231	5,441	5,230	5,200	5,889
6,697	6,679	7,115	8,287	7,954	7,706
1,885	1,756	1,856	2,343	2,629	2,470
1,998	1,836	2,153	2,587	2,626	3,275
17,682	19,203	20,442	23,522	24,527	26,445
69,503	75,950	73,977	86,799	92,687	98,672
59,718	65,535	63,109	75,179	78,373	97,724
9,785	10,415	10,868	11,620	14,314	948
37,363	37,606	40,459	44,389	52,838	58,194
96,418	105,870	112,015	130,005	136,284	133,058
5,521	5,109	4,977	5,052	6,001	6,147
3,692	3,413	3,516	3,736	4,151	4,086
57	1,579	1,085	(545)	2,974	2,647

Source: Office of Management and Budget, "The Budget of the United States Government" (Annually).
NOTE: Data in parentheses are credit items.
   a Includes all items in the DoD military budget; excludes the DoD civil budget for the Army Corps of Engineers and other non-defense related activities.
   b Beginning in 1978, DoD combined Navy Missiles Procurement with torpedoes and other related products into Navy Weapons Procurement. Missiles comprise approximately 80 percent of the value of this category.
   c Includes Communications and Electronics.

FEDERAL PRICE DEFLATORS FOR GDP, DEFENSE, PPI, AND CPI
Calendar/Fiscal Years 1973-2004

Year	GDP FY GDP (FY 1996 =100)	GDP CY GDP (CY 1996 =100)	Federal Government Defense Purchases Goods & Services (CY 1996 =100)	Federal Government Defense Purchases Equipment Investment (CY 1996 =100)	PPI, Capital Equipment (CY 1982 =100)	CPI, (Urban) All Items (CY 82-84 =100)
1973	33.2	33.6	32.9	NA	44.2	44.4
1974	35.8	36.6	35.8	NA	50.5	49.3
1975	39.5	40.0	39.2	NA	58.2	53.8
1976	41.9	42.3	42.0	NA	62.1	56.9
1977	44.5	45.0	45.2	NA	66.1	60.6
1978	47.6	48.2	48.3	NA	71.3	65.2
1979	51.4	52.2	52.2	NA	77.5	72.6
1980	56.0	57.1	57.9	NA	85.8	82.4
1981	61.4	62.4	63.7	NA	94.6	90.9
1982	65.7	66.3	68.4	NA	100.0	96.5
1983	68.6	68.9	70.9	NA	102.8	99.6
1984	71.1	71.4	76.0	NA	105.2	103.9
1985	73.5	73.7	77.2	NA	107.5	107.6
1986	75.3	75.3	77.3	NA	109.7	109.6
1987	77.3	77.6	78.0	89.5	111.7	113.6
1988	79.9	80.2	79.7	88.8	114.3	118.3
1989	82.9	83.3	81.9	89.9	118.8	124.0
1990	86.0	86.5	84.6	91.4	122.9	130.7
1991	89.4	89.7	87.7	93.4	126.7	136.2
1992	91.7	91.8	90.8	93.9	129.1	140.3
1993	93.9	94.1	92.5	95.9	131.4	144.5
1994	96.0	96.0	94.5	98.1	134.1	148.2
1995	98.0	98.1	96.9	100.2	136.7	152.4
1996	100.0	100.0	100.0	100.0	138.3	156.9
1997	102.0	101.9	101.4	97.9	138.2	160.5
1998	103.4	103.2	102.2	95.8	137.6	163.0
1999	104.8ʳ	104.7	104.5	96.0	137.6	166.6
2000	106.8ʳ	106.9ʳ	107.5	95.7	138.8	172.2
2001	109.4	109.4	109.3	94.4	139.7	177.1
2002	110.8	110.7	111.9	93.3	139.1	179.9
2003 E	112.2	112.1	NA	NA	NA	183.8
2004 E	113.9	113.8	NA	NA	NA	187.6

Source: Bureau of Economic Analysis, Price Measurement Branch; Bureau of Labor Statistics; and Office of Management and Budget, "The Budget of the United States Government" (Annually).

Key: PPI = Producer Price Index for Capital Equipment.
CPI = Consumer Price Index, All Items, All Urban Consumers for 1978 and subsequent years. Previous years, All Urban Wage Earners.
GDP = Gross Domestic Product.

PRICE DEFLATORS FOR AEROSPACE INDUSTRY
Calendar Years 1974-2002

Year	Aerospace Deflators (1987 = 100)					
	Composite	SIC 3721	SIC 3724	SIC 3728	SIC 3761	SIC 3764,9
1972	33.7	39.9	30.1	36.6	39.7	34.4
1973	37.7	41.2	30.9	38.1	39.4	35.6
1974	41.5	44.8	34.9	44.0	41.6	40.5
1975	46.6	48.3	42.3	51.6	45.2	49.2
1976	51.0	52.8	45.9	56.5	50.4	53.8
1977	54.6	56.2	49.1	58.7	55.6	58.2
1978	57.5	59.3	54.6	55.2	60.7	63.6
1979	63.5	65.3	60.9	58.9	69.7	70.0
1980	70.6	72.9	66.3	65.3	78.9	78.5
1981	79.5	80.8	77.0	74.9	87.1	89.5
1982	87.9	89.8	85.2	84.3	93.4	97.2
1983	92.2	94.4	89.5	87.9	98.6	101.5
1984	99.8	105.9	98.1	93.6	100.7	102.9
1985[a]	98.7	100.7	99.2	94.4	102.4	103.2
1986	99.8	100.6	99.3	97.9	103.5	102.4
1987	100.0	100.0	100.0	100.0	100.0	100.0
1988	101.5	102.2	103.0	103.5	98.6	98.4
1989	105.5	111.0	105.8	106.8	97.1	97.7
1990	108.6	116.8	111.7	109.8	93.4	98.2
1991	111.4	121.3	117.0	113.6	90.5	101.9
1992[b]	116.9	125.2	122.7	118.0	88.4	104.8
1993	120.2	129.5	124.7	120.9	90.9	109.6
1994	122.7	133.9	128.0	123.5	88.0	107.1
1995	124.5	138.3	129.9	124.4	84.3	104.2
1996	126.7	141.5	132.4	128.8	81.8	103.6
1997	127.8	143.4	133.7	131.4	77.8	103.5
1998	128.5	143.8	134.7	133.0	78.3	102.4
1999	129.4	145.1	135.7	134.3	76.8	103.1
2000	133.3	151.6	138.6	135.4	78.1	102.8
2001[r]	136.9	156.9	142.9	138.5	77.1	103.6
2002	138.6	160.0	144.6	139.9	74.6	103.6

Source: Aerospace Industries Association, based on data from: Bureau of Labor Statistics, Producer Price Indexes; Bureau of Economic Analysis, Chain-Type Price Indexes and Implicit Price Deflators; and International Trade Administration.

a The International Trade Administration has discontinued its reporting of the Aerospace Deflators with 1986. Subsequent composite deflators computed by AIA and deflators for 1985 and 1986 revised for consistency.

b The Bureau of Economic Analysis discontinued its reporting in 1995 of the National Defense Purchases Deflators (used in AIA's Composite calculations). 1992-1994 revised using 1992 fixed weights and BEA's Chain-Type Price Indexes for National Defense Investment and Consumption Expenditures.

Key: SIC = Standard Industrial Classification, SIC 3721 = Aircraft; SIC 3724 = Aircraft Engines and Engine Parts; SIC 3728 = Aircraft Parts; SIC 3761 = Missiles and Space Vehicles; SIC 3764 = Space Propulsion; SIC 3769 = Space Equipment not elsewhere classified.

AIRCRAFT PRODUCTION

Sales of new aircraft, engines, and parts fell $7.9 billion from 2001's level to $67 billion, led by declines in the civil sector. Data compiled by the U.S. Census Bureau showed military sales grew by $3.4 billion to $25 billion, while civil sales fell sharply—down 22% to $41 billion following a one-year up tick. Hidden in the aircraft sector's overall decline was a strong gain in sales of military engines and parts—up 43%, or $1.7 billion, from year-earlier levels of $4.0 billion.

Military aircraft production, as measured by acceptances, increased to its highest level in three years. Manufacturers delivered 355 aircraft of which 37% were destined to customers other than the U.S. government. The number of military aircraft exported declined for the fifth straight year—down 19 to 130—and those exported through the FMS program rebounded somewhat from their lowest level on record (29). Encouragingly, aircraft acceptances by the services for their own use increased for the third straight year.

Aircraft acceptances (including FMS) increased by 56 to 281. All categories showed gains except tanker/transport. Flyaway costs also increased overall—rising 14% to $9.5 billion. Despite increased fighter/attack acceptances, their corresponding flyaway costs declined.

The civil aircraft industry produced and delivered 659 fewer aircraft in 2002 than it had in 2001. Each category—transports, helicopters, and general aviation—posted declines. The majority of the decline came from general aviation aircraft, whose shipments dropped by 415 to 2,203. The weak economy and at least partially-satiated demand in the fractional sector ended a six-year string of rising shipments and billings. Transport aircraft production fell by 147, or 28%, to 379. Lastly, production of civil helicopters subsided from 415 to 318. Likewise, domestic shipments dropped by 528 while exports fell by only 131. For example, Boeing shipped 57% fewer jetliners domestically than last year and only 45% of what it did overseas—exporting 262 versus delivering 117 transports domestically.

Net new orders in 2002 fell by $4.6 billion from year-earlier levels. Military orders grew $6.9 billion—meaning that civil orders dropped $11.5 billion or 28%. Similarly, the aircraft sector's unfilled order backlog fell $9 billion to $133 billion. While the military backlog increased $3.2 billion, civil registered declining backlogs, civil was responsible for the entirety of the drop—down $12.6 billion.

Three programs dominated new aircraft procurement in FY 2002: the Air Force's C-17 Globemaster III cargo aircraft remained the largest, big-ticket item with 15 planes worth $3.7 billion, followed by the Navy's 48 F/A-18E/F Super Hornet fighters costing $3.1 billion, and the Air Force's 13 F-22 Raptor fighters costing $3.0 billion. Eleven V-22 Osprey tiltrotor aircraft for $840 million logged a distant fourth. Scheduled for significant procurement funding increases in FY 2003 are the Air Force's C-17, F-22, and C-130J variants and the Navy's V-22.

SALES OF AIRCRAFT, ENGINES, AND PARTS
Calendar Years 1988-2002
(Millions of Dollars)

Year	GRAND TOTAL	TOTAL		Complete Aircraft & Parts		Aircraft Engines & parts	
		Mili-tary	Non-Mil.	Mili-tary	Non-Mil.	Mili-tary	Non-Mil.
CURRENT DOLLARS							
1988	$50,742	$25,068	$25,674	$19,030	$16,681	$6,038	$ 8,993
1989	53,825	24,287	29,538	18,256	20,140	6,031	9,398
1990	66,289	27,667	38,622	22,023	27,872	5,644	10,750
1991	68,540	25,385	43,155	19,710	33,215	5,675	9,940
1992	67,669	23,509	44,160	18,411	35,595	5,098	8,565
1993	61,086	20,099	40,987	16,118	32,780	3,981	8,207
1994	54,553	23,652	30,901	20,127	23,176	3,525	7,725
1995	55,029	22,944	32,085	19,596	22,897	3,348	9,188
1996	57,526	24,804	32,722	20,822	20,993	3,982	11,729
1997	66,558	23,944	42,614	21,297	33,206	2,647	9,408
1998	76,503	23,795	52,708	21,154	42,541	2,641	10,167
1999	82,449	26,043	56,406	22,917	45,107	3,126	11,299
2000	69,673	23,196	46,477	19,650	37,538	3,546	8,939
2001[r]	74,637	22,133	52,504	18,176	40,548	3,957	11,956
2002	66,691	25,498	41,193	19,849	32,071	5,649	9,122
CONSTANT DOLLARS[a]							
1988	$49,992	$24,698	$25,295	$18,749	$16,434	$5,949	$8,860
1989	51,019	23,021	27,998	17,304	19,090	5,717	8,908
1990	61,040	25,476	35,564	20,279	25,665	5,197	9,899
1991	61,526	22,787	38,739	17,693	29,816	5,094	8,923
1992	57,886	20,110	37,776	15,749	30,449	4,361	7,327
1993	50,820	16,721	34,099	13,409	27,271	3,312	6,828
1994	44,460	19,276	25,184	16,403	18,888	2,873	6,296
1995	44,200	18,429	25,771	15,740	18,391	2,689	7,380
1996	45,403	19,577	25,826	16,434	16,569	3,143	9,257
1997	52,080	18,736	33,344	16,664	25,983	2,071	7,362
1998	59,535	18,518	41,018	16,462	33,106	2,055	7,912
1999	63,716	20,126	43,590	17,710	34,859	2,416	8,732
2000	52,268	17,401	34,866	14,741	28,161	2,660	6,706
2001[r]	54,519	16,167	38,352	13,277	29,619	2,890	8,733
2002	48,118	18,397	29,721	14,321	23,139	4,076	6,582

Source: Bureau of the Census, "Aerospace Industry (Orders, Sales, and Backlog)" (Annually).
a Based on AIA's aerospace composite price deflator, 1987=100.

ORDERS AND BACKLOG OF AIRCRAFT, ENGINES, AND PARTS
Calendar Years 1988-2002
(Millions of Dollars)

Year	GRAND TOTAL	TOTAL		Complete Aircraft & Parts		Aircraft Engines & Parts	
		Mili-tary	Non-Mil.	Mili-tary	Non-Mil.	Mili-tary	Non-Mil.

NET NEW ORDERS

Year	GRAND TOTAL	Military	Non-Mil.	Military	Non-Mil.	Military	Non-Mil.
1988	$ 82,148	$24,242	$ 57,906	$17,493	$ 41,762	$6,749	$16,144
1989	96,591	28,818	67,773	23,569	52,619	5,249	15,154
1990	82,386	17,735	64,651	12,766	52,371	4,969	12,280
1991	67,490	26,675	40,815	22,140	30,745	4,535	10,070
1992	49,741	19,631	30,110	16,391	20,548	3,240	9,562
1993	35,608	19,518	16,090	15,853	11,238	3,665	4,852
1994	43,518	23,352	20,166	19,806	12,854	3,546	7,312
1995	56,321	19,854	36,467	16,248	27,156	3,606	9,311
1996	70,624	25,343	45,281	21,755	33,802	3,588	11,479
1997	71,100	21,424	49,676	19,102	41,439	2,322	8,237
1998	64,483	16,870	47,613	14,051	37,362	2,819	10,251
1999	73,027	25,009	48,018	21,422	35,529	3,587	12,489
2000	96,855	31,396	65,459	27,440	54,335	3,956	11,124
2001 ʳ	62,493	21,762	40,731	18,144	27,525	3,618	13,206
2002	57,863	28,653	29,210	21,135	23,116	7,518	6,094

BACKLOG AS OF DECEMBER 31

Year	GRAND TOTAL	Military	Non-Mil.	Military	Non-Mil.	Military	Non-Mil.
1988	$111,280	$35,515	$ 75,765	$28,186	$ 59,679	$7,329	$16,086
1989	159,150	44,026	115,124	36,888	95,108	7,138	20,016
1990	172,940	33,788	139,152	27,259	119,123	6,529	20,029
1991	173,676	39,149	134,527	32,795	116,139	6,354	18,388
1992	168,577	44,255	124,322	39,748	107,686	4,507	16,636
1993	142,405	46,177	96,228	41,732	82,772	4,445	13,456
1994	129,929	44,624	85,305	40,206	72,295	4,418	13,010
1995	136,871	44,642	92,229	39,673	77,802	4,969	14,427
1996	153,976	47,635	106,341	42,788	91,851	4,847	14,490
1997	155,546	43,615	111,931	40,562	100,022	3,053	11,909
1998	143,696	37,530	106,166	34,866	94,161	2,664	12,005
1999	133,161	36,565	96,596	33,374	83,412	3,191	13,184
2000	156,491	41,250	115,241	37,650	99,942	3,600	15,299
2001 ʳ	142,503	39,623	102,880	36,456	86,172	3,167	16,708
2002	133,091	42,791	90,300	37,754	76,618	5,037	13,682

Source: Bureau of the Census, "Aerospace Industry (Orders, Sales, and Backlog)" (Annually).

U.S. AIRCRAFT PRODUCTION—CIVIL
Calendar Years 1969-2002
(Number of Aircraft)

Year	TOTAL	Domestic Shipments			Export Shipments		
		Trans-ports	Heli-copters	General Aviation	Trans-ports	Heli-copters	General Aviation
1969	13,505	332	282	9,996	182	252	2,461
1970	8,076	127	150	5,246	184	332	2,037
1971	8,158	50	171	5,900	173	298	1,566
1972	10,576	79	319	7,702	148	256	2,072
1973	14,709	143	342	10,482	151	428	3,163
1974	15,326	91	433	9,903	241	395	4,263
1975	15,251	127	528	10,804	188	336	3,268
1976	16,429	64 [a]	442	12,232	158	315	3,218
1977	17,913	54	527	13,441	101	321	3,469
1978	18,962	130	536	14,346	111	368	3,471
1979	18,460	176	570	13,177	200	459	3,878
1980	13,634	150	841	8,703	237	525	3,178
1981	10,916	132	619	6,840	255	453	2,617
1982	5,085	111	333	3,326	121	254	940
1983	3,356	133	187	2,172	129	216	519
1984	2,999	102	143	2,013	83	233	425
1985	2,691	126	247	1,545	152	137	484
1986	2,156	171	120	1,031	159	210	464
1987	1,800	187	116	598	170	242	487
1988	1,949	206	103	500	217	280	643
1989	2,448	138	221	225	260	294	1,310
1990	2,268	215	254	335	306	349	809
1991	2,181	204	253	487	385	318	534
1992	1,790	180	112	541	387	212	358
1993	1,630	130	83	631	278	175	333
1994	1,545	87	154	543	222	154	385
1995	1,625	119	82	714	137	210	363
1996	1,662	97	64	732	172	214	383
1997	2,269	122	87	1,140	252	259	409
1998	3,115	184	125	1,794	375	238	399
1999	3,456	279	180	1,972	341	181	503
2000	3,780	217	189	2,391	268	304	411
2001	3,559	273	106	2,172	253	309	446
2002	2,900	117	24	1,882	262	294	321

Source: Aerospace Industries Association, based on company reports; General Aviation Manufacturers Association; and Department of Commerce, International Trade Administration.

a Prior to 1976, includes the C-130 military transport.

U.S. AIRCRAFT PRODUCTION—MILITARY
Calendar Years 1969-2002
(Number of Aircraft)

Year	TOTAL	U.S. Military Agencies	Exports		
			TOTAL	FMS[a]	Direct[b]
1969	4,290	3,644	646	NA	NA
1970	3,720	3,085	635	NA	NA
1971	2,914	2,232	682	NA	NA
1972	2,530	1,993	537	124	413
1973	1,821	1,243	578	129	449
1974	1,513	799	714	365	349
1975	1,779	844	935	525	410
1976	1,318	625	693	518	175
1977	1,134	454	680	408	272
1978	996	467	529	256	273
1979	837	531	306	203	103
1980	1,047	625	422	194	228
1981	1,062	703	359	215	144
1982	1,159	690	469	68	401
1983	1,053	766	287	70	217
1984	936	561	375	71	304
1985	919	643	276	134	142
1986	1,107	708	399	110	289
1987	1,210	725	485	133	352
1988	1,305	687	618	138	480
1989	1,261	614	647	92	555
1990	1,053	664	387	99	290
1991	911	556	355	94	261
1992	753	422	331	122	209
1993	955[c]	437	518	146	372[c]
1994	764	418	346	69	277
1995	811[d]	354	457	108	349
1996	558	242	316	106	210
1997	488	151	337	181	156
1998	418	149	269	175	94
1999	359	133	226	114	112
2000	333	138	195	42	153
2001[r]	345	196	149	29	120
2002	355	225	130	56	74

Source: Aerospace Industries Association, based on USAF, USA, and USN survey responses and Department of Commerce, International Trade Administration.
  a Also includes acceptances of NATO AWACS aircraft.
  b Military aircraft exported via commercial contracts, directly from manufacturers to foreign governments.
  c The number of small (450 kg–2000 kg), new aircraft exported doubled in 1993 to 340 worth $18 million.
  d Includes 358 small (450 kg–2000 kg), new aircraft worth $14.7 million.

CIVIL AIRCRAFT SHIPMENTS
Calendar Years 1988-2002

Year	TOTAL	Transport Aircraft[a]	Helicopters	General Aviation
NUMBER OF AIRCRAFT SHIPPED				
1988	1,949	423	383	1,143
1989	2,448	398	515	1,535
1990	2,268	521	603	1,144
1991	2,181	589	571	1,021
1992	1,790	567	324	899
1993	1,630	408	258	964
1994	1,545	309	308	928
1995	1,625	256	292	1,077
1996	1,662	269 [a]	278	1,115
1997	2,269	374	346	1,549
1998	3,115	559	363	2,193
1999	3,456	620	361	2,475
2000	3,780	485	493	2,802
2001	3,559	526	415	2,618
2002	2,900	379	318	2,203
VALUE (Millions of Dollars)				
1988	$15,855	$13,603	$334	$1,918
1989	17,129	15,074	251	1,804
1990	24,477	22,215	254	2,008
1991	29,035	26,856	211	1,968
1992	30,728	28,750	142	1,836
1993	26,389	24,133	113	2,144
1994	20,666	18,124 [E]	185	2,357
1995	18,299	15,263 [E]	194	2,842
1996	20,805	17,564 [E]	193	3,048
1997	31,753	26,929	231	4,593
1998	41,449	35,663	252	5,534
1999	45,161	38,171	187	6,803
2000	38,637	30,327	270	8,040
2001	42,399	34,155	247	7,997
2002	35,072	27,574	157	7,341

Source: Aerospace Industries Association, based on company reports and General Aviation Manufacturers' Association.

a U.S.-manufactured fixed-wing aircraft over 33,000 pounds empty weight, including all jet transports plus the four-engine turboprop-powered Lockheed L-100.

SHIPMENTS OF CIVIL TRANSPORT AIRCRAFT[a]
Calendar Years 1988-2002

Company and Model	1998	1999	2000	2001	2002
TOTAL					
Number of Aircraft	559	620	485	526	379
Value (Millions of Dollars).............	$35,663	$38,171	$30,327	$34,155	$27,547
Boeing—TOTAL	505	561	446	475	359
B-737	281	320	278	298	221
B-747	53	47	24	31	27
B-757	50	67	45	45	29
B-767	47	44	44	40	35
B-777	74	83	55	61	47
Douglas[b] —TOTAL.....................	54	59	39	51	20
MD-11	12	8	4	2	—
MD-80	8	26	—	—	—
MD-90	34	13	3	—	—
MD-95 (B-717)	—	12	32	49	20

Source: Aerospace Industries Association, based on company reports.
   a U.S.-manufactured fixed-wing aircraft over 33,000 lbs.
   b Formerly reported as McDonnell Douglas.

SPECIFICATIONS OF U.S. CIVIL JET TRANSPORT AIRCRAFT[a]
On Order or in Production as of 2002

Number of Engines and Crew, and Model Designation[b]	Initial Service	Standard Mixed Class	Operating Empty Weight (000's lbs)	Maximum Takeoff Gross Weight (000's lbs)	Range (Nautical Miles)[c]	Engine Manufacturer[d] and Model
FOUR ENGINES/CREW OF 2						
747-400*	1989	416-524	39-9	875	7,260	GE CF6-80C2, P&W PW4000, or RR RB211-524
747-400ER*	TBD	416-524	407	910	7,670	GE GE CF6-80C2 or P&W PW4000
TWO ENGINES/CREW OF 2						
MD-95 (717)	1999	106	69	121	2,060	RR BR715
737-600	1998	110-132	81	144	3,260	CFMI CFM56-7B
737-700	1997	126-149	84	155	3,260	CFMI CFM56-7B
737-800	1998	162-189	92	174	2,940	CFMI CFM56-7B
737-900	2001	177-189	95	174	2,745	CFMI CFM56-7B
757-200	1983	200-228	130	255	3,900	RR RB211-535 or P&W PW2000
757-300	1999	243-280	142	273	3,395	RR RB211-535 or P&W PW2000
767-200ER*	1984	181-255	187	395	6,600	P&W PW4000 or GE CF6-80C2
767-300*	1986	218-351	196	412	5,344	P&W PW4000, GE CF6-80C2, or RR RB211-524
767-300ER*	1997	218-351	202	412	6,105	P&W PW4000, GE CF6-80C2, or RR RB211-524
767-400ER*	2000	245-375	229 226	450	5,645	P&W PW4000 or GE CF6-80C2
777-200*	1995	305-440	302	545	5,210	RR Trent, GE GE90, or P&W PW4000
777-200ER*	1997	301-440	320	656	7,730	RR Trent, GE GE90, or P&W PW4000
777-200LR*	2003	301	344	766	9,170	GE GE90
777-300*	1998	368-550	343	660	5,955	RR Trent, GE GE90, or P&W PW4000
777-300ER*	2003	365	373	760	7,420	GE GE90

Source: Aerospace Industries Association, based on company reports.
  a All jet-powered passenger transport aircraft 33,000 pounds or more empty weight.
  b The Boeing Company manufactures models: 737, 747, 757, 767, & 777 and its Douglas Products Division manufactures MD-95 (renamed the 717).
  c Full passenger load and baggage.
  d P&W = Pratt & Whitney; GE = General Electric; RR = Rolls-Royce; CFMI = General Electric/Snecma; IAE = International Aero Engines; BMW = Bayerische Motoren Werke.
  TBD To be determined.
  * Wide-body aircraft.

CIVIL TRANSPORT AIRCRAFT BACKLOG[a]
As of December 31, 1988-2002

Company and Model	1998	1999	2000	2001	2002
TOTAL AIRCRAFT ON ORDER					
Number of Aircraft	1,786	1,512 [b]	1,612 [b]	1,357 [b]	1,152 [b]
Value (Millions of Dollars)	$86,057	$72,972	$89,780	$75,850	$68,159
Boeing—TOTAL	1,595	1,385	1,503	1,313	1,112
B-737	978	916	1,016	902	798
B-747	102	77	77	62	52
B-757	130	81	79	57	28
B-767	134	122	84	76	39
B-777	251	189	247	216	195
Douglas[c]—TOTAL	191	127	109	44	40
MD-11	14	6	2	—	—
MD-80/90	62	3	—	—	—
MD-95 (B-717)	115	118	107	44	40
TOTAL FOREIGN ORDERS					
Number of Aircraft	687	493	477	444	440
Value[E] (Millions of Dollars)	$38,726	$29,939	$38,972	$34,891	$34,079
Boeing—TOTAL	625	458	450	423	426
B-737	344	258	227	229	249
B-747	75	65	64	47	41
B-757	40	15	9	8	5
B-767	21	14	19	21	16
B-777	145	106	131	118	115
Douglas[c]—TOTAL	62	35	27	21	26
MD-11	11	6	2	—	—
MD-80/90	36	3	—	—	—
MD-95 (B-717)	15	26	25	21	26

Source: Aerospace Industries Association, based on company reports.

a   Unfilled announced orders excluding options for U.S.-manufactured transport aircraft over 33,000 pounds. Includes new transports contracted for lease from the manufacturer.

b   Includes 84 unidentified orders in 1999, 64 in 2000, 156 in 2001, and 69 in 2002.

c   Formerly reported as McDonnell Douglas.

SPECIFICATIONS OF U.S. CIVIL HELICOPTERS
In Production as of 2002

Company	Commercial Model	Number of Places	Useful Load (Lbs.)	Range with Useful Load (N. Miles)	External Cargo Payload (Lbs.)
Bell/Agusta Aerospace	BA609	10-11	5,500	750	—
Brantly International	B-2B	2	620	174	—
Enstrom Helicopter	F-28 Series	3	1,030	241	1,000
	280 Series	3	1,015	260	1,000
	480 Series	5	1,305	375	1,000
Hiller Aircraft	UH-12E3	3	1,341	232	1,000
	UH-12E3T	3	1,460	172	1,000
Kaman	K-1200	1–3	500	267	6,000 [r]
MD Helicopters	500 Series	5	1,484 [r]	290 [r]	2,069
	520 Series	5	1,764	243 [r]	2,364
	530F	5	1,509	268 [r]	2,159
	600 Series	8	2,000	383	3,000
	900 Series	8	2,875	223 [r]	3,525 [r]
Robinson Helicopter	R22	2	515	180	—
	R44	4	980	365	—
Schweizer Aircraft	300C	3	950	201	1,050
	300CB	2–3	662	NA	—
	330/333	4	1,300	310	—
Sikorsky Aircraft	S-76C	14	4,803 [r]	439	3,300
	S-92	21	10,250 [r]	538 [r]	10,000

Source: Helicopter Association International, "2003 Helicopter Annual" (Annually).

CIVIL HELICOPTER SHIPMENTS[a]
Calendar Years 1998-2002

Company and Model	1998	1999	2000	2001	2002
CIVIL SHIPMENTS					
Number of Aircraft	363	361	493	415	318
Value (Millions of Dollars)	$252	$187	$270	$247	$157
Brantly—TOTAL	2	=	6	2	1
B-2B	2	—	6	2	1
Enstrom—TOTAL	14	8	7	8	12
F-28/280 series	3	5	2	4	4
480 series	11	3	5	4	8
Hiller—TOTAL	=	=	1	2	=
UH12E	—	—	1	2	—
Kaman—TOTAL	2	=	3	6	=
K-1200	2	—	3	6	—
MD Helicopters[b]—TOTAL	37	33	41	28	12
500 series	5	5	11	4	5
520N series	2	5	4	2	3
530 series	5	6	4	—	—
600 series	21	6	8	2	—
900 series	4	11	14	20	4
Robinson—TOTAL	251	278	390	328	255
R22	117	128	126	134	107
R44	134	150	264	194	148
Schweizer—TOTAL	41	35	36	33	32
300C	17	23	13	17	13
300CB	21	11	17	12	17
330/333	3	1	6	4	2
Sikorsky—TOTAL	6	7	9	8	6
S-70	—	—	2	—	—
S-76	16	7	7	8	6

Source: Aerospace Industries Association, based on company reports.
NOTE: All data exclude production by foreign licensees.
  a Domestic and export helicopter shipments for non-military use. Helicopters in military configuration exported to foreign governments and purchased under commercial contract are reported elsewhere. Please note that shipments from Bell Helicopter's Canadian facilities are excluded as are other foreign-produced helicopters, but reported separately below for information purposes only.
  b Formerly reported as McDonnell Douglas.

Bell—TOTAL	197	146	143	122	92
206B	24	28	14	14	10
206L/LT	16	12	27	10	12
212	1	—	—	—	—
230	2	—	—	—	—
407	104	62	62	47	33
412	35	26	24	22	25
427	—	—	5	15	5
430	15	18	11	14	7

GENERAL AVIATION AIRCRAFT SHIPMENTS
BY SELECTED MANUFACTURERS
Calendar Years 1998-2002

	1998	1999	2000	2001	2002
NUMBER OF AIRCRAFT SHIPPED	2,193	2,475	2,802	2,618	2,203
Single-Engine, Piston	1,434	1,634	1,810	1,581	1,366
Multi-Engine, Piston.....................	94	114	103	147	130
Turboprop	259	239	315	306	187
Turbojet	406	488	574	584	520
VALUE[a] OF SHIPMENTS					
(Millions of Dollars)......................	$5,534	$6,803	$8,040	$7,997	$7,341
Piston	$ 330	$ 385	$ 446	$ 471	$ 283
Turboprop.....................................	763	658	935	742	487
Turbojet	4,441	5,760	6,659	6,784	6,572
Number of Aircraft Shipped by					
Selected Manufacturer					
American Champion	74	91	96	56	53
Aviat..	85	83	91	57	38
Bellanca..	1	1	1	1	—
Cessna	1,072	1,202	1,256	1,202	944
Cirrus Design................................	—	9	95	183	397
Commander...................................	13	13	20	11	7
Gulfstream	61	70	71	71	61
Lancair..	—	—	5	27	24
Learjet..	61	99	133	109	60
Maule..	63	69	57	57	46
Micco	—	—	6	10	—
Mooney...	93	97	100	29	10
Piper	295	341	395	441	290
Raytheon[b]	375	400	476	364	259
Tiger..	—	—	—	—	14

Source: General Aviation Manufacturers' Association.
 a   Manufacturers' net billing price.
 b   Formerly reported as Beech.

DIRECT EXPORT SHIPMENTS OF MILITARY HELICOPTERS[a]
Calendar Years 1998-2002

Manufacturer and Model	1998	1999	2000	2001	2002
TOTAL					
Number of Aircraft	50	28	39	10	10
Value (Millions of Dollars)	$757	$484	$699	$164[b]	$300[b]
Boeing AH-64[c]	1	6	1	—	—
Boeing Vertol CH-47/414/352.............	17	10	7	—	—
Sikorsky S-70C	32	12	31	10	10

Source: Aerospace Industries Association, company reports.
    a Shipments of helicopters in military configuration exported directly from U.S. manufacturers to foreign governments. Military helicopters exported via Foreign Military Sales (FMS) are reported with Dept. of Defense (DoD) aircraft acceptance data elsewhere in this chapter. Some models reported on this page may be shipped in either military or civil configuration; see Civil Helicopter Shipments table for additional data.
    b Estimated by AIA using trade statistics.
    c Formerly reported as McDonnell Douglas.

SPECIFICATIONS OF U.S. MILITARY AIRCRAFT
On Order or in Production as of 2002

Primary Mission, DoD Designation, & Popular Name	Manufacturer	U.S. Military Service	Crew	Empty Weight (000's lbs.)	Engines	Performance Typical for Primary Mission	Remarks
FIGHTERS							
F-15E Eagle	Boeing	USAF	2	37	2xP&W F100	Mach 2.5 class	Dual role fighter/long range interdiction
F-16C/D Fighting Falcon	LM	USAF	1-2	19	1xP&W F100/ 1xGE F110	Mach 2+ class	Multirole fighter
F/A-18E/F Hornet	Boeing/NGC	USN/USMC	1-2	31	2xGE F414	Mach 1.8 class	Multi-mission strike fighter
F/A-22A Raptor	LM/Boeing	USAF	1	NA	2xP&W F119	Mach 2+ class	Air superiority with near-precision ground attack
COMMAND/CONTROL AND PATROL							
E-2C Hawkeye 2000	NGC	USN	5	40	2xRR T56	6+ hr. mission duration	AEW command & control; active & passive detection
E-8C Joint STARS	NGC	USAF/Army	21+	171	4xP&W JT3D	11-20+ hr. loiter	Ground surveillance/battle mgmt.
RC-12 P/Q	Raytheon	Army	2	9	2xP&W PT6A	4 hr. loiter	Electronic intercept
YAL-1A Airborne Laser	Boeing	USAF	6	TBD	4xGE CF6	TBD	Airborne high-energy chemical laser system
CARGO-TRANSPORT							
C-12R	Raytheon	Army	2	8	2xP&W PT6A	268 mph; 788 n.m.	Utility/transport
C-17A Globemaster III	Boeing	USAF	3	277	4xP&W F117	Mach 0.77; 2,400 n.m.	102 troops or 170,000 lbs.
C-20F/G/H	Gulfstream	All	3-5	42-43	2xRR Tay	Mach 0.80; 4,200 n.m.	Versions of Gulfstream IV
C-37A	Gulfstream	All	3-5	48	2xBR 710	Mach 0.80; 6,500 n.m.	Version of Gulfstream V
C-40A	Boeing	USN	3-7	92	2xCFM 56-7	Mach 0.79; 3,000 n.m.	Navy Unique Fleet Essential Aircraft
C-40B	Boeing	USAF	3-7	92	2xCFM 56-7	Mach 0.79; 5,000 n.m.	Special air mission aircraft
C/EC/WC-130J	LM	USAF/ANG	3	97	4xRR AE2100	396 mph; 3,260 mi.	41,000 lbs.
KC-130J	LM	USMC	3	97	4xRR AE2100	12,100 gals.	Tanker
MV/CV-22 Osprey	Bell/Boeing	USMC/USAF	3-4	33	2xRR AE1107C	Max 316 mph; 2,100 n.m.	With internal fuel tanks, engine nacelles tilt for STOL
TRAINING							
T-1A Jayhawk	Raytheon	USAF	2	10	2xP&W JT-15D	Max 538 mph	Tanker/transport trainer
T-6A Texan II	Raytheon	USN/USAF	2	5	1xP&W PT6A-68	Max 368 mph	Primary trainer
T-45C Goshawk	Boeing/BAe	USN	2	11	1xRR F405	Mach 0.85, 675 mph	Next generation trainer
TH-57 Sea Ranger	Bell	USN	1	2	1xRR 250	Max 135 mph; 405 mi.	Rotary wing trainer
TH-67 Creek	Bell	Army	1	2	1xRR 250	Max 135 mph; 405 mi.	Rotary wing trainer
HELICOPTERS							
AH-1Z	Bell	USMC	2	12	2xGE T700	Max 253 mph; 398 mi.	Attack helicopter
AH-64D Apache	Boeing	Army	2	11	2xGE T700	Max 226 mph; 445 mi.	Attack helicopter
CH-53E	Sikorsky	USN	3-8	33-36	3xGE T64	Max 196 mph; 710 mi.	55 passengers, aux. tanks/ minesweeping
HH/SH-60 Seahawk	Sikorsky	USN	4-12	14	2xGE T700	Max 184 mph; 500 mi.	Combat search and rescue, SOF
HH/MH-60G Pave Hawk	Sikorsky	USAF	3	12	2xGE T700	Max 184 mph; 1,380 mi.	11 troops; combat; search; rescue
MH-60S	Sikorsky	USN	4	11	2xGE T700	Max 184 mph; 373 mi.	Vertical replenishment
RAH-66 Comanche	Boeing/Sikorsky	Army	2	9	2xLHTEC T801	Max 201 mph; 400 mi.	Armed recon./light attack
UH-1Y	Bell	USMC	2	12	2xGE T700	Max 219 mph; 373 mi.	Utility assault helicopter
UH-60L Black Hawk	Sikorsky	Army	3	11	2xGE T700	Max 184 mph; 373 mi.	Utility assault helicopter

Source: Aerospace Industries Association, based on company reports.

KEY: BAe = BAE Systems; BR = BMW-Rolls Royce; GE = General Electric; LHTEC = Light Helicopter Turbine Engine Co.; LM = Lockheed Martin; NGC = Northrop Grumman; P&W = Pratt & Whitney; RR = Rolls-Royce.

TBD To be determined.

MILITARY AIRCRAFT PROGRAM PROCUREMENT[a]
Fiscal Years 2002, 2003, and 2004
(Costs in Millions of Dollars)

Agency and Model	2002		2003[E]		2004[E]	
	No.	Cost	No.	Cost	No.	Cost
AIR FORCE						
B-2 Stealth Bomber	—	$ 34.5	—	$ 96.8	—	$ 83.4
C-17 Globemaster III	15	3,745.1	15	4,276.4	11	3,502.3
C-32B	1	103.2	—	30.4	—	—
C-130J Hercules	1	218.9	—	452.1	5	641.7
Civil Air Patrol Aircraft	27	7.4	27	5.2	27	2.5
E-8C JSTARS	1	364.4	1	287.2	—	36.0
F-15E Eagle	—	247.7	—	281.4	—	204.9
F-16 Falcon	—	236.0	—	290.1	—	314.5
F-22 Raptor	13	3,031.0	20	4,468.5	22	4,233.7
JPATS[b]	47	253.7	39	231.6	52	283.0
Unmanned Aerial Vehicles[c]	37	310.5	37	394.1	28	520.3
ARMY						
AH-64 Apache Mods	60	$ 895.7	74	$ 880.2	64	$ 776.7
C-XX Medium Range Aircraft	1	44.8	—	8.2	—	—
CH-47 Mods	—	267.8	—	442.6	—	516.0
OH-58D Kiowa Warrior	—	45.1	—	33.9	—	45.1
TH-67 Creek	15	24.9	6	9.5	—	—
UH-60 Black Hawk	12	206.6	19	291.8	10	167.0
NAVY						
C-40A	—	$ —	1	$ 61.6	1	$ 64.0
E-2C Hawkeye	5	273.6	5	288.0	2	228.5
EA-6B Prowler	—	216.6	—	257.1	—	207.1
F-5	—	—	4	2.0	4	1.9
F/A-18E/F Hornet	48	3,100.3	46	3,208.1	42	3,031.2
KC-130J	2	154.9	4	308.1	—	79.2
MH-60R	—	14.4	—	117.0	6	398.6
MH-60S	13	251.5	15	352.8	13	431.5
T-39	—	—	—	—	1	22.0
T-45 Goshawk	6	180.6	8	214.1	15	339.2
UC-35	1	7.4	1	8.1	2	15.6
UH-1Y/AH-1Z	—	—	—	—	9	310.8
V-22 Osprey[b]	11[d]	839.9	11	1,155.2	11	1,110.1

Source: Department of Defense Budget, "Program Acquisition Costs by Weapon System" (Annually) and "Procurement Programs (P-1)" (Annually).

NOTE: See Research and Development Chapter for aircraft program RDT&E authorization data.

a Total Obligational Authority for procurement, excluding initial spares and mods (except where noted).

b Air Force and Navy funding.

c Air Force and Army funding.

d Includes 2 test aircraft funded under RDT&E.

DEPARTMENT OF DEFENSE OUTLAYS FOR AIRCRAFT PROCUREMENT BY AGENCY

Fiscal Years 1969–2004
(Millions of Dollars)

Year	TOTAL	Air Force	Army	Navy
1969	$ 9,177	$ 5,230	$1,126	$ 2,821
1970	7,948	4,623	2,488	837
1971	6,631	3,960	546	2,125
1972	5,927	3,191	389	2,347
1973	5,066	2,396	113	2,557
1974	5,006	2,078	122	2,806
1975	5,484	2,211	136	3,137
1976	6,520	3,323	136	3,061
Tr.Qtr.	1,557	859	26	672
1977	6,608	3,586	301	2,721
1978	6,971	3,989	380	2,602
1979	8,836	5,138	558	3,140
1980	11,124	6,647	787	3,689
1981	13,193	7,941	855	4,397
1982	16,793	9,624	1,297	5,872
1983	21,013	11,799	1,724	7,490
1984	23,196	12,992	2,165	8,040
1985	26,586	15,619	2,705	8,263
1986	30,828	18,919	2,987	8,922
1987	32,956	20,036	3,306	9,614
1988	28,246	15,961	2,878	9,407
1989	27,569	14,662	2,834	10,073
1990	26,142	14,303	2,808	9,031
1991	25,689	13,794	2,840	9,055
1992	23,581	13,154	2,520	7,907
1993	20,359	11,438	1,675	7,246
1994	18,840	10,303	1,711	6,826
1995	16,125	8,891	1,549	5,685
1996	14,331	7,862	1,435	5,034
1997	14,663	7,799	1,542	5,322
1998	15,473	8,236	1,392	5,845
1999	16,484	8,928	1,532	6,024
2000	17,991	8,979	1,268	7,744
2001	17,979	8,217	1,358	8,404
2002	20,546	10,424	1,633	8,489
2003 [E]	20,284	10,639	1,754	7,891
2004 [E]	22,118	11,655	2,058	8,405

Source: Office of Management and Budget, "Budget of the United States Government" (Annually).

MILITARY AIRCRAFT ACCEPTED BY U.S. MILITARY AGENCIES
Calendar Years 1988–2002

Year	TOTAL	Bomber/ Patrol/ Command/ Control	Fighter/ Attack	Trans- port/ Tanker	Trainer	Heli- copter	Other
NUMBER OF AIRCRAFT							
1988	842	55	509	31	—	247	—
1989	706	24	408	21	—	253	—
1990	763	24	454	25	—	260	—
1991	650	17	395	23	—	215	—
1992	544	10	312	30	37	155	—
1993	583	11	293	25	56	198	—
1994	487	6	167	40	114	157	3
1995	462	4	133	32	102	176	15
1996	348	4	116	28	54	146	—
1997	332	4	202	19	26	81	—
1998	324	10	188	30	33	63	—
1999	247	6	153	45	12	31	—
2000	180	2	82	30	33	33	—
2001 r	225	3	77	36	52	48	9
2002	281	4	84	28	57	90	18
FLYAWAY VALUE (Millions of Dollars)							
1988	$16,031	$2,911	$8,953	$2,314	$ —	$1,853	$ —
1989	11,968	1,423	7,735	743	—	2,067	—
1990	13,036	1,499	8,731	605	—	2,201	—
1991	11,754	1,023	8,517	437	—	1,777	—
1992	11,482	613	7,673	1,346	267	1,583	—
1993	12,101	1,530	6,400	1,553	484	2,134	—
1994	13,000	3,861	3,661	3,298	477	1,686	17
1995	12,369	3,585	3,547	2,759	460	1,922	98
1996	11,383	3,596	3,524	2,350	337	1,576	—
1997	10,945	1,921	5,653	2,336	270	766	—
1998	15,099	4,831	6,240	2,890	319	835	—
1999	10,731	415	6,164	3,588	219	345	—
2000	8,366	140	3,810	3,651	356	409	—
2001 r	8,334	218	4,026	2,962	376	691	61
2002	9,496	291	3,898	3,531	369	1,278	130

Source: Aerospace Industries Association, based on USAF, USA, and USN survey responses.
NOTE: Data represent new U.S.-manufactured aircraft, excluding gliders and targets. Values include spares, spare parts, and support equipment that are procured with the aircraft. Includes aircraft accepted for shipment to foreign governments for military assistance programs and foreign military sales.

MILITARY AIRCRAFT ACCEPTANCES BY UNITED STATES AIR FORCE[a]
Calendar Years 2001–2002
(Costs in Millions of Dollars)

Type and Model	Number of Aircraft		Flyaway Cost[b]		Weapon System Cost[c]	
	2001	2002	2001	2002	2001	2002
TOTAL	72[r]	96	$2,909[r]	$4,260	$3,661[r]	$5,351
Fighter/Attack—TOTAL	8[r]	21	$ 406[r]	$ 873	$ 520[r]	$1,294
F-15	—	3	—	121	—	140
F-16	5	13	123	280	123	491
F/A -22	3[r]	5	283[r]	472	398[r]	663
Transports/Tankers—TOTAL	18	16	2,330	3,150	2,920	3,761
C-17	10	16	1,930	3,150	2,250	3,761
C-37	2[d]	—	88	—	92	—
C-130 variants...................	6	—	312	—	578	—
Trainers—TOTAL	37	41	112	107	159	166
T-6.....................................	37	41	112	107	159	166
Other—TOTAL	9[r]	18	61[r]	130	61[r]	130
Predator	9[r]	18	61[Er]	130[E]	61[Er]	130[E]

Source: Aerospace Industries Association, based on USAF survey responses.
  a Air Force acceptances for own use; excludes FMS/MAP shipments.
  b Flyaway Cost includes airframe, engines, electronics, communications, armament, other installed equipment, and non-recurring costs associated with the manufacture of aircraft.
  c Weapon System Cost includes flyaway costs, peculiar ground equipment, training equipment, and technical data.
  d Under lease.

MILITARY AIRCRAFT ACCEPTANCES BY UNITED STATES ARMY[a]
Calendar Years 2001–2002
(Costs in Millions of Dollars)

Type and Model	Number of Aircraft		Flyaway Cost[b]		Weapon System Cost[c]	
	2001	2002	2001	2002	2001	2002
TOTAL	27[r]	32	$218[r]	$257	$255[r]	$320
Transports/Tankers—TOTAL	5[r]	2	$ 25[r]	$ 50	$ 25[r]	$ 50
C-37	—	1	—	43	—	43
UC-35	5[r]	1	25[r]	7	25[r]	7
Helicopters—TOTAL	22	30	193	207	230	270
TH-67	—	10	—	13	—	14
UH-60L	22	20	193	194	230	256

Source: Aerospace Industries Association, based on USA survey responses.

a Army acceptances for own use; excludes FMS/MAP shipments.
b Flyaway Cost includes airframes, engines, electronics, communications, armament and other installed equipment.
c Weapon System Cost includes flyaway cost, initial spares, ground equipment, training equipment and other support items.

MILITARY AIRCRAFT ACCEPTANCES BY UNITED STATES NAVY[a]
Calendar Years 2001–2002
(Costs in Millions of Dollars)

Type and Model	Number of Aircraft		Flyaway Cost[b]		Weapon System Cost[c]	
	2001	2002	2001	2002	2001	2002
TOTAL	97[r]	97	$4,410[r]	$3,925	$5,393[r]	$5,033
Patrol—TOTAL	3[r]	4	$ 218[r]	$ 291	$ 288[r]	$ 518
E-2..	3[r]	4	218[r]	291	288[r]	518
Fighter/Attack—TOTAL	50	55	3,075[r]	2,814	3,808[r]	3,560
AV-8B	14	15	287[r]	311	439[r]	383
F/A-18	36	40	2,788[r]	2,503	3,369[r]	3,176
Transports/Tankers—TOTAL	13[r]	6	606[r]	310	654[r]	343
C-37	—	1	—	43	—	50
C-40	4	2	199	107	207	108
KC-130....................................	7[r]	1	397[r]	65	436[r]	77
UC-35	2	1	10	7	12[r]	8
V-22	—	1	—	88	—	101
Trainers—TOTAL	15	16	264	262	307	313
T-6..	—	2	—	5	—	9
T-45A	15	14	264	256	307	304
Helicopters—TOTAL	16	16	247[r]	249	336[r]	299
MH-60S	16	16	247[r]	249	336[r]	299

Source: Aerospace Industries Association, based on USN survey responses.
  a Navy acceptances for own use; excludes FMS shipments.
  b Flyaway Cost includes airframe, engines, electronics, communications, armament, other installed equipment, non-recurring costs, and ancillary equipment.
  c Weapons System Cost (Investment Cost) includes flyaway cost, initial spares, ground equipment, training equipment, and other support items.

MILITARY AIRCRAFT ACCEPTANCES FOR REIMBURSABLE PROGRAMS[a]
Calendar Years 2001–2002
(Costs in Millions of Dollars)

Accepting Agency, Type, and Model	Number of Aircraft		Flyaway Cost[b]	
	2001	2002	2001	2002
TOTAL...................................	29[r]	56	$797[r]	$1,055
AIR FORCE—TOTAL	19	8	$546	$ 211
Fighter/Attack—TOTAL	19	8	546	211
F-16	19	8	546	211
ARMY—TOTAL	7[r]	48	$210[r]	$ 844
Helicopters—TOTAL	7[r]	44	210[r]	822
AH-64	—	14	—	300
CH-47	7[r]	7	210[r]	280
UH-60	—	23	—	242
Transports/Tankers—TOTAL	=	4	=	22
B200 (C-12)..........................	—	4	—	22
NAVY—TOTAL	3	—	$ 41	$ —
Helicopters—TOTAL	3	=	41	=
AH-1	3	—	41	—

Source: Aerospace Industries Association, based on USAF, USA, and USN survey responses.
  a Foreign government aircraft purchases through the Department of Defense Foreign Military Sales program.
  b Flyaway Cost includes airframes, engines, electronics, communications, armament, other installed equipment, and non-recurring costs associated with the manufacture of the aircraft.

MISSILE PROGRAMS

Sales of missile systems and parts reached a nine-year high in 2002, coming in at $7.7 billion. The Census Bureau also reported that new orders jumped 75%. The year-end 2002 backlog of unfilled orders stood at $11.0 billion.

DoD outlays for missile procurement fell in FY 2002. Despite the second highest level in five years at $5.2 billion, procurement spending remained much lower than in the late 1980s and early 1990s. Ballistic Missile Defense continued to dominate missile RDT&E. Funding totaled $6.9 billion in FY 2002 and is scheduled to increase to $7.7 billion in 2004.

Each service funded procurement in excess of $200 million for a few programs. For instance, the Air Force's largest program was the Joint Direct Attack Munition (JDAM) with $1.0 billion in combined USAF/USN funding. The joint procurement totaled 42,746 units, which use a low-cost Global Positioning System unit and some additional fins to turn a simple gravity bomb into a precision-guided munition. The Navy's Trident II, with $535 million of funding for 12 submarine-launched ballistic missiles, constituted its largest missile procurement program. The Army had two large programs: Javelin, a surface-to-surface anti-armor missile, with $409 million and Longbow Hellfire, a joint Army/Navy missile, with $238 million in combined funding. Finally, the BMDO funded the purchase of 72 Patriots with joint BMDO/Army money totaling $754 million.

Procurement of several smaller programs continued. The Air Force had five other missile procurements underway in FY 2002: 245 Advanced Medium Range Air-to-Air Missiles (AMRAAM) costing $137 million; 6,917 Wind-Corrected Munitions Dispensers (WCMD), $115 million; 270 Sensor-Fused Weapons (SFW), $109 million; 243 AIM-9X air-to-air missiles, $64 million; and 76 Joint Air-to-Surface Stand-off Missiles (JASSM), $43 million. The Navy had five other programs in active procurement including: 96 Standard missiles costing $155 million; 25 Tomahawk cruise missiles, $73 million; 90 Rolling Airframe Missiles, $46 million; 13 Evolved SeaSparrow Missiles (ESSM) for $41 million; and 30 Sea-Launched Attack Missile-Extended Range (SLAM-ER), $26 million. The Army bought 24 Army TACtical Missile Systems (ATACMS) for $76 million and 300 Stingers worth $29 million.

In FY 2003, five programs begin or return to unit procurement: 3,474 Army Multiple Launch Rocket System/Guided MLRS (MLRS/GMLRS) rockets costing $187 million; 28 Army HIgh Mobility Artillery Rocket System(s) (HIMARS) for $129 million; 183 joint Air Force/ Navy Joint Stand-Off Weapon(s) (JSOW) for $114 million; 445 Navy Short Range Attack Weapon(s) (SRAW) for $36 million; and 137 Air Force Predator Hellfires for $10 million.

ORDERS, SALES, AND BACKLOG OF MISSILE SYSTEMS AND PARTS[a]
Calendar Years 1988-2002
(Millions of Dollars)

Year	SALES—Current Dollars	SALES—Constant Dollars[b]
1988	$9,485	$ 9,345
1989	9,283	8,799
1990	9,102	8,381
1991	8,989	8,069
1992	9,032	7,726
1993	7,713	6,417
1994	5,294	4,315
1995	4,688	3,765
1996	4,792	3,782
1997	4,024	3,149
1998	4,356	3,390
1999	4,521	3,494
2000	5,567	4,176
2001 [r]	6,241	4,559
2002	7,679	5,540

Year	NET NEW ORDERS	BACKLOG AS OF DECEMBER 31
1988	$9,437	$14,255
1989	8,998	14,005
1990	7,917	12,956
1991	8,072	12,571
1992	9,234	11,814
1993	4,775	9,305
1994	2,785	5,823
1995	3,164	4,833
1996	8,672	6,563
1997	4,239	5,828
1998	4,884	6,539
1999	3,753	5,342
2000	9,738	9,389
2001 [r]	5,215	9,538
2002	9,128	10,998

Source: Bureau of the Census, "Aerospace Industry (Orders, Sales, and Backlog)" (Annually).
  a Excludes engines and propulsion units where separable.
  b Based on AIA's aerospace composite price deflator, 1987=100.

DEPARTMENT OF DEFENSE OUTLAYS FOR MISSILE PROCUREMENT BY AGENCY

Fiscal Years 1969–2004
(Millions of Dollars)

Year	TOTAL	Air Force	Army	Navy
1969	$ 2,509	$1,382	$ 593	$ 534
1970	2,912	1,467	743	702
1971	3,140	1,497	852	791
1972	3,009	1,334	844	831
1973	3,023	1,454	941	628
1974	2,981	1,537	903	541
1975	2,889	1,602	672	615
1976	2,296	1,549	163	584
Tr.Qtr.	402	347	(93)	148
1977	2,781	1,501	374	905
1978	3,096[a]	1,376	418	1,302[a]
1979	3,786	1,537	547	1,702
1980	4,434	1,810	651	1,973
1981	5,809	2,366	1,146	2,297
1982	6,782	3,069	1,269	2,444
1983	7,795	3,383	1,600	2,812
1984	9,527	4,640	2,079	2,809
1985	10,749	5,409	2,399	2,941
1986	11,731	6,473	2,478	2,780
1987	11,473	6,002	2,314	3,157
1988	11,676	6,046	2,239	3,392
1989	14,503	7,349	2,709	4,445
1990	14,851	7,951	2,453	4,446
1991	14,400	6,906	2,540	4,954
1992	13,504	6,409	2,401	4,694
1993	11,404	5,424	2,187	3,794
1994	8,934	4,312	1,384	3,238
1995	7,513	3,845	974	2,694
1996	6,199	3,235	919	2,045
1997	5,225	2,743	936	1,546
1998	4,907	2,543	964	1,400
1999	4,080	2,299	783	998
2000	4,231	2,243	926	1,062
2001	5,441	2,982	1,248	1,211
2002	5,230	2,719	1,256	1,255
2003[E]	5,200	2,702	1,282	1,216
2004[E]	5,889	3,391	1,127	1,371

Source: Office of Management and Budget, "The Budget of the United States Government" (Annually).

  a Beginning 1978, DoD combined Navy Missile Procurement with torpedoes and other related products into Navy Weapons Procurement. Missiles comprise approximately 80 percent of the value of this category.

MAJOR MISSILE PROGRAMS
IN RESEARCH, DEVELOPMENT, OR PRODUCTION
As of 2002

Program	Agency	Status	Systems Contractor	Propulsion Manufacturer	Guidance Manufacturer
AIR-TO-AIR					
AMRAAM-120B/C	USAF/USN	P	Raytheon	ATK	Raytheon/NGC
Sidewinder-9M	USN/USAF	P	NASC	ATK	Raytheon
Sidewinder-9X	USN/USAF	P	Raytheon	ATK	Raytheon
AIR-TO-SURFACE					
AGM-142	USAF	P	LM/Rafael	Rafael	NGC/BAE
EGBU 15	USAF	P	Raytheon	—	HI
GATS/GAM	USAF	P	NGC	—	Honeywell
HARM-88A/B	USN/USAF	P	Raytheon	ATK	Raytheon
*Harpoon-84A/C/ D/G	USN	P	Boeing	TCM/ATK	Ray/Kearfott/ IBM/LSI
*Harpoon-84L	USN	P	Boeing	TCM/ATK	HI/IBM/LSI/Ray/ Kearfott
JASSM	USN/USAF	D	LM	TCM	HI/BAE
JDAM	USAF/USN	D	Boeing	—	HI/Boeing
JSOW-154	USN/USAF	D	Raytheon	—	HI/Kearfott
Maverick-65D/G/H/K	USAF	P	Raytheon	ATK	Raytheon
Maverick-65F	USN	P	Raytheon	ATK	Raytheon
Maverick-65J	USN/USMC	D	Raytheon	ATK	Raytheon
Paveway-Enhanced	USN/USAF	P	Raytheon	—	Raytheon/HI
SLAM-ER-84H/K	USN	P	Boeing	TCM	Boeing/Ray/HI
Small Diameter Bomb	USAF	D	Boeing	—	HI
WCMD	USAF	P	LM	—	LM/BAE/HI
ANTI-SUBMARINE					
VLA-44A	USN	P	LM	ATK	LM
BATTLEFIELD SUPPORT AND ANTIARMOR					
ATACMS	Army	P	LM	ARC	Honeywell
BAT	Army	P	NGC	—	NGC/Ray/BAE
GMLRS	Army	D	LM	ARC	HI
HELLFIRE II-114K	Army/USMC	P	LM	ATK	LM
Longbow HELLFIRE 114L	Army	P	LM/NGC	ATK	LM/NGC/BAE
HELLFIRE-114M	USN/USMC	P	LM	ATK	LM
LOSAT	Army	D	LM	ATK	HI/ARC
Javelin	Army/USMC	P	Ray/LM	ARC	LM/Ray/BAE
MLRS-26	Army	P	LM	ARC	—
PGMM	Army	D	LM	—	HI/Draper
Predator	USMC	P	LM	ATK	LM
TOW2A-71E	Army	P	Raytheon	ATK	Raytheon
TOW2B-71F	Army	P	Raytheon	ATK	Raytheon

* Also Surface-to-Surface

(Continued on next page)

MAJOR MISSILE PROGRAMS
IN RESEARCH, DEVELOPMENT, OR PRODUCTION
As of 2002, continued

Program	Agency	Status	Systems Contractor	Propulsion Manufacturer	Guidance Manufacturer
SURFACE-TO-AIR					
GMD	Army	R,D	Boeing	ATK/UTC	Boeing/Aerojet
PAC-3	Army	P	LM	ARC	LM/HI/Boeing
RAM-116A	USN	P	Raytheon	ARC	Ray/RAMSYS
RAM-116B	USN	P	Raytheon	ARC	Ray/RAMSYS
SeaSparrow-7M	USN	P	Raytheon	ATK	Raytheon
SeaSparrow-Evolved	USN	D	Raytheon	ATK/Raufoss	Raytheon/HI
Standard 2 MR	USN	P	Raytheon	ARC	Raytheon/HI
Standard 2-IV	USN	P	Raytheon	ARC/UTC	Raytheon/HI
Standard 3	USN	D	Raytheon	ARC/UTC/ATK	Raytheon/HI
Stinger-92D/E	All	P	Raytheon	ARC	Raytheon/HI
THAAD	Army	D	LM	UTC/Boeing	LM/HI
SURFACE-TO-SURFACE					
Advanced Gun System	USN	D	LM	—	HI
Excalibur	USA	D	Raytheon	—	HI/L-3
*Harpoon-84A/C/D	USN	P	Boeing	TCM/ATK	Ray/IBM/LSI/HI/Kearfott
*Harpoon-84L	USN	D	Boeing	TCM/ATK	HI/IBM/LSI/Ray/Kearfott
Minuteman III	USAF	P	TRW	ATK/UTC/ARC	Boeing
NLOS-LS	USA	D	LM/Raytheon	Aerojet	LM/Raytheon
Tomahawk Tactical	USN	D	Raytheon	WI/ARC	Ray/HI
Trident 2 (D-5)	USN	P	LM	ATK/ARC	LM/Draper/Ray/Boeing/Kearfott

Source: Aerospace Industries Association, based on company reports.
Status: R-Research; D-Development; P-Production.
 * Also Air-to-Surface

Abb: ARC — Atlantic Research Corp. LSI — Lear Siegler Ray — Raytheon
 ATK — Alliant Techsystems LM — Lockheed Martin TCM — Teledyne Continental Motors
 BAE — BAE Systems NASC — Naval Air Systems Command UTC — United Technologies
 HI — Honeywell NGC — Northrop Grumman WI — Williams International

MISSILE PROGRAM PROCUREMENT[a]
Fiscal Years 2002, 2003, and 2004
(Costs in Millions of Dollars)

Agency and Model	2002		2003[E]		2004[E]	
	No.	Cost	No.	Cost	No.	Cost
AIR FORCE						
AIM-9X[b]	243	$ 64.2	570	$108.1	553	$104.9
AMRAAM[b]	245	136.7	258	137.9	254	142.8
JASSM	76	42.7	100	53.8	250	102.5
JDAM[b]	42,746	1,047.5	35,153	752.3	32,570	705.9
Predator Hellfire	—	—	137	9.9	280	23.1
SFW	270	108.5	310	124.1	294	117.8
WCMD	6,917	115.0	3,262	70.0	2,516	72.4
ARMY						
ATACMS	24	$ 75.6	16	$ 28.5	50	$ 50.3
Avenger	—	11.5	—	—	—	—
Longbow Hellfire	2,200	238.3	1,797	181.4	—	33.1
HIMARS	—	—	28	128.6	24	124.2
Javelin	4,139	408.7	1,478	219.2	901	104.7
LOSAT	—	—	—	—	76	43.2
MLRS/GMLRS	—	130.6	3,474	186.9	3,720	162.6
Stinger[d]	300	28.8	160	25.4	—	2.9
TOW 2	—	—	—	—	200	26.4
BMDO						
Patriot[f]	72	$ 754.4	100	$740.9	108	$774.2
NAVY						
ESSM	13	$ 41.3	23	$ 42.7	105	$112.8
JSOW[b]	—	4.2	183	113.5	754	218.5
RAM	90	46.4	90	64.1	90	48.3
SLAM-ER	30	25.7	120	82.2	84	54.1
SRAW/Predator	—	—	445	35.7	526	36.4
Standard	96	155.4	93	153.4	75	148.3
Tomahawk	25	73.0	167	244.1	267	277.6
Trident II	12	534.9	12	574.7	12	675.2

Source: Department of Defense, "Program Acquisition Costs by Weapon System" (Annually) and "Procurement Programs (P-1)" (Annually).
 a Total Obligational Authority excluding initial spares and RDT&E.
 b Navy and Air Force funding.
 c Army and Navy funding.
 d Army and Marine Corps funding.
 f Army and BMDO funding.

MISSILE PROGRAMS RESEARCH, DEVELOPMENT, TEST, AND EVALUATION[a] BY AGENCY AND MODEL
Fiscal Years 2002, 2003, and 2004
(Millions of Dollars)

Agency and Model	2002	2003[E]	2004[E]
AIR FORCE			
ACM/ALCM	$ 12.3	$ 22.7	$ 43.2
AMRAAM[b]	63.2	43.4	41.7
HIMARS	102.2	112.8	87.4
ICBM	44.4	62.1	67.6
JASSM[b]	85.7	65.6	56.3
Longbow Hellfire	17.6	13.0	10.0
WCMD	—	3.5	15.8
ARMY			
AAWS-M	$ 2.8	$ 0.5	$ 1.0
BAT (ATACMS)	106.9	42.9	55.1
LOSAT	24.8	13.6	30.8
MEADS	—	—	276.3
MLRS	101.6	94.6	84.8
Patriot	9.4	41.8	219.0
MDA			
BMD	$6,909.9	$6,718.9	$7,728.9
NAVY			
AIM-9X Sidewinder[b]	$ 24.8	$ 4.8	$ 2.7
HARM	31.0	60.3	49.4
JDAM[b]	75.3	64.0	67.1
JSOW	30.3	16.3	0.8
Standard	13.6	20.8	76.9
Tomahawk	72.6	97.4	71.4
Trident II	43.1	39.3	104.8

Source: Department of Defense Budget, "Program Acquisition Costs by Weapon System" (Annually) and "RDT&E Programs (R-1)" (Annually).
  a Total Obligational Authority.
  b Navy and Air Force funding.

Missile Program Acronyms:

AAWS-M	—Advanced Anti-tank Weapon System-Medium	ACM/ALCM	—Advanced & Air Launched Cruise Missile
AIM	—Air Intercept Missile	AMRAAM	—Advanced Medium Range Air-to-Air Missile
ATACMS	—Army TACtical Missile System	BAT	—Brilliant Anti-Tank submunition
BMD	—Ballistic Missile Defense	HARM	—High-speed Anti-Radiation Missile
HIMARS	—HIgh Mobility Artillery Rocket System	ICBM	—Inter-Continental Ballistic Missile
JASSM	—Joint Air-to-Surface Stand-off Missile	JDAM	—Joint Direct Attack Munition
JSOW	—Joint Stand-Off Weapon	LOSAT	—Line Of Sight Anti-Tank
MEADS	—Medium Extended Air Defense System	MRLS	—Multiple Launch Rocket Systems
SFW	—Sensor-Fused Weapon	WCMD	—Wind-Corrected Munitions Dispenser

BALLISTIC MISSILE DEFENSE FUNDING
Fiscal Years 2000-2004
(Millions of Dollars)

Category and Title	Program Element	2000	2001	2002	2003E	2004E
TOTAL		$4,711	$5,888	$7,775	$7,411	$8,743
BMDO Programs—TOTAL		$3,669	$4,755	$7,775	$7,411	$7,731
Procurement—TOTAL		$ 416	$ 444	$ 737	$ 492	$ —
TMD BMC3.............................	0208864C	—	4	—	—	—
PAC-3	0208865C	361	365	737	492	—
Navy Area	0208867C	55	—	—	—	—
National Missile Defense	0208871C	—	75	—	—	—
Military Construction—TOTAL		17	104	8	23	3
National Missile Defense	0603871C	17	104	—	—	—
BMD System	0603880C	—	—	8	—	—
Terminal	0603881C	—	—	1	23	—
BMD Test & Targets	0603888C	—	—	—	—	3
RDT&E—TOTAL		3,236	4,207	7,030	6,896	7,729
TMD—TOTAL..........................		1,830	1,653	1,101	1,211	—
THAAD System	0603861C	528	—	—	—	—
Navy Theater Wide...............	0603868C	420	463	—	—	—
MEADS	0603869C	49	53	—	118	—
Joint Theater Missile Defense	0603872C	201	—	—	—	—
THAAD System	0604861C	—	550	872	912	—
PAC-3	0604865C	181	81	129	181	—
Navy Area............................	0604867C	310	274	100	—	—
Family of Systems E&I	0603873C	142	231	—	—	—

(Continued on next page)

54

BALLISTIC MISSILE DEFENSE FUNDING
Fiscal Years 2000-2004, continued
(Millions of Dollars)

Category and Title	Program Element	2000	2001	2002	2003^E	2004^E
RDT&E (continued)						
NMD	0603871C	$ 852	$1,875	$ —	$ —	$ —
Support Technology/Applied Research	0602173C	84	40	—	—	—
Support Technology/Advanced Development	0603173C	214	122	—	—	—
Support Technology/Space Based Laser	0603174C	—	75	—	—	—
BMD Technology	0603175C	—	—	141	155	241
International Cooperative Programs	0603875C	37	125	—	—	—
BMD Technical Operations	0603874C	204	291	—	—	—
Threat and Countermeasures	0603876C	16	23	—	—	—
Advanced Concepts Evaluation & Systems	0603879C	—	—	—	—	152
BMD System	0603880C	—	—	819	1,073	—
Terminal Defense Segment	0603881C	—	—	203	140	810
Midcourse Defense Segment	0603882C	—	—	3,821	3,186	3,613
Boost Defense Segment	0603883C	—	—	609	737	626
Sensors Segment	0603884C	—	—	341	359	438
BMD System Interceptors	0603886C	—	—	—	—	301
BMD Test & Targets	0603888C	—	—	—	—	612
BMD Products	0603889C	—	—	—	—	344
BMD System Core	0603890C	—	—	—	—	484
Pentagon Reservation Maintenance Fund	0901585C	—	5	7	7	14
Headquarters Management	0901598C	—	—	28	28	93
BMD-Related Programs—TOTAL		$1,042	$1,133	$ —	$ —	$1,012
Air Force SBIR (SMTS)	0603441F	$ 229	$ —	$ —	$ —	$ —
Air Force SBIRS-High	0604441F	421	569	—	—	—
Air Force SBIRS-Low	0604442F	—	241	—	—	—
Air Force ABL	0603319F	309	234	—	—	—
Air Force SBL	0603876F	74	73	—	—	—
Army THEL	0602307A	10	16	—	—	—
Army PAC-3	C49200	—	—	—	—	562
Army PAC-3	0604865A	—	—	—	—	174
Army MEADS	0603869A	—	—	—	—	276

Source: Ballistic Missile Defense Organization.

SPACE PROGRAMS

Sales of space vehicle systems (including propulsion units) fell $1.9 billion in 2002 to $7.1 billion, according to figures compiled by the U.S. Census Bureau. Both military and civil sales declined—$1.2 billion and $0.8 billion, respectively.

Net new orders skyrocketed 47% to $10.7 billion solely on the strength of military orders. Civil orders declined 19% to $2.9 billion. The resulting backlog of unfilled orders rose $3.6 billion to $28 billion with a 46/54 split between military and civil work.

Federal outlays on space programs totaled $29 billion in FY 2002, with DoD accounting for $14.9 billion and NASA $13.4 billion. The federal government's space spending at all other agencies increased a combined $110 million to a total of $1.1 billion.

A variety of unclassified military space programs received funding in FY 2002. The Air Force led the majority of major DoD space programs, including: SBIRS-High, $525 million; Advanced EHF, $460 million; Wideband Gapfiller, $458 million; NAVSTAR GPS, $456 million; EELV, $322 million; Titan Launch Vehicles, $261 million; and Milstar, $226 million. The Army's DSCS received $118 million and the Navy's Sat Comm Systems and Mobile User Objective System (MOUS) programs received $235 million and $34 million, respectively. Of the above-mentioned programs, SBIRS-High, Advanced EHF, NAVSTAR GPS, Titan

Launch Vehicles, Sat Comm Systems, and MOUS are scheduled to receive increased funding in FY 2003.

Operating the Space Shuttle and building the International Space Station (ISS) dominated NASA's FY 2002 budget, accounting for 34% of NASA's $14.9 billion in budget authority for the year. The Station accounted for $1.7 billion while operating the Shuttle cost $3.3 billion, according to NASA budget summaries. Space science funding totaled $2.9 billion and aerospace technology received $2.5 billion. NASA's FY 2003 budget should total $15.0 billion. Program comparisons with prior year data are difficult due to NASA's conversion to full cost accounting. However, the Space Shuttle is budgeted for $3.8 billion; Space Science, $3.5 billion; and the ISS, $1.9 billion.

While the pace of launching has decreased from 2001 overall, European Space Agency flights rebounded and Israel and Japan logged launches after a hiatus for a number of years.

Orders for commercial geosynchronous (GEO) satellites plummeted in 2002, according to figures supplied by the Futron Corporation. The world's manufacturers received ten orders worth $1.0 billion in 2002—down from 25 worth $2.4 billion in 2001. The unfilled order backlog was estimated at 83 commercial GEO satellites worth $9.0 billion.

ORDERS, SALES, AND BACKLOG OF SPACE VEHICLE SYSTEMS[a]
Calendar Years 1988–2002
(Millions of Dollars)

Year	SALES—Current Dollars			SALES—Constant Dollars[b]		
	TOTAL	Military	Non-Military	TOTAL	Military	Non-Military
1988	$ 8,622	$6,190	$ 2,432	$ 8,495	$ 6,099	$ 2,396
1989	9,758	6,457	3,301	9,249	6,120	3,129
1990	9,691	6,556	3,135	8,924	6,037	2,887
1991	10,515	6,770	3,745	9,439	6,077	3,362
1992	9,266	5,887	3,379	7,926	5,036	2,891
1993	7,317	4,175	3,142	6,087	3,473	2,614
1994	10,594	5,707	4,887	8,634	4,651	3,983
1995	11,314	4,782	6,532	9,088	3,841	5,247
1996	11,698	5,613	6,085	9,233	4,430	4,803
1997	14,643	4,919	9,724	11,458	3,849	7,609
1998	9,491	4,227	5,264	7,396	3,289	4,096
1999	9,022	5,107	3,915	6,972	3,947	3,026
2000	8,164	3,723	4,441	6,125	2,793	3,332
2001[cr]	9,032	4,413	4,619	6,598	3,224	3,374
2002[c]	7,086	3,261	3,825	5,113	2,353	2,760

Year	NET NEW ORDERS			BACKLOG AS OF DECEMBER 31		
	TOTAL	Military	Non-Military	TOTAL	Military	Non-Military
1988	$ 7,296	$4,561	$ 2,735	$10,838	$ 7,880	$ 2,958
1989	11,709	8,107	3,602	13,356	9,192	4,164
1990	9,598	6,256	3,342	12,462	8,130	4,332
1991	11,222	5,468	5,754	11,664	6,221	5,443
1992	10,491	6,773	3,718	12,809	7,622	5,187
1993	8,436	5,106	3,330	13,663	7,384	6,279
1994	9,041	4,896	4,145	12,888	6,732	6,156
1995	13,212	4,679	8,533	15,650	5,872	9,778
1996	16,527	8,888	7,639	23,004	9,125	13,879
1997	15,078	4,584	10,494	23,189	8,848	14,341
1998	12,420	4,563	7,857	20,372	7,970	12,402
1999	11,175	7,912	3,263	22,356	10,666	11,690
2000	7,205	2,310	4,895	21,395	8,942	12,453
2001[cr]	7,267	3,719	3,548	24,425	8,355	16,070
2002[c]	10,717	7,843	2,874	27,988	12,923	15,065

Source: Bureau of the Census, "Aerospace Industry (Orders, Sales, and Backlog)" (Annually).
   a   Excludes engines and propulsion units where separable.
   b   Based on AIA's aerospace composite price deflator, 1987=100.
   c   Due to disclosure limitations, space propulsion units combined with space vehicle systems.

ORDERS, SALES, AND BACKLOG OF ENGINES AND PROPULSION UNITS FOR MISSILES AND SPACE VEHICLES
Calendar Years 1988–2002
(Millions of Dollars)

Year	SALES—Current Dollars			SALES—Constant Dollars[a]		
	TOTAL	Military	Non-Military	TOTAL	Military	Non-Military
1988	$3,407	$1,830	$1,577	$3,357	$1,803	$1,554
1989	3,602	1,771	1,831	3,414	1,679	1,736
1990	3,247	1,911	1,336	2,990	1,760	1,230
1991	3,807	1,869	1,938	3,417	1,678	1,740
1992	3,051	1,577	1,474	2,610	1,349	1,261
1993	3,104	1,619	1,485	2,582	1,347	1,235
1994	2,518	1,123	1,395	2,052	915	1,137
1995	2,364	1,035	1,329	1,899	831	1,067
1996	2,016	635	1,381	1,591	501	1,090
1997	2,687	558	2,129	2,103	437	1,666
1998	2,262	496	1,766	1,760	386	1,374
1999	2,118	525	1,593	1,637	406	1,231
2000	1,872	683	1,189	1,404	512	892
2001 [br]	239	239	—	175	175	—
2002 [b]	246	246	—	177	177	—

Year	NET NEW ORDERS			BACKLOG AS OF DECEMBER 31		
	TOTAL	Military	Non-Military	TOTAL	Military	Non-Military
1988	$3,507	$1,623	$1,884	$3,985	$1,998	$1,987
1989	6,113	2,475	3,638	6,410	2,595	3,815
1990	2,692	1,891	801	6,230	2,887	3,343
1991	5,661	1,087	4,574	8,422	2,327	6,095
1992	3,124	2,097	1,027	8,310	2,729	5,581
1993	1,708	710	998	6,543	1,903	4,640
1994	1,879	484	1,395	6,035	1,390	4,645
1995	2,805	444	2,361	6,630	1,065	5,565
1996	1,868	745	1,123	5,873	1,108	4,765
1997	2,009	477	1,532	5,568	1,023	4,545
1998	2,395	655	1,740	4,263	1,102	3,161
1999	3,896	687	3,209	6,182	1,017	5,165
2000	1,425	493	932	5,499	816	4,683
2001 [br]	245	245	—	486	486	—
2002 [b]	415	415	—	590	590	—

Source: Bureau of the Census, "Aerospace Industry (Orders, Sales, and Backlog)" (Annually).

a Based on AIA's aerospace composite price deflator, 1987=100.

b Due to disclosure limitations, space propulsion units combined with space vehicle systems. See page 58.

WORLDWIDE SPACE LAUNCHINGS[a]
WHICH ATTAINED EARTH ORBIT OR BEYOND
Calendar Years 1957–2002

Country	Total 1957-2002	1998	1999	2000	2001	2002[c]
TOTAL	5,242	80	74	82	66	46
U.S.S.R./C.I.S	3,680	25	29	36	31	15
United States	1,254	36	30	29	25	14
European Space Agency	149	11	10	12	8	11
People's Republic of China	66	6	4	5	1	2
Japan	56	2	—	—	—	2
India	13	—	1	—	1	1
Israel	4	—	—	—	—	1
Other[b]	20	—	—	—	—	—

Source: NASA, "Aeronautics and Space Report of the President" (Annually).
  a Number of launchings rather than spacecraft; some launches orbited multiple spacecraft.
  b Includes 10 by France, 8 by Italy (5 were U.S. spacecraft), 1 by Australia, and 1 by the United Kingdom.
  c Through September 30.

U.S. GOVERNMENT SPACECRAFT RECORD[a]
Calendar Years 1957–2002

Year	Earth Orbit[b] Success	Failure	Earth Escape[b] Success	Failure	Year	Earth Orbit[b] Success	Failure	Earth Escape[b] Success	Failure
1957	—	1	—	—	1982	21	—	—	—
1958	5	8	—	4	1983	31	—	—	—
1959	9	9	1	2	1984	35	3	—	—
1960	16	12	1	2	1985	37	1	—	—
1961	35	12	—	2	1986	11	4	—	—
1962	55	12	4	1	1987	9	1	—	—
1963	62	11	—	—	1988	16	1	—	—
1964	69	8	4	—	1989	24	—	2	—
1965	93	7	4	1	1990	40	—	1	—
1966	94	12	7	1[c]	1991	32[d]	—	—	—
1967	78	4	10	—	1992	26[d]	—	1	—
1968	61	15	3	—	1993	28[d]	1	1	—
1969	58	1	8	1	1994	31[d]	1	1	—
1970	36	1	3	—	1995	24[d]	2	1	—
1971	45	2	8	1	1996	30[d]	1	3	—
1972	33	2	8	—	1997	22	—	1	—
1973	23	2	3	—	1998	23	—	2	—
1974	27	2	1	—	1999	35	4	2	—
1975	30	4	4	—	2000	31	—	—	—
1976	33	—	1	—	2001	23	—	3	—
1977	27	2	2	—	2002[f]	14	—	—	1[c]
1978	34	2	7	—					
1979	18	—	—	—	TOTAL	1,520	153	97	16
1980	16	4	—	—					
1981	20	1	—	—					

Source: NASA, "Aeronautics and Space Report of the President" (Annually).
  a Payloads, rather than launchings; some launches account for multiple spacecraft. Includes spacecraft from cooperating countries launched on U.S. launch vehicles.
  b The criterion of success is attainment of Earth orbit or Earth escape rather than judgement of mission success. "Escape" flights include all that were intended to go at least an altitude equal to the lunar distance from the Earth.
  c This Earth-escape failure did attain Earth orbit and therefore is included in the Earth-orbit success totals.
  d Excludes commercial satellites.
  f Through September 30.

U.S. SPACE LAUNCH VEHICLES

As of 2002

Vehicle and Initial Launch & First Launch of This Modification	Stages	Thrust (Kilonewtons)	Maximum Payload (Kg)[a]		
			185-Km Orbit	Geosynch.-Transfer Orbit	Circular Sun-synch. Orbit
Athena (1995)	1. Athena*	1,450.0	520	245	—
Atlas E (1958; 1968)	1. Atlas MA-3	1,739.5	820[b] 1,860[bc]	—	910[c]
Atlas I (1966; 1990)	1. Atlas MA-5 2. 2 Centaur I	1,952.0 146.8	—	2,255	—
Atlas II (1966; 1991)	1. Atlas MA-5A 2. 2 Centaur II	2,110.0 146.8	6,580 5,510[b]	2,810	4,300
Atlas IIA (1966; 1992)	1. Atlas MA-5A 2. 2 Centaur II	2,110.0 185.1	6,828 6,170[b]	3,062	4,750
Atlas IIAS (1966; 1993)	1. Atlas MA-5A plus 4 Castor IV* 2. 2 Centaur II	2,110.0 1,734.4 185.1	8,640 7,300[b]	3,606	5,800
Delta II 7900 Series (1960; 1990)	1. RS-270/A plus 9 Hercules GEM* 2. AJ10-118K 3. Star 48B*	1,043.0 4,388.4 42.4 66.4	5,089 3,890[b]	1,842[d]	3,175
Delta III (1998)[f]	1. RS-27 plus 9 Alliant GEM* 2. RL-10B 3. Star 48B*	1,043.0 5,479.2 110.0 66.4	8,292	3,810	6,768
Pegasus (1990)	1. Orion 50S* 2. Orion 50* 3. Orion 38*	484.9 118.2 31.9	380 280[b]	—	210
Pegasus XL (1994)[f]	1. Orion 50S-XL* 2. Orion 50-XL* 3. Orion 38*	743.3 201.5 31.9	460 350[b]	—	335
Space Shuttle (reusable) (1981)	0. 3 main engines (SSMEs) fire in parallel with solid-fueled rocket boosters (SRBs) 1. 2 SRBs mounted on external tank (ET) fire in parallel with SSMEs 2. 2 OMS	5,006.1 23,580.0 53.4	24,900[g]	5,900[h]	—
Taurus (1994)	0. Castor 120* 1. Orion 50S* 2. Orion 50* 3. Orion 38*	1,687.7 580.5 138.6 31.9	1,400 1,080[b]	255	1,020

(Continued on next page)

U.S. SPACE LAUNCH VEHICLES
As of 2002, continued

Vehicle and Initial Launch & First Launch of This Modification	Stages	Thrust (Kilo-newtons)	Maximum Payload (Kg)[a]		
			185-Km Orbit	Geo-synch.-Transfer Orbit	Circular Sun-synch. Orbit
Titan II (1964; 1988)	1. 2 LR-87 2. LR-91	2,090.0 440.0	1,905[b]	—	—
Titan III (1964; 1989)	0. 2 5 1/2-segment, 3.05-m. dia* 1. 2 LR-87 2. LR-91	12,420.0 2,429.0 462.8	14,515	5,000[i]	—
Titan IV (1989)	0. 2 7-segment, 3.05-m. dia* 1. 2 LR-87 2. LR-91	14,000.0 2,429.0 462.8	17,700 14,110[b]	6,350[i]	—
Titan IV/Centaur (1994)	0. 2 7-segment, 4.3-m. dia* 1. 2 LR-87 2. LR-91 3. Centaur 4. SRMU	14,000.0 2,429.0 462.5 73.4 7,690.0	—	5,760	—

Source: NASA, "Aeronautics and Space Report of the President" (Annually).
* Solid propellant; all others are liquid.
a Due east launch except as indicated.
b Polar launch.
c With TE-M-364-4 upper stage.
d With Star 48B.
f First launch was a failure.
g In full performance configuration (280–420 km orbit).
h With IUS or TOS.
i With appropriate upper stage.

FEDERAL SPACE ACTIVITIES BUDGET AUTHORITY
Fiscal Years 1964-2003
(Millions of Dollars)

Year	TOTAL	NASA[a]	DoD	Commerce	Energy	Other[b]
1964	$ 6,828	$ 5,016	$ 1,599	$ 3	$210	$ —
1965	6,953	5,138	1,574	12	229	—
1966	6,968	5,065	1,689	27	187	—
1967	6,707	4,830	1,664	29	184	—
1968	6,526	4,430	1,922	28	145	1
1969	6,005	3,822	2,013	20	118	32
1970	5,366	3,547	1,678	8	103	30
1971	4,775	3,101	1,512	27	95	40
1972	4,611	3,071	1,407	31	55	47
1973	4,863	3,093	1,623	40	54	53
1974	4,683	2,759	1,766	60	42	56
1975	4,965	2,915	1,892	64	30	64
1976	5,376	3,225	1,983	72	23	73
Tr.Qtr.	1,352	849	460	22	5	16
1977	6,046	3,440	2,412	91	22	81
1978	6,587	3,623	2,738	103	34	89
1979	7,314	4,030	3,036	98	59	91
1980	8,759	4,680	3,848	93	40	98
1981	10,054	4,992	4,828	87	41	106
1982	12,520	5,528	6,679	145	61	107
1983	15,674	6,328	9,019	178	39	110
1984	17,448	6,858	10,195	236	34	125
1985	20,277	6,925	12,768	423	34	127
1986	21,768	7,165	14,126	309	35	133
1987	26,562	9,809	16,287	278	48	140
1988	26,742	8,322	17,679	352	241	148
1989	28,563	10,097	17,906	301	97	162
1990	27,582	11,460	15,616	243	79	184
1991	27,999	13,046	14,181	251	251	270
1992	29,020	13,199	15,023	327	223	248
1993	27,901	13,064	14,106	324	165	242
1994	26,820	13,022	13,166	312	74	246
1995	23,946	12,543	10,644	352	60	347
1996	24,911	12,569	11,514	472	46	310
1997	24,973	12,457	11,727	448	35	306
1998	25,519	12,321	12,359	435	103	301
1999	26,644	12,459	13,203	575	105	302
2000	26,518	12,521	12,941	575	164	317
2001	28,692	13,304	14,326	577	145	340
2002	30,791	13,871	15,740	644	166	370
2003[E]	33,954	14,224	18,448	647	184	431

Source: NASA, "Aeronautics and Space Report of the President" (Annually).
   a Excludes amounts for air transportation.
   b Departments of Interior, Transportation, and Agriculture, the National Science Foundation, and the Environmental Protection Agency.

FEDERAL SPACE ACTIVITIES OUTLAYS
Fiscal Years 1964-2002
(Millions of Dollars)

Year	TOTAL	NASA[a]	DoD	Commerce	Energy	Other[b]
1964	$ 5,930	$ 4,131	$ 1,564	$ 12	$220	$ 3
1965	6,886	5,035	1,592	24	232	3
1966	7,719	5,858	1,637	28	188	7
1967	7,237	5,337	1,673	39	184	5
1968	6,667	4,595	1,890	29	147	6
1969	6,326	4,078	2,095	31	118	5
1970	5,453	3,565	1,756	24	103	5
1971	4,999	3,171	1,693	30	97	8
1972	4,772	3,195	1,470	37	60	10
1973	4,719	3,069	1,557	29	51	13
1974	4,854	2,960	1,777	64	39	14
1975	4,891	2,951	1,831	64	34	11
1976	5,314	3,336	1,864	71	26	16
Tr.Qtr.	1,361	869	458	23	8	4
1977	5,559	3,600	1,833	87	22	18
1978	6,188	3,582	2,457	101	29	20
1979	6,808	3,744	2,892	97	55	21
1980	7,734	4,340	3,162	89	49	94
1981	9,238	4,877	4,131	81	47	102
1982	10,542	5,463	4,772	142	60	106
1983	12,668	6,101	6,247	178	40	103
1984	14,813	6,461	8,000	209	33	109
1985	17,353	6,607	10,441	155	34	115
1986	18,683	6,756	11,449	317	35	127
1987	21,948	7,254	14,264	262	37	130
1988	23,521	8,451	14,397	334	199	140
1989	25,255	10,195	14,504	306	97	153
1990	25,788	12,292	12,962	279	79	177
1991	28,484	13,351	14,432	266	251	184
1992	27,998	12,838	14,437	298	223	202
1993	27,537	13,092	13,779	295	165	206
1994	23,929	12,363	10,973	297	83	213
1995	24,700	12,593	11,494	330	70	213
1996	24,675	12,694	11,353	354	46	228
1997	25,620	13,055	11,959	336	37	233
1998	25,827	12,866	12,230	326	97	308
1999	25,771	12,466	12,453	431	103	318
2000	26,633	12,427	13,207	517	165	317
2001	27,226	13,197	13,046	525	143	315
2002	29,448	13,449	14,906	579	167	347

Source: NASA, "Aeronautics and Space Report of the President" (Annually).
   a Excludes amounts for air transportation.
   b Departments of Interior, Transportation, and Agriculture, the National Science Foundation, and the Environmental Protection Agency.

NATIONAL AERONAUTICS AND SPACE ADMINISTRATION
BUDGET AUTHORITY
Fiscal Years 1976-2004
(Millions of Dollars)

Year	TOTAL	Research and Development	Space Flight Control and Data Communications[a]	Contruction of Facilities	Research & Program Management[b]
1976	$ 3,552	$2,678	$ —	$ 82	$ 792
Tr.Qtr.	932	700	—	11	221
1977	3,819	2,856	—	118	845
1978	4,064	3,012	—	162	890
1979	4,559	3,477	—	148	934
1980	5,243	4,088	—	159	996
1981	5,522	4,334	—	117	1,071
1982	6,020	4,772	—	114	1,134
1983	6,875	5,539	—	139	1,197
1984	7,316	2,064[a]	3,772	223	1,256
1985	7,573	2,468	3,594	178	1,332
1986	7,807	2,619	3,670	176	1,342
1987	10,923	3,154	6,100	217	1,453
1988	9,062	3,280	3,806	213	1,763
1989	10,969	4,213	4,555	275	1,927
1990	12,324	5,225	4,645	218	2,023
1991	14,016	6,024	5,271	498	2,212
1992	14,317	6,848	5,352	525	1,576
1993	14,310	7,074	5,059	526	1,652
1994	14,570	7,534	4,835	493	1,708

Year	TOTAL	Science, Aeronautics, & Technology	Human Space Flight	Other[b]	Mission Support
1995[c]	$13,854	$5,936	$5,515	$(130)	$2,533
1996	13,886	5,929	5,457	17	2,483
1997	13,711	5,590	5,540	19	2,562
1998	13,649	5,690	5,560	19	2,380
1999	13,655	5,654	5,480	21	2,500
2000	13,602	5,582	5,488	21	2,511
2001	14,361	6,235	5,496	28	2,602
2002[d]	14,893	8,095	6,773	25	—
2003[E]	15,001	8,844	6,131	26	—

Year	TOTAL	Science, Aeronautics, & Exploration	Space Flight Capabilities	Other[b]	Mission Support
2004[E]	$15,470	$7,661	$7,782	$ 27	$ —

Source: Office of Management and Budget, "Budget of the United States Government" (Annually).
   a   Separate budget category beginning in 1984; funds formerly included under Research and Development.
   b   Includes trust funds, Office of the Inspector General, National Space Grant Program, & GSA building delegation.
   c   1995 features major budget account restructuring.
   d   Mission Support, as a separate category, discontinued; funds merged into other categories.

NATIONAL AERONAUTICS AND SPACE ADMINISTRATION OUTLAYS
Fiscal Years 1985-2004
(Millions of Dollars)

Year	TOTAL	Research and Development	Space Flight Control and Data Communications[a]	Contruction of Facilities	Research & Program Management[b]
1985	$ 7,318	$2,118	$3,707	$170	$1,323
1986	7,404	2,615	3,267	189	1,332
1987	7,591	2,436	3,597	149	1,409
1988	9,092	2,916	4,362	166	1,648
1989	11,052	3,922	5,030	190	1,909
1990	12,429	5,094	5,117	218	2,000
1991	13,878	5,765	5,590	326	2,196
1992	13,961	6,579	5,118	463	1,802
1993	14,305	7,086	5,025	557	1,638
1994	13,695	6,758	4,899	371	1,666
1995[c]	5,098	3,286	1,409	305	98
1996[c]	1,022	510	241	265	6
1997[c]	317	101	92	122	2
1998[c]	138	40	34	64	—
1999[c]	47	18	2	27	—
2000[c]	31	18	1	12	—

Year	TOTAL	Science, Aeronautics, & Technology	Human Space Flight	Other[b]	Mission Support
1995[c]	$ 8,280	$2,708	$3,528	$ 15	$2,029
1996[c]	12,858	5,017	5,452	16	2,373
1997[c]	14,043	5,891	5,656	19	2,477
1998[c]	14,068	6,015	5,551	19	2,483
1999[c]	13,617	5,785	5,417	20	2,395
2000[c]	13,411	5,477	5,497	21	2,416
2001[d]	14,199	5,752	5,829	32	2,586
2002[f]	14,430	7,532	6,337	27	534
2003[Ef]	14,599	8,275	6,150	29	145
2004[Efg]	5,958	4,048	1,821	—	89

Year	TOTAL	Science, Aeronautics, & Exploration	Space Flight Capabilities	Other[b]	Mission Support
2004[Eg]	$ 9,297	$3,985	$5,285	$ 27	$ —

Source: Office of Management and Budget, "Budget of the United States Government" (Annually).
  a Separate budget category beginning in 1984; funds formerly included under Research and Development.
  b Includes trust funds, Office of Inspector General, National Space Grant Program, & GSA building delegation.
  c 1995 featured major budget account restructuring. Note: 1995–2000 outlays split between old and new account structure.
  d Continuing minimal outlays reported under old account structure included under Other beginning in 2001.
  f Mission Support, as a separate category, is being discontinued; funds merged into other categories.
  g 2004 featured another budget account restructuring. 2004 outlays split between old and new account structure.

NATIONAL AERONAUTICS AND SPACE ADMINISTRATION
BUDGET AUTHORITY BY MAJOR BUDGET ACCOUNT
FOR SELECTED PROGRAMS
Fiscal Years 2002-2004
(Millions of Dollars)

	2002	2003ᴱ	2004ᴱ
TOTAL	$14,902	$15,000	$15,469
HUMAN SPACE FLIGHT/			
SPACE FLIGHT CAPABILITIES	$ 6,830	$ 7,875	$ 7,782
International Space Station	$ 1,722	$ 1,851	$ 1,707
Space Shuttle	3,273	3,786	3,968
Space Flight Support	NA	471	434
Space Launch Initiative	NA	1,150	1,065
Mission & Science Measurement Tech.	NA	434	438
Innovative Tech. Transfer Partnerships	NA	183	169
Payload & ELV Support	91	NA	NA
Investments and Support	1,215	NA	NA
Space Communications & Data Systems	482	NA	NA
Safety, Mission Assurance, & Engineering	48	NA	NA
SCIENCE, AERONAUTICS, & TECHNOLOGY/			
SCIENCE, AERONAUTICS, & EXPLORATION	$ 8,048	$ 7,101	$ 7,661
Space Science	$ 2,867	$ 3,468	$ 4,007
Biological & Physical Research	820	913	973
Earth Science	1,626	1,610	1,552
Aeronautics Technology	NA	949	959
Education	NA	160	170
Aerospace Technology	2,508	NA	NA
Academic Programs	227	NA	NA
INSPECTOR GENERAL	$ 24	$ 25	$ 26

Source: NASA.

DEPARTMENT OF DEFENSE SPACE PROGRAMS
PROCUREMENT[a] AND RDT&E
Fiscal Years 2002, 2003, and 2004
(Millions of Dollars)

Agency and Program	2002		2003E		2004E	
	Pro-cure-ment	RDT&E	Pro-cure-ment	RDT&E	Pro-cure-ment	RDT&E
AIR FORCE						
Advanced EHF	$ —	$ 459.6	$ —	$822.5	$ —	$778.1
Defense Satellite Comm Sys	28.0	3.6	20.5	2.0	12.5	—
Defense Space Reconn Pgm	—	44.8	281.6	41.6	292.0	232.3
Defense Support Program	97.6	5.9	113.5	2.0	113.1	—
DMSP	42.6	12.8	59.6	3.8	68.0	0.9
EELV	—	321.8	165.6	57.0	609.3	8.0
Medium Launch Vehicles	39.3	—	47.8	—	91.1	—
MilSat Com, Polar	—	21.4	—	19.3	—	6.6
Milstar	—	226.4	—	147.8	—	1.4
NAVSTAR GPS	161.9	294.4	226.4	426.2	258.8	247.1
NPOESS	—	145.6	—	232.1	—	267.7
NUDET Detection System	18.2	21.4	—	20.9	—	35.8
Satellite Control Network	28.3	47.4	44.6	16.8	48.2	18.6
SBIRS-High	—	524.5	—	775.4	95.4	617.2
Space-Based Radar	—	70.2	—	274.1	—	358.7
Spacelift Range System	128.4	65.6	102.4	85.5	80.6	63.2
Titan Launch Vehicles	244.3	16.9	288.7	—	91.5	—
Wideband Gapfiller	361.2	96.4	188.2	13.8	34.6	36.7
ARMY						
DSCS	$104.8	$ 12.7	$ 87.4	$ 11.6	$ 98.3	$ 13.5
NAVY						
Fleet Sat Comm	$ 76.8	$ NA	$ —	$ NA	$ —	$ NA
MUOS	—	34.4	—	59.0	—	315.8
Sat Comm Systems	180.1	54.7	131.8	113.0	257.4	379.5

Source: Department of Defense, "Program Acquisition Costs by Weapon System" (Annually) and "Procurement Programs (P-1)" (Annually).

  a Total Obligational Authority for procurement including initial spares.
  b Air Force and BMDO funding.
  c Army and Air Force funding.

KEY: DMSP   = Defense Meteorological Satellite Program
       DSCS   = Defense Satellite Communications System
       EELV   = Evolved Expendable Launch Vehicle
       EHF   = Extremely High Frequency
       GPS   = Global Positioning System
       MUOS   = Mobile User Objective System
       NPOESS = National Polar-orbiting Operational Environmental Satellite System
       SBIRS   = Space-Based InfraRed System

ORDERS AND BACKLOG OF COMMERCIAL GEOSYNCHRONOUS SATELLITES BY MANUFACTURER[a]

Calendar Years 1998–2002

	1998	1999	2000	2001	2002
ORDERS					
Value[b] (Millions of Dollars)...........	$2,247	$1,847	$3,287	$2,380	$1,010
Number of Satellites—TOTAL ...	19	16	31	25	10
Alcatel	1	2	6	2	2
Alenia Aerospazio	—	—	1	—	—
Astrium	1	1	6	2	2
Boeing Satellite Systems	11	7	4	5	1
Chinese Academy of Space Technology	—	—	—	—	2
Israel Aircraft Industries.............	—	—	—	1	—
Lockheed Martin Commercial Space Systems	4	3	2	5	2
NPO PM	—	—	3	—	—
Orbital Sciences	—	2	—	4	1
Space Systems Loral	2	1	9	6	—
BACKLOG[c]					
Value[b] (Millions of Dollars)...........	$7,034	$7,884	$9,311	$9,235	$9,039
Number of Satellites—TOTAL ...	62	67	80	84	83
Alcatel	8	9	12	13	13
Alenia Aerospazio	—	—	1	1	1
Astrium	5	3	9	8	10
Boeing Satellite Systems	23	24	23	19	16
Chinese Academy of Space Technology	—	—	—	—	2
Israel Aircraft Industries.............	—	—	—	1	1
Lockheed Martin Commercial Space Systems	11	13	10	10	11
NPO PM	—	—	3	3	3
Orbital Sciences	—	2	2	6	5
Space Systems Loral	15	16	20	23	21

Source: Futron Corporation.
    a Excludes canceled orders and orders on hold, without firm funding or business commitment, or with extended construction delay.
    b Estimated using best available public information; where not available, used Futron estimates.
    c Includes satellites on order during year and may include satellites that have been launched.

ORDERS AND BACKLOG OF COMMERCIAL LAUNCHES BY PROVIDER-COUNTRY
Calendar Years 1998–2002

	1998	1999	2000	2001	2002
ORDERS—TOTAL	20	28	38	35	21
China	2	1	—	—	—
India	—	—	—	—	—
Japan	—	—	—	—	—
Russia	2	9	—	5	5
United States	2	6	17	15	5
Europe	14	12	16	13	10
Other multinational[a]	—	—	5	2	1
BACKLOG—TOTAL	140	141	129	163	155
China	6	7	7	7	7[E]
India	—	—	—	—	—
Japan	8	8	—	—	—
Russia	4	13	13	18	15
United States	58	55	47	68	60
Europe	46	40	46	53	55
Other multinational[a]	18	18	16	17	18

Source: Futron Corporation.
  a Sea Launch.

71

AIR TRANSPORTATION

The world's airlines suffered another disastrous year in 2002, posting near-record losses and declining passenger traffic. Operating losses improved by $4.5 billion from a $12 billion loss in 2001 to a $7 billion loss! Taking into account non-operating expenses such as interest and taxes, the industry's net loss totaled $12 billion, or -3.7% of revenue, down from a $13 billion loss. International Civil Aviation Organization statistics show that the airlines carried nine million less passengers in 2002; but flew seven million more passenger-miles. Load factors rose too to historic high levels, reflecting airlines' adjustment to lower traffic by grounding aircraft.

The United States and U.S. airlines lie at the epicenter of this downturn. Enplanements fell by nine million, passenger revenue ton-miles fell again (by 1.6%), and operating losses totaled $8.6 billion. Operating expenses decreased 8.3% or $10.4 billion as carriers matched capacity to traffic and otherwise cut costs. Fuel prices, which remain high, have fallen 6% or 4.6 cents per gallon. Fuel cost as a percentage of cash operating expenses fell from 13% to 12% or $2.2 billion, according to data from the Air Transport Association of America. Consequently, U.S. scheduled airline operating losses declined somewhat—falling $1.8 billion from $10.3 billion in 2001 to $8.6 billion in 2002. Despite this improvement, 2002's losses exceeded the combined losses posted in the 1990–1992 downturn.

The world's turbine-engined airline fleet continued to grow in 2002, albeit by fewer than recent years, reaching 26,112 aircraft in service according to Air BP's "Turbine-Engined Fleets of the World's Airlines." While the number of jets increased from 17,291 to 17,609, the numbers of turboprops and helicopters declined. Among the jet aircraft fleet, the number of Boeing 727s fell by 155 to 922 and DC-9s fell by 89 to 538. Approximately 20% of the DC-10s left the fleet. Perhaps not too surprisingly, smaller aircraft models lead the unit growth: the Airbus A320 family (A319/A320/A321) grew by 202 to 1,809; Boeing's 737s grew by 147 to 3,814; but regional jet manufacturers showed both large unit gains and large percentage increases. In particular, Canadair RJ grew by 176 or 31% and Embraer ERJ family grew by 119 or 24%.

The number of installed turbojet engines grew by 425 to 44,375 in 2002. Accounting for the growth: CFM International engines increased 645; General Electric, 324; International Aero Engines, 193; "Other", 70; and Rolls-Royce, 69. The number of Pratt & Whitney engines declined by 876 to 13,910. Pratt & Whitney retains the dominant share with 31.3% of the installed turbine engines in the world's airline fleet.

Based on the latest available data, the number of hours flown by general aviation aircraft in the United States decreased by 5.9% to 29 million in 2001. Similarly, the number of active general aviation aircraft also decreased. However, since the enactment of the General Aviation Revitalization Act of 1994, the number of active single-engine aircraft has increased 18,200 to approximately 146,000 despite the decline of the last two years.

73

OPERATING REVENUES, EXPENSES, AND RESULTS
OF WORLD SCHEDULED AIRLINES
Calendar Years 1999–2002
(Millions of Dollars)

	1999	2000	2001	2002[p]
OPERATING REVENUES:				
Scheduled Services:				
Passenger	$231,410	$248,940	$232,410	
Freight	30,400	33,840	32,990	
Mail	2,240	2,140	2,150	
				NA
Scheduled Services—Total	$264,050	$284,920	$267,550	
Non-Scheduled Services	11,440	11,710[r]	10,470	
Incidental	30,010	31,870[r]	29,480	
Operating Revenues—Total	$305,500	$328,500	$307,500	$312,500
OPERATING EXPENSES:				
Flight Operations	$82,240	$98,790	$ 97,020	
Maintenance & Overhaul	31,670	33,710	36,120	
Depreciation & Amortization	19,280	20,780	22,670	
User Charges & Station				NA
Expenses	51,760	54,720	54,000	
Passenger Services	31,520	31,780	32,670	
Ticketing, Sales & Promotion	40,130	40,450	35,650	
General, Administrative & Other	36,600	37,570	41,170	
Operating Expenses—Total	$293,200	$317,800	$319,300	$319,800
OPERATING RESULT	$ 12,300	$ 10,700	($ 11,800)	($ 7,300)
Percent of Revenue	4.0%	3.3%	−3.8%	−2.3%
NET RESULT[a]	$ 8,500	$ 3,700	($ 13,000)	($ 11,700)
Percent of Revenue	2.8%	1.1%	−4.2%	−3.7%

Source: International Civil Aviation Organization, "Civil Aviation Statistics of the World" (Annually).

a Net Result equals Operating Result minus non-operating items, including interest, income taxes, retirement of property and equipment, affiliated companies, and subsidies.

OPERATING REVENUES AND EXPENSES OF U.S. AIR CARRIERS[a]
DOMESTIC AND INTERNATIONAL OPERATIONS
Calendar Years 1968–2002
(Millions of Dollars)

Year	TOTAL			Domestic Operations			International Operations		
	Operating Revenues	Operating Expenses	Operating Profit (or Loss)	Operating Revenues	Operating Expenses	Operating Profit (or Loss)	Operating Revenues	Operating Expenses	Operating Profit (or Loss)
1968	$ 7,753	$ 7,248	$ 505	$ 5,691	$ 5,397	$ 295	$ 2,062	$ 1,852	$ 210
1969	8,791	8,403	387	6,936	6,613	322	1,855	1,790	65
1970	9,290	9,247	43	7,180	7,181	(1)	2,109	2,066	44
1971	10,046	9,717	328	7,753	7,496	257	2,292	2,221	71
1972	11,163	10,578	584	8,652	8,158	493	2,512	2,420	91
1973	12,419	11,834	585	9,694	9,200	494	2,725	2,633	91
1974	14,703	13,978	725	11,546	10,761	785	3,157	3,218	(60)
1975	15,356	15,229	128	12,020	11,903	117	3,336	3,326	11
1976	17,503	16,781	721	13,899	13,324	575	3,605	3,457	147
1977	19,926	19,018	908	15,822	15,166	657	4,104	3,852	252
1978	22,892	21,527	1,366	18,189	17,172	1,018	4,703	4,355	348
1979	27,227	27,028	199	21,652	21,523	129	5,575	5,505	69
1980	33,728	33,949	(222)	26,404	26,409	(6)	6,543	6,766	(223)
1981	36,211	36,612	(401)	28,788	29,051	(264)	6,390	6,574	(184)
1982	36,066	36,804	(739)	28,728	29,478	(750)	6,435	6,452	(17)
1983	38,593	38,231	362	31,014	31,186	(171)	7,163	6,693	470
1984	44,060	41,946	2,114	35,394	33,812	1,582	7,975	7,485	490
1985	48,580	47,207	1,372	37,629	36,611	1,018	8,302	7,984	319
1986	50,086	48,855	1,231	41,001	39,984	1,060	8,621	8,458	163
1987	56,787	54,339	2,448	45,658	43,925	1,733	10,925	10,226	698
1988	63,679	60,236	3,443	50,187	47,739	2,448	13,402	12,403	998
1989	69,225	67,413	1,812	54,314	52,460	1,855	14,911	14,954	(43)
1990	75,984	77,898	(1,913)	57,994	58,983	(989)	17,990	18,914	(924)
1991	75,158	76,943	(1,785)	56,230	56,758	(528)	18,928	20,185	(1,257)
1992	78,140	80,585	(2,444)	57,654	58,801	(1,147)	20,486	21,784	(1,298)
1993	84,559	83,121	1,438	63,233	61,157	2,076	21,326	21,964	(637)
1994	88,313	85,600	2,713	65,949	63,758	2,191	22,364	21,842	522
1995	94,318	88,455	5,863	70,885	66,120	4,765	23,433	22,335	1,098
1996	101,937	95,728	6,209	76,891	71,573	5,317	25,047	24,155	892
1997	109,568	100,981	8,587	82,250	75,731	6,518	27,318	25,250	2,068
1998	113,465	104,137	9,328	86,494	78,389	8,105	26,971	25,749	1,223
1999	119,038	110,635	8,403	90,931	84,328	6,603	28,107	26,307	1,800
2000	130,299	123,314	6,985	98,896	93,579	5,317	31,403	29,736	1,668
2001	115,227	125,550	(10,323)	86,511	94,892	(8,380)	28,716	30,658	(1,943)
2002[p]	106,609	115,176	(8,567)	79,131	86,592	(7,462)	27,479	28,584	(1,105)

Source: Department of Transportation, Office of Airline Information, "Air Carrier Financial Statistics Quarterly" (Quarterly).
a Scheduled and non-scheduled service for all certificated route air carriers. Excludes supplemental air carriers, commuters, and air taxis.

SOURCES OF OPERATING REVENUES OF U.S. AIR CARRIERS[a]
DOMESTIC AND INTERNATIONAL OPERATIONS
Calendar Years 1988–2002
(Millions of Dollars)

Year	TOTAL	Passenger Service[b]	Mail	Freight[b] & Air Express	Excess Baggage	Other[c]
DOMESTIC OPERATIONS						
1988	$50,187	$41,002	$ 789	$5,807	$ 72	$ 2,518
1989	54,314	43,670	767	5,408	70	4,399
1990	57,994	46,282	747	4,276	76	6,613
1991	56,230	44,594	734	4,487	78	6,337
1992	57,654	45,246	937	4,655	87	6,729
1993	63,233	49,289	974	5,266	91	7,612
1994	65,949	50,504	971	5,844	98	8,531
1995	70,885	53,971	1,050	6,546	92	9,227
1996	76,891	59,381	1,024	7,029	94	9,362
1997	82,250	62,549	1,087	7,497	99	11,017
1998	86,494	64,847	1,423	7,711	105	12,408
1999	90,931	67,777	1,475	8,053	118	13,509
2000	98,896	74,744	1,688	8,804	123	13,537
2001	86,511	64,324	824	8,170	111	13,082
2002[p]	79,131	57,782	430	8,139	133	12,647
INTERNATIONAL OPERATIONS						
1988	$13,402	$10,357	$ 183	$2,150	$ 39	$ 672
1989	14,911	11,181	188	2,417	47	1,078
1990	17,990	13,468	223	2,602	43	1,654
1991	18,928	14,103	223	3,134	50	1,419
1992	20,486	15,664	247	2,980	47	1,547
1993	21,326	15,915	237	3,220	49	1,905
1994	22,364	16,300	212	3,606	46	2,201
1995	23,433	16,788	216	3,994	48	2,387
1996	25,047	17,337	255	4,664	47	2,743
1997	27,318	18,320	275	5,156	56	3,511
1998	26,971	17,667	285	5,278	50	3,692
1999	28,107	18,011	264	5,921	46	3,865
2000	31,403	20,419	283	6,566	47	4,089
2001	28,716	18,227	240	6,444	42	3,763
2002[p]	27,479	17,089	228	7,122	48	2,992

Source: Department of Transportation, Office of Airline Information, "Air Carrier Financial Statistics Quarterly" (Quarterly).
 a Scheduled and non-scheduled service for all certificated route air carriers. Excludes supplemental air carriers, commuters, and air taxis.
 b Scheduled and charter.
 c Includes subsidy, reservation cancellation fees, miscellaneous operating revenues, and other transport-related revenues.

OPERATING EXPENSES OF U.S. AIR CARRIERS[a]
DOMESTIC AND INTERNATIONAL OPERATIONS
Calendar Years 1988–2002
(Millions of Dollars)

Year	TOTAL	Flying Opera- tions	Mainte- nance	Passen- ger Service	Aircraft & Traffic Ser- vicing	Promo- tion and Sales	Depreci- ation & Amorti zation	Other[b]
DOMESTIC OPERATIONS								
1988	$47,739	$13,176	$ 5,643	$4,444	$ 9,527	$ 8,235	$2,977	$ 3,737
1989	52,460	14,749	6,184	4,775	9,449	8,718	3,078	5,507
1990	58,983	18,166	6,921	5,220	9,094	9,102	3,273	7,207
1991	56,758	16,831	6,682	5,068	9,140	8,856	3,217	6,964
1992	58,801	17,203	6,884	5,327	9,783	8,936	3,340	7,328
1993	61,157	17,622	7,025	5,241	10,172	9,387	3,621	8,089
1994	63,758	17,912	7,312	5,305	10,543	9,882	3,782	9,023
1995	66,120	18,926	7,656	5,281	11,103	9,974	3,762	9,417
1996	71,573	21,515	8,292	5,577	11,569	10,414	3,878	10,328
1997	75,731	22,156	9,475	5,854	12,058	10,780	3,940	11,469
1998	78,389	21,044	10,311	6,252	12,699	10,743	4,144	13,195
1999	84,328	22,820	11,161	6,763	13,796	10,760	4,657	14,372
2000	93,579	28,565	12,062	7,355	14,827	10,089	5,122	15,558
2001	94,892	27,908	12,113	7,219	15,390	8,949	6,230	17,081
2002[p]	86,592	25,791	11,049	7,087	14,892	6,726	4,988	16,060
INTERNATIONAL OPERATIONS								
1988	$12,403	$ 3,230	$ 1,332	$1,280	$ 2,193	$ 2,742	$ 618	$ 1,009
1989	14,954	3,919	1,724	1,454	2,483	3,108	746	1,520
1990	18,878	5,454	2,051	1,738	2,657	3,833	887	2,295
1991	20,185	5,636	2,152	1,861	2,831	4,602	892	2,210
1992	21,784	5,843	2,148	2,204	3,255	5,229	1,033	2,073
1993	21,964	5,928	1,967	2,175	3,072	5,339	1,077	2,406
1994	21,842	5,842	2,064	2,311	3,336	4,335	1,237	2,716
1995	22,335	6,181	2,273	2,467	3,748	3,527	1,106	3,033
1996	24,155	7,279	2,616	2,596	3,736	3,354	1,483	3,091
1997	25,250	7,462	2,899	2,736	3,823	3,476	1,281	3,571
1998	25,749	7,158	2,955	2,920	3,978	3,374	1,438	3,926
1999	26,307	7,472	2,902	3,067	4,207	3,201	1,614	3,845
2000	29,736	9,504	3,093	3,211	4,565	3,282	1,751	4,329
2001	30,658	9,652	3,196	3,254	4,599	2,828	2,168	4,960
2002[p]	28,584	9,179	3,125	3,100	4,586	2,239	1,925	4,430

Source: Department of Transportation, Office of Airline Information, "Air Carrier Financial Statistics Quarterly" (Quarterly).
  a Scheduled and non-scheduled service for all certificated route air carriers. Excludes supplemental air carriers, commuters, and air taxis.
  b General and administrative and other transport-related expenses.

JET FUEL COSTS AND CONSUMPTION BY U.S. AIR CARRIERS[ar]
Calendar Years 1971–2002

Year	Total Jet Fuel Cost (Millions of Dollars)	Gallons Consumed (Millions)	Cost Per Gallon (Cents)	Cost Index (1982 = 100)	Cost of Fuel as Percent of Cash Operating Expenses
1971	$ 1,121.1	9,836.5	11.4 ¢	11.4	11.8%
1972	1,163.9	9,979.2	11.7	11.7	11.2
1973	1,337.3	10,489.5	12.7	12.8	11.4
1974	2,341.2	9,377.3	25.0	25.1	16.7
1975	2,783.3	9,312.5	29.9	30.0	18.3
1976	3,117.4	9,631.6	32.4	32.5	18.7
1977	3,740.6	10,063.4	37.2	37.3	19.7
1978	4,178.6	10,352.2	40.4	40.5	19.5
1979	6,491.7	11,032.5	58.8	59.1	23.8
1980	9,739.7	10,630.2	91.6	92.0	29.7
1981	10,494.2	9,838.7	106.7	107.1	29.6
1982	9,695.9	9,737.4	99.6	100.0	27.2
1983	9,006.7	10,225.3	88.1	88.5	24.5
1984	9,324.1	11,182.5	83.4	83.7	23.4
1985	9,352.7	10,324.9	90.6	91.0	21.7
1986	7,054.9	10,722.0	65.8	66.1	15.9
1987	7,607.5	11,542.2	65.9	66.2	15.5
1988	7,551.6	12,059.4	62.6	62.9	14.0
1989	8,572.7	14,255.4	60.1	60.4	14.4
1990	11,768.8	15,265.6	77.1	77.4	16.9
1991	9,694.7	14,441.8	67.1	67.4	14.4
1992	9,257.7	14,852.2	62.3	62.6	13.0
1993	8,850.4	14,969.0	59.1	59.4	12.3
1994	8,279.5	15,237.8	54.3	54.6	11.4
1995	8,465.7	15,492.0	54.6	54.9	11.4
1996	10,329.1	15,950.2	64.8	65.0	13.0
1997	10,313.7	16,324.7	63.2	63.4	12.5
1998	8,408.5	16,751.4	50.2	50.4	10.0
1999	9,048.9	17,397.5	52.0	52.2	10.1
2000	14,146.0	18,401.9	76.9	77.2	14.1
2001	13,220.4	17,299.5	76.4	76.7	12.8
2002	11,025.5	15,345.5	71.8	72.2	11.7

Source: Air Transport Association of America, "Airline Cost Index" (Quarterly).
 a Majors and Nationals.

TOTAL ASSETS AND INVESTMENT IN EQUIPMENT BY U.S. AIR CARRIERS
Calendar Years 1969–2002
(Millions of Dollars)

Year	Total Assets	Value of Flight Equipment	Value of Ground Property & Equipment & Other[a]	Less: Reserves for Depreciation & Overhaul	Equals: Net Value of Owned Operating Property & Equipment	Investment in Operating Property and Equipment as a Percent of Total Assets
1969	$ 12,069	$ 9,943	$ 1,516	$ 3,560	$ 7,899	65.4%
1970	12,913	10,950	1,951	4,120	8,782	68.0
1971	12,998	11,221	2,028	4,649	8,600	66.2
1972	13,635	11,918	2,225	5,115	9,028	66.2
1973	14,464	12,908	2,424	5,693	9,639	66.6
1974	15,200	13,538	2,539	6,252	9,826	64.6
1975	15,064	14,035	2,635	6,823	9,847	65.4
1976	15,454	14,399	2,792	7,585	9,605	62.2
1977	16,869	14,822	2,997	8,141	9,679	57.4
1978	20,745	16,127	3,367	8,799	10,696	51.6
1979	24,907	18,561	3,985	9,746	12,800	51.4
1980	28,900	20,859	4,682	10,309	15,233	52.7
1981	30,513	22,375	5,175	11,028	16,521	54.1
1982	31,525	23,786	5,424	11,405	17,804	56.5
1983	35,213	26,588	6,191	12,910	19,868	56.4
1984	36,769	28,509	6,061	14,043	20,527	55.8
1985	40,978	30,402	6,772	15,467	21,707	53.0
1986	47,105	31,750	8,468	14,764	25,454	54.0
1987	51,436	33,177	9,223	15,580	26,820	52.1
1988	56,047	35,781	10,248	17,450	28,579	51.0
1989	62,454	38,812	11,903	19,018	31,697	50.8
1990	67,769	40,215	13,523	20,593	33,144	48.9
1991	70,332	42,897	14,285	22,009	35,173	50.0
1992	75,426	48,563	15,219	24,445	39,337	52.2
1993	82,399	51,513	15,438	24,949	42,003	51.0
1994	84,442	51,951	15,844	26,476	41,319	48.9
1995	89,782	56,018	16,804	29,056	43,766	48.7
1996	95,184	59,206	16,661	30,029	45,838	48.2
1997	105,226	66,523	17,643	32,789	51,377	48.8
1998	118,308	75,385	19,980	35,992	59,373	50.2
1999	133,711	86,269	21,826	39,060	69,035	51.6
2000	146,300	98,404	22,095	41,880	78,620	53.7
2001	158,516	103,508	23,092	42,666	83,934	52.9
2002[p]	158,191	106,300	24,226	44,371	86,155	54.5

Source: Department of Transportation, Office of Airline Information, "Air Carrier Financial Statistics Quarterly" (Quarterly).
a Includes land and construction in progress

TRAFFIC STATISTICS
WORLD AIRLINE SCHEDULED SERVICE[a]
Calendar Years 1970–2002

Year	Passen-gers Carried	Freight Tons Carried	Passen-ger-Miles Per-formed	Seat-Miles Avail-able	Passen-ger Load Factor	Total (Passen-gers & Baggage, Freight, Mail)	Freight	Mail
	(Millions)		(Billions)		(Percent)	(Billions)		
1970	383	6.7	286	522	55%	38.82 [r]	8.23	2.10
1971	411	7.4	307	568	54	41.42	9.06	1.99
1972	450	8.0	348	609	57	46.69	10.29	1.90
1973	489	9.1	384	667	58	51.91	12.01	1.97
1974	514	9.5	408	688	59	55.27	13.03	1.98
1975	534	9.6	433	733	59	58.08	13.27	1.99
1976	576	10.3	475	789	60	63.88	14.75	2.08
1977	610	11.1	508	837	61	68.79	16.19	2.17
1978	679	11.7	582	902	65	77.77	17.77	2.24
1979	754	12.1	659	999	66	86.89	19.19	2.35
1980	748	12.2	677	1,071	63	89.72 [r]	20.12	2.52
1981	752	12.0	695	1,092 [r]	64	92.81	21.15	2.60
1982	766	12.8	710	1,115	64	94.84	21.60	2.65
1983	798	13.5	739	1,151	64	100.28 [r]	24.05	2.74
1984	848	14.8	794	1,226	65	109.05	27.17	2.95
1985	899	15.1	850	1,293	66	114.86	27.29	3.01
1986	960	16.2	902	1,389	65	122.47	29.58	3.11
1987	1,028	17.7	988	1,471	67	134.57	33.10	3.22
1988	1,082	19.0	1,060	1,568	68	145.29 [r]	36.48	3.31
1989	1,109	19.9	1,102	1,621	68	152.73	39.14	3.46
1990	1,165	20.3	1,177	1,740	68	161.12 [r]	40.27	3.65
1991	1,135	19.3	1,147	1,727	66	158.04 [r]	40.11	3.48
1992	1,146	19.5	1,199	1,821	66	165.86 [r]	42.90	3.51
1993	1,142	19.9	1,211	1,873 [r]	65	171.67	46.88	3.58
1994	1,233	22.6	1,305	1,969	66	187.29 [r]	52.89	3.71
1995	1,304	24.5	1,397	2,087	67	201.34 [r]	56.94	3.86
1996	1,391	25.6	1,511	2,214	68	217.24	61.10	3.97
1997	1,457	29.1	1,599	2,317 [r]	69	235.76 [r]	70.47	4.10
1998	1,471	29.2	1,633	2,385	68	238.78 [r]	69.74	3.94
1999	1,562	31.0	1,739	2,517	69	253.73 [r]	74.43 [r]	3.92
2000	1,656	33.3	1,875	2,646	71	274.79 [r]	80.80	4.14
2001	1,624	31.6	1,821	2,638	69	264.02	75.83	3.63
2002 [p]	1,615	32.6	1,828	2,569	71	268.37	79.89	3.10

Source: International Civil Aviation Organization (ICAO).
   a Includes international and domestic traffic on scheduled service performed by the airlines of the 185 states which were members of ICAO in 2002.

TRAFFIC STATISTICS
U.S. AIR CARRIER SCHEDULED SERVICE[a]
Calendar Years 1968–2002

Year	Revenue Ton-Miles (Millions)			Total Available Ton-Miles (Millions)	Total Revenue Load Factor (Percent)	Aircraft Revenue Miles (Millions)	Average Overall Flight Stage Length (Miles)	Average Available Seats per Aircraft Mile
	TOTAL	Passenger	Cargo[b]					
1968	15,249	11,023	4,226	33,221	45.9%	2,146	401	107
1969	16,898	12,197	4,701	38,664	43.7	2,385	443	112
1970	18,166	13,171	4,994	41,693	43.6	2,426	473	117
1971	18,685	13,565	5,120	44,139	42.3	2,378	476	125
1972	20,746	15,241	5,506	45,583	45.5	2,376	471	129
1973	22,242	16,196	6,046	49,019	45.4	2,448	477	135
1974	22,425	16,292	6,133	46,848	47.9	2,258	478	140
1975	22,186	16,281	5,905	47,254	46.9	2,241	476	143
1976	24,121	17,899	6,222	49,325	48.9	2,320	480	146
1977	25,909	19,322	6,587	52,284	49.6	2,419	490	149
1978	29,679	22,678	7,001	54,765	54.2	2,520	502	152
1979	33,390	26,202	7,189	60,844	54.9	2,791	517	154
1980	32,603	25,519	7,084	62,983	51.8	2,816	526	158
1981	31,949	24,889	7,060	61,186	52.2	2,703	519	161
1982	32,850	25,964	6,886	62,401	52.6	2,699	544	167
1983	35,756	28,183	7,573	65,385	54.7	2,809	558	169
1984	38,697	30,512	8,185	72,223	53.6	3,134	575	168
1985	41,329	33,640	7,689	76,059	54.3	3,320	569	168
1986	45,681	36,655	9,026	85,140	53.7	3,725	580	168
1987	50,469	40,453	10,016	92,209	54.7	3,988	606	167
1988	53,800	42,330	11,469	97,899	55.0	4,141	618	169
1989	55,458	43,271	12,187	100,082	55.4	4,193	633	169
1990	58,342	45,793	12,549	107,559	54.2	4,491	649	170
1991	56,925	44,795	12,130	105,599	53.9	4,416	651	169
1992	61,054	47,855	13,199	112,749	54.2	4,661	661	169
1993	63,088	48,968	14,120	115,473	54.6	4,846	669	166
1994	67,989	51,938	16,052	120,798	56.3	5,033	668	163
1995	70,987	54,066	16,921	126,154	56.3	5,293	657	160
1996	75,621	57,866	17,754	131,381	57.6	5,501	668	160
1997	80,852	60,342	20,510	137,544	58.8	5,659	696	160
1998	82,304	61,809	20,496	141,722	58.1	5,838	704	159
1999	86,817	65,205	21,613	149,561	58.0	6,168	715	157
2000	93,163	69,276	23,888	159,441	58.4	6,574	728	154
2001	87,173	65,170	22,003	158,975	54.8	6,514	745	143
2002[p]	88,696	64,105	24,591	158,785	55.9	6,552	757	136

Source: Department of Transportation, Office of Airline Information, "Air Carrier Traffic Statistics Monthly" (Monthly).
a Includes international and domestic operations.
b Includes freight, air express, U.S. and foreign mail.

PASSENGER STATISTICS
U.S. AIR CARRIER SCHEDULED SERVICE
DOMESTIC AND INTERNATIONAL OPERATIONS
Calendar Years 1988–2002

Year	Revenue Passenger Enplanements (Thousands)	Average Passenger Trip-Length (Miles)	Revenue Passenger Miles (Millions)	Available Seat Miles (Millions)	Revenue Passenger Load Factor[a]
DOMESTIC OPERATIONS					
1988	419,210	786	329,309	536,663	61.4
1989	416,331	793	329,975	530,079	62.3
1990	423,565	803	340,231	563,065	60.4
1991	412,360	806	332,566	543,638	61.2
1992	431,693	806	347,931	557,989	62.4
1993	443,172	799	354,177	571,489	62.0
1994	481,755	787	378,990	585,438	64.7
1995	499,000	791	394,708	603,917	65.4
1996	530,708	802	425,596	626,389	67.9
1997	542,001	817	442,640	640,319	69.1
1998	559,653	812	454,430	649,362	70.0
1999	582,880	824	480,134	687,502	69.8
2000	610,601	833	508,403	714,454	71.2
2001	570,125	843	480,348	695,200	69.1
2002[p]	559,906	850	475,956	676,870	70.3
INTERNATIONAL OPERATIONS					
1988	35,404	2,655	93,992	140,140	67.1
1989	37,361	2,750	102,739	154,297	66.6
1990	41,995	2,803	117,695	170,310	69.1
1991	39,941	2,889	115,389	171,561	67.3
1992	43,415	3,009	130,622	194,784	67.1
1993	45,348	2,988	135,508	200,151	67.7
1994	47,093	2,981	140,391	198,893	70.6
1995	48,773	2,992	145,948	203,160	71.8
1996	50,526	3,029	153,067	208,682	73.3
1997	52,724	3,049	160,779	216,913	74.1
1998	53,232	3,074	163,656	224,728	72.8
1999	53,079	3,239	171,913	230,917	74.4
2000	55,549	3,319	184,354	242,496	76.0
2001	52,003	3,295	171,352	235,311	72.8
2002[p]	52,769	3,129	165,098	215,606	76.6

Source: Department of Transportation, Office of Airline Information, "Air Carrier Traffic Statistics Monthly" (Monthly).
a Revenue passenger miles as a percent of available seat miles.

AIR CARGO STATISTICS
U.S. COMMERCIAL AIR CARRIERS
Fiscal Years 1970–2002
(Millions of Revenue-Ton-Miles)

| Year | TOTAL | Freight/Express/Mail | |
		Domestic	International
1970	4,606	2,679	1,927
1971	4,758	2,653	2,105
1972	5,857	3,050	2,808
1973	5,839	3,310	2,530
1974	6,167	3,550	2,617
1975	5,725	3,309	2,416
1976	6,112	3,470	2,643
1977	6,315	3,676	2,639
1978	7,003	4,083	2,920
1979	7,211	4,217	2,994
1980	7,255	4,105	3,150
1981	6,979	4,078	2,901
1982	6,895	3,847	3,048
1983	7,715	4,539	3,177
1984	8,857	5,228	3,629
1985	8,653	4,994	3,659
1986	10,311	5,989	4,322
1987	12,130	7,010	5,119
1988	14,136	8,075	6,061
1989	15,954	8,821	7,133
1990	16,229	8,987	7,242
1991	16,327	8,913	7,414
1992	16,793	9,474	7,319
1993	18,420	10,374	8,046
1994	20,790	11,323	9,467
1995	23,228	12,416	10,812
1996	24,217	12,782	11,435
1997	26,954	13,455	13,499
1998	28,347	13,830	14,517
1999	28,102	13,975	14,127
2000	30,044	14,686	15,358
2001	28,463	13,916	14,547
2002[E]	27,732	12,936	14,796

Source: Federal Aviation Administration, Office of Aviation Policy & Plans.

WORLD AIRLINE FLEET OF TURBINE-ENGINED AIRCRAFT BY MODEL
Calendar Years 1998–2002

	1998	1999	2000	2001	2002
TOTAL	23,002	24,128	25,173	25,963	26,112
Turbojets—TOTAL	14,621	15,453	16,405	17,291	17,609
Aerospatiale SE-210 Caravelle	12	12	9	5	5
Aerospatiale Corvette	—	2	2	2	2
Airbus A300	383	389	408	396	388
Airbus A310	227	220	217	216	206
Airbus A319	118	206	309	398	475
Airbus A320	685	773	880	994	1,090
Airbus A321	109	143	165	215	244
Airbus A330	87	131	170	201	242
Airbus A340	138	161	181	200	208
Antonov 72/74	9	9	15	19	20
Antonov 124	18	17	17	17	17
Antonov 225	1	1	1	1	1
Avro RJ-70/85/100	120	138	158	163	162
B.Ae./Aerospatiale Concorde	13	13	12	12	12
B.Ae. 146	206	203	206	195	176
B.Ae. One-Eleven	105	101	97	88	86
B.Ae. (HS) 125	17	11	13	15	16
Beech 400 Beechjet	3	3	3	3	2
Boeing 707/720	98	94	86	76	59
Boeing 717	—	11	44	92	108
Boeing 727	1,263	1,189	1,144	1,077	922
Boeing 737	2,968	3,176	3,431	3,667	3,814
Boeing 747	1,042	1,041	1,027	1,029	1,018
Boeing 757	818	879	924	952	974
Boeing 767	710	752	799	816	845
Boeing 777	174	261	313	373	419
Canadair CL-601 Challenger	2	2	1	1	1
Canadair Regional Jet	258	351	451	559	735
Cessna Citation I/II/III	35	34	41	39	37
Dassault Falcon 10/20/50	61	71	69	73	69
Embraer ERJ-135/140/145	91	186	345	497	616
Fairchild 328 Jet	—	11	43	67	79
Fokker F-28 Fellowship	160	169	172	148	146
Fokker 70	42	42	42	42	44
Fokker 100	278	277	271	257	267
Gulfstream II/III/IV G-1159	14	14	14	12	12
Ilyushin IL-62	86	83	85	105	100
Ilyushin IL-76	215	226	257	285	297
Ilyushin IL-86	75	79	81	87	83
Ilyushin IL-96	7	8	8	9	9
Israel Aircraft 1121/1124	18	10	8	8	9
Learjet	49	85	86	85	85
Lockheed L-1011 Tristar	156	135	117	102	93
Lockheed L-1329 Jetstar	1	1	1	1	1
MBB Hansa HFB-320	17	9	9	6	6
McDonnell Douglas DC-8	261	225	227	200	171
McDonnell Douglas DC-9	749	714	676	627	538
McDonnell Douglas DC-10	354	340	319	317	255
McDonnell Douglas MD-11	180	187	188	191	182

(Continued on next page)

WORLD AIRLINE FLEET OF TURBINE-ENGINED AIRCRAFT BY MODEL
Calendar Years 1998–2002, continued

	1998	1999	2000	2001	2002
Turbojets (continued)					
McDonnell Douglas MD-80	1,154	1,180	1,164	1,141	1,118
McDonnell Douglas MD-90	97	109	110	106	105
Tupolev Tu-134	189	188	193	202	188
Tupolev Tu-154	438	446	439	482	453
Tupolev Tu-204	7	9	11	14	14
Yakolev Yak-40/42	303	326	356	406	385
Turbine-Powered					
Helicopters—TOTAL	1,371	1,449	1,438	1,429	1,381
Aerospatiale SA-315 Lama	2	2	—	—	—
Aerospatiale SA-316 Alouette III ..	5	5	5	2	1
Aerospatiale SA-318 Alouette II ...	1	1	1	1	1
Aerospatiale (Nurtanio)					
SA-330 Puma	18	22	19	3	6
Aerospatiale AS-332 Super Puma	73	72	74	92	93
Aerospatiale AS-350 Ecureuil/					
Astar	112	125	124	124	119
Aerospatiale AS-355 Ecureuil 2/					
Twinstar..................................	23	28	26	23	32
Aerospatiale SA-365 Dauphin II	26	36	43	45	34
Agusta A109	—	—	—	2	3
Bell (Agusta/Fuji) 204.................	2	4	4	4	4
Bell 205	11	15	14	14	14
Bell 206 Jetranger/Longranger	361	363	353	323	308
Bell 212	112	120	115	115	108
Bell 214	17	14	13	11	11
Bell 222 UT.................................	3	2	2	1	1
Bell 230	3	—	—	—	—
Bell 407	44	53	54	74	70
Bell 412	55	56	59	71	75
Boeing 107	15	15	15	15	15
Boeing Vertol BV-234	9	9	9	9	9
Eurocopter EC-120	—	—	2	2	5
Hughes (Kawasaki) 500/369D	16	13	12	9	9
Kamov Ka-26	16	19	16	16	16
MBB BK-117	13	10	8	7	7
MBB/Nurtanio Bo.105	103	101	100	106	85
MD Helicopters MD-900	—	—	—	—	4
Mil Mi-2	32	28	26	26	26
Mil Mi-6	6	6	6	—	6
Mil Mi-8	83	107	102	96	88
Mil Mi-14....................................	1	1	1	1	1
Mil Mi-26....................................	7	5	8	8	8
Sikorsky S-55T	6	—	1	—	—
Sikorsky S-58T	1	1	—	1	1
Sikorsky S-61	65	79	81	85	74
Sikorsky S-62	1	—	—	—	—
Sikorsky S-64	5	22	24	5	5
Sikorsky S-76	124	115	121	138	139

(Continued on next page)

WORLD AIRLINE FLEET OF TURBINE-ENGINED AIRCRAFT BY MODEL
Calendar Years 1998–2002, continued

	1998	1999	2000	2001	2002
Turboprops—TOTAL....................	7,010	7,226	7,330	7,243	7,122
Aerospatiale N.262/Mohawk 298	11	12	12	14	10
Aerospatiale/Aeritalia ATR 42	299	296	311	306	245
Aerospatiale/Aeritalia ATR 72	202	222	223	255	267
Airtech CN-235	24	33	23	23	17
Antonov An-8	—	6	4	6	6
Antonov An-12	83	81	114	112	114
Antonov An-22	3	1	1	1	1
Antonov An-24/26/30/32	499	475	526	582	566
B.Ae. ATP..................................	57	55	49	28	33
B.Ae. Viscount	12	12	12	—	3
B.Ae. (HP-137) Jetstream 31......	233	258	223	190	186
B.Ae. Jetstream 41	92	92	93	90	91
B.Ae. HS-748	124	118	109	110	93
Beech 18 Turbo	18	9	9	8	8
Beech 90 King Air	39	46	39	39	34
Beech 99	139	110	142	146	142
Beech 100 King Air	39	47	51	48	47
Beech 200/300 Super King Air....	111	112	131	134	136
Beech 1300................................	6	9	8	7	6
Beech 1900C/D	467	469	490	397	426
Canadair CL-44	—	4	3	3	1
CASA/Nurtanio C-212 Aviocar....	105	110	109	108	95
Cessna 208 Caravan I	601	647	661	705	746
Cessna F406 Caravan II	31	30	29	33	29
Cessna 425/441 Conquest I/II	19	19	15	15	15
Convair 580/600/640..................	107	106	104	103	104
DHC-2/3 Turbo Beaver/Otter	20	24	28	35	36
DHC-5 Buffalo	1	1	1	1	1
DHC-6 Twin Otter	371	365	349	345	348
DHC-7 Dash 7	71	69	67	68	63
DHC-8 Dash 8	444	489	523	557	556
Dornier DO-228..........................	118	121	103	105	107
Dornier DO-328..........................	73	83	91	89	85
Douglas DC-3T Turbo Express ...	1	3	3	3	5
Embraer EMB-110 Bandeirante ..	199	199	181	181	176
Embraer EMB-120 Brasilia	316	307	300	290	281
Embraer EMB-121 Xingu	2	3	1	1	1
Fokker/Fairchild F-27/FH-227 Friendship	278	276	257	251	218
Fokker 50...................................	167	188	184	170	167
GAF Nomad	15	16	12	12	11
Grumman G-73 Turbo Mallard....	5	6	6	6	6
Grumman G-159 Gulfstream I	27	27	17	14	4

(Continued on next page)

WORLD AIRLINE FLEET OF TURBINE-ENGINED AIRCRAFT BY MODEL

Calendar Years 1998–2002, continued

	1998	1999	2000	2001	2002
Turboprops (continued)					
Handley Page Herald	1	1	1	1	—
Harbin YU-12 II	48	48	46	47	43
IAI Arava	3	4	3	2	1
Ilyushin IL-18	32	41	38	44	38
Ilyushin IL-114	2	3	3	3	3
LET L-410	118	141	178	186	197
Lockheed L-188 Electra............	44	43	40	35	34
Lockheed L-100/L-382 Hercules	35	44	43	41	43
Mitsubishi MU-2B	16	21	18	22	19
Nihon AMC YS-11	49	46	37	33	35
Piaggio P-180 Avanti	—	—	—	1	1
Pilatus Britten-Norman BN-2T					
Turbo Islander	6	5	5	4	4
Pilatus PC-6 Turbo Porter	24	23	27	25	25
Pilatus PC-XII	14	21	22	22	29
Piper PA-31T/42 Cheyenne	20	22	19	18	14
Piper T-1040	13	13	9	9	6
PZL (Antonov) An-28	3	27	43	42	51
Rockwell Turbo Commander	9	8	8	9	7
Saab SF-340A/B	432	414	447	380	376
Saab 2000	45	43	48	48	51
Shorts SC-5 Belfast	2	2	2	1	—
Shorts SC-7 Skyliner/Skyvan ...	30	27	26	25	28
Shorts 330	42	37	39	39	33
Shorts 360	93	102	101	106	102
Swearingen Merlin	55	58	50	52	51
Swearingen Metro	379	398	392	385	371
Transall C-160	—	6	6	6	6
Xian (Antonov) Y-7/Y-8/MA-60...	66	65	65	66	68
TOTAL AIRCRAFT IN SERVICE	23,002	24,128	25,173	25,963	26,112
Number Manufactured in U.S. ...	13,139	13,537	13,857	13,988	13,842
Percent Manufactured in U.S. ...	57.1%	56.1%	55.0%	53.9%	53.0%
Turbojet Aircraft in Service	14,621	15,453	16,405	17,291	17,609
Number Manufactured in U.S. ...	10,126	10,430	10,714	10,906	10,758
Percent Manufactured in U.S. ...	69.3%	67.5%	65.3%	63.1%	61.1%
Turboprop Aircraft in Service	7,010	7,226	7,330	7,243	7,122
Number Manufactured in U.S. ...	2,165	2,226	2,266	2,207	2,234
Percent Manufactured in U.S. ...	30.9%	30.8%	30.9%	30.5%	31.4%
Turbine-Powered Helicopters					
in Service	1,371	1,449	1,438	1,429	1,381
Number Manufactured in U.S. ...	848	881	877	875	850
Percent Manufactured in U.S. ...	61.9%	60.8%	61.0%	61.2%	61.5%

Source: Air BP Lubricants, "Turbine-Engined Fleets of the World's Airlines," compiled by Aviation Data Service, Inc. (Annually).
NOTE: "Turbine-Engined Fleets of the World's Airlines" covers aircraft in airline service as of December 31. Excludes air taxi operators.

NUMBER AND PERCENT OF CIVIL TURBOJET ENGINES
IN WORLD AIRLINE FLEET BY MANUFACTURER AND AIRCRAFT MODEL
As of December 2002

Aircraft Manufacturer and Model	Total Installed Engines	Engine Manufacturers					
		P&W	GE	RR	CFM	IAE	Other
TOTAL ENGINES	44,375	13,910	6,679	4,454	9,611	1,679	8,042
PERCENT OF TOTAL ...	100.0%	31.3%	15.1%	10.0%	21.7%	3.8%	18.1%
Airbus A300[a]	540	22%	78%	–%	–%	–%	–%
Airbus A300B4-600R	318	54	46	–	–	–	–
Airbus A310	446	41	59	–	–	–	–
Airbus A319	944	–	–	–	69	31	–
Airbus A320[a]	36	–	–	–	100	–	–
Airbus A320-200	2,154	–	–	–	57	43	–
Airbus A321[a]	174	–	–	–	48	52	–
Airbus A321-200	324	–	–	–	58	42	–
Airbus A330-200	236	39	17	44	–	–	–
Airbus A330-300	232	45	14	41	–	–	–
Airbus A340[a]	332	–	–	6	94	–	–
Airbus A340-300X...........	540	–	–	–	100	–	–
Antonov AN-72	16	–	–	–	–	–	100
Antonov AN-74	28	–	–	–	–	–	100
Antonov AN-124	72	–	–	–	–	–	100
AS Corvette	4	100	–	–	–	–	–
AS Caravelle	12	83	–	17	–	–	–
AS/BAe Concorde	48	–	–	100	–	–	–
Avro Int'l RJ	652	–	–	–	–	–	100
BAe 1-11	184	–	–	100	–	–	–
BAe 146	816	–	–	–	–	–	100
BAe/HS 125	32	6	–	13	–	–	81
Beech 400 Beechjet	18	100	–	–	–	–	–
Boeing B-707	416	100	–	–	–	–	–
Boeing B-717	224	–	–	100	–	–	–
Boeing B-720	4	100	–	–	–	–	–
Boeing B-727 series[a]	1,152	87	–	13	–	–	–
Boeing B-727-200 Adv F	684	100	–	–	–	–	–
Boeing B-727-200 ADV...	1,401	100	–	–	–	–	–
Boeing B-737[a]................	558	57	–	–	43	–	–
Boeing B-737-200 ADV...	1,246	100	–	–	–	–	–
Boeing B-737-300	2,110	–	–	–	100	–	–
Boeing B-737-400	944	–	–	–	100	–	–
Boeing B-737-500	768	–	–	–	100	–	–
Boeing B-737-700	810	–	–	–	100	–	–
Boeing B-737-800	1,350	–	–	–	100	–	–
Boeing B-747[a]	2,088	45	44	11	–	–	–
Boeing B-747-200B	512	70	11	19	–	–	–
Boeing B-747-400	1,696	41	34	25	–	–	–
Boeing B-757[a]	398	23	–	77	–	–	–
Boeing B-757-200	1,598	46	–	54	–	–	–
Boeing B-767[a]	324	15	85	–	–	–	–
Boeing B-767-200ER......	272	46	54	–	–	–	–
Boeing B-767-300	202	25	75	–	–	–	–
Boeing B-767-300ER......	930	37	57	6	–	–	–
Boeing B-777a	238	53	8	39	–	–	–
Boeing B-777-200ER......	606	22	36	41	–	–	–

(Continued on next page)

NUMBER AND PERCENT OF CIVIL TURBOJET ENGINES
IN WORLD AIRLINE FLEET BY MANUFACTURER AND AIRCRAFT MODEL
As of December 2002, continued

Canadair CL 600/601	8	–%	50%	–%	–%	–%	50%
Canadair RJ series[a]	132	–	100	–	–	–	–
Canadair Regional Jet[b]	464	–	100	–	–	–	–
Canadair Regional Jet 300	894	–	100	–	–	–	–
Cessna 500s	86	95	–	5	–	–	–
Cessna 650	6	–	–	–	–	–	100
Cessna 750	2	–	–	–	–	–	100
Dassault Falcon	154	–	86	–	–	–	14
Embraer ERJ-135	182	–	–	–	–	–	100
Embraer ERJ-140	114	–	–	–	–	–	100
Embraer ERJ-145	926	–	–	–	–	–	100
Fairchild Dornier 328 Jet	158	100	–	–	–	–	–
Fokker F-28	308	–	–	100	–	–	–
Fokker 70	84	–	–	100	–	–	–
Fokker 100	536	–	–	100	–	–	–
Gulfstream II/III/IV	26	–	–	100	–	–	–
IAI 1124/1125	18	–	–	–	–	–	100
Ilyushin IL-62	412	–	–	–	–	–	100
Ilyushin IL-76[a]	108	–	–	–	–	–	100
Ilyushin IL-76MD	492	–	–	–	–	–	100
Ilyushin IL-76TD	556	–	–	–	–	–	100
Ilyushin IL-86	332	–	–	–	–	–	100
Ilyushin IL-96	36	–	–	–	–	–	100
Learjet 23/24/25	126	–	100	–	–	–	–
Learjet 35/36/45/55/60	96	8	–	–	–	–	92
Lockheed JetStar	4	–	–	–	–	–	100
Lockheed L-1011	333	–	–	100	–	–	–
MBB HFB-320 Hansa Jet	12	–	100	–	–	–	–
Douglas DC-8	820	57	–	–	43	–	–
Douglas DC-9[a]	482	100	–	–	–	–	–
Douglas DC-9-30	740	100	–	–	–	–	–
Douglas DC-10	819	8	92	–	–	–	–
MDC MD-11 series[a]	273	23	77	–	–	–	–
MDC MD-11[b]	309	52	48	–	–	–	–
MDC MD-80s[a]	294	100	–	–	–	–	–
MDC MD-82	1,132	100	–	–	–	–	–
MDC MD-83	530	100	–	–	–	–	–
MDC MD-88	314	100	–	–	–	–	–
MDC MD-90-30	232	–	–	–	–	100	–
Raytheon 800XP	8	–	–	–	–	–	100
Rockwell Sabreliner	2	–	100	–	–	–	–
Tupolev TU-134[a]	170	–	–	–	–	–	100
Tupolev TU-134A3	236	–	–	–	–	–	100
Tupolev TU-154[a]	171	–	–	–	–	–	100
Tupolev TU-154B2	540	–	–	–	–	–	100
Tupolev TU-154M	717	–	–	–	–	–	100
Tupolev TU-204	24	–	–	33	–	–	67
Yakolev YAK-40	978	–	–	–	–	–	100
Yakolev YAK-42	294	–	–	–	–	–	100

Source: Aerospace Industries Association, based on data from Aviation Data Service.
a Data for major (100 or more aircraft) series excluded and reported separately.
b Series bearing same designation as model number, but qualifies for separate reporting as a major series.
KEY: AS = Aerospatiale; BAe = British Aerospace; CFM = CFM International; GE = General Electric;
IAE = International Aero Engines; IAI = Israel Aircraft Industries; MBB = Messerschmitt Bolkow Blohm;
MDC = McDonnell Douglas; P&W = Pratt & Whitney; RR = Rolls-Royce.

ACTIVE[a] U.S. AIR CARRIER FLEET
BY TYPE OF AIRCRAFT, NUMBER OF ENGINES, AND MODEL
As of December 1998–2002

	1998	1999	2000	2001	2002
TOTAL...	8,111	8,228	8,055	8,497	8,194
Turbojets—TOTAL.............................	5,411	5,630	5,956	6,296	6,383
Four-Engine—TOTAL	447	441	432	419	365
Boeing 707	—	1	—	1	—
Boeing 747	201	188	190	209	175
B.Ae./AVRO 146..............................	18	46	54	54	53
McDonnell Douglas DC-8................	228	206	188	155	137
Three-Engine—TOTAL	1,238	1,181	1,061	996	790
Boeing 727	882	811	720	674	514
Lockheed L-1011	70	66	52	24	20
McDonnell Douglas DC-10/MD-11 ...	286	304	289	298	256
Twin-Engine—TOTAL	3,726	4,008	4,463	4,881	5,228
Airbus A-300	61	68	85	113	119
Airbus A-310	39	39	39	46	46
Airbus A-319	23	40	111	170	218
Airbus A-320	143	162	207	231	278
Airbus A-321	—	—	—	23	28
Airbus A-330	—	—	5	9	9
BAe HS-125	—	1	—	—	—
Beech 400	1	1	—	1	—
Boeing 717	—	2	22	57	83
Boeing 737	1,080	1,179	1,280	1,359	1,396
Boeing 757	510	555	585	599	647
Boeing 767	261	278	315	340	366
Boeing 777	36	53	89	96	129
Canadair CL-600............................	152	187	251	324	459
Cessna C500/C501/C525	10	9	—	—	1
Dassau AMD	27	27	—	26	—
Embraer ERJ-135	—	7	39	69	123
Embraer ERJ-145	55	95	151	217	275
Fokker F-28	147	145	145	133	86
Israel Aircraft 1124.........................	1	1	—	1	—
Learjet LR-25	7	8	6	2	1
Learjet LR-31	1	1	—	—	—
Learjet LR-35	11	11	11	2	1
McDonnell Douglas DC-9/MD-80/ MD-90	1,158	1,133	1,122	1,060	963
Mitsubishi MU-300	2	5	—	2	—
North American NA-265	1	1	—	1	—
Turboprops—TOTAL	1,832	1,788	1,475	1,494	1,250
Four-Engine—TOTAL	39	28	29	24	17
De Havilland DHC-7.........................	7	6	7	4	2
Lockheed 188 Electra	17	14	14	12	9
Lockheed 382	15	8	8	8	6

(Continued on next page)

ACTIVE[a] U.S. AIR CARRIER FLEET
BY TYPE OF AIRCRAFT, NUMBER OF ENGINES, AND MODEL
As of December 1998–2002, continued

	1998	1999	2000	2001[r]	2002
Twin-Engine—TOTAL	1,789	1,759	1,440	1,470	1,233
Airtech CN-235	—	1	1	1	1
Beech BE90	8	6	1	3	1
Beech BE99	36	38	9	14	9
Beech BE100	2	4	3	3	3
Beech BE200	19	19	7	8	6
Beech BE300	—	—	—	2	—
Beech BE1900	325	239	224	185	163
B.Ae. ATP	—	9	—	—	—
B.Ae. Jetstream	203	184	145	100	89
CASA C212 Aviocar	3	4	4	4	9
Cessna CE208B	137	167	44	159	38
Cessna C441	4	2	1	—	—
Convair 580/600/640	15	12	10	5	5
Curtis C-46	—	—	1	2	2
DeHavilland DHC-6	54	54	38	51	27
DeHavilland DHC-8	169	180	183	190	183
Dornier DO328	35	39	65	85	87
Embraer EMB110	1	1	1	1	1
Embraer EMB120	218	225	197	176	160
Fairchild/Fokker F-27/FH-227	38	38	38	38	38
Grumman G-73	5	3	5	5	5
Gulfstream 695	—	—	—	—	1
Gulfstream GA1159	—	—	—	3	—
Mitsubishi MU-2	13	14	13	—	—
Piper PA31T	6	6	4	4	4
Piper 42	2	2	—	—	—
Saab-Fairchild SF340	271	275	272	255	232
Shorts SC-7	3	3	3	3	3
Shorts SD-3	15	20	10	13	6
SNAIS ATR-42	83	79	69	66	64
SNAIS ATR-72	60	60	70	65	63
Swearingen SA-226	4	3	1	2	2
Swearingen SA-227	60	72	27	27	27
Single-Engine—TOTAL	4	1	—	—	—
Piston-Engine—TOTAL	751	688	585	580	528
Four-Engine—TOTAL	17	19	17	16	12
Douglas DC-6	17	19	17	16	12
Three-Engine—TOTAL	3	3	3	3	3
Pilatus Britten-Norman BN2A-MK-3 Turbo Islander	3	3	3	3	3
Twin-Engine—TOTAL	391	292	255	173	154
Single-Engine—TOTAL	340	374	310	388	359
Helicopters—TOTAL	117	122	39	127	33

Source: Federal Aviation Administration.
NOTE: Includes certificated route air carriers, supplemental air carriers (charters), multi-engine aircraft in passenger service of commuters, and all aircraft over 12,500 pounds operated by Part 121 and Part 135 commuter operators.
a "Active aircraft" equals the average number of aircraft reported in operation during the last quarter of the year.

ACTIVE U.S. MILITARY AIRCRAFT[a]
Fiscal Years 1980–2002

Year	TOTAL[a]	Fixed-Wing Aircraft				Helicopters
		TOTAL	Jet	Turboprop	Piston	
1980	18,969	11,362	8,794	1,869	699	7,607
1981	19,363	11,645	9,111	1,943	591	7,718
1982	21,728	12,063	9,647	1,900	516	9,665
1983	18,652	11,603	9,495	1,745	363	7,049
1984	18,833	11,661	9,551	1,777	333	7,172
1985	19,333	11,929	9,640	1,881	408	7,404
1986	20,157	11,919	9,730	1,803	386	8,238
1987	20,514	12,054	9,819	1,865	370	8,460
1988	21,010	12,481	9,954	2,222	305	8,529
1989	19,223	11,893	9,501	2,131	261	7,330
1990	20,017	12,817	10,360	2,199	258	7,200
1991	19,966	12,587	10,221	2,119	247	7,379
1992	19,210	11,936	9,672	2,035	229	7,274
1993	17,231	9,681	7,651	1,852	178	7,550
1994[E]	17,018	9,803	7,786	1,835	182	7,215
1995[E]	16,207	9,277	7,294	1,754	229	6,930
1996[b]	20,554	10,154	7,798	2,199	157	10,400
1997	20,245	9,677	7,364	2,151	162	10,568
1998	15,585	9,187[c]	7,082	1,951	120	6,398
1999	16,062	9,015[d]	6,981	1,908	115	7,047
2000	15,902	8,777[d]	6,738	2,023	5	7,125
2001	16,155	9,024[f]	6,790	2,084	118	7,131
2002	16,037	8,993[f]	6,748	2,092	121	7,044

Source: Aerospace Industries Association.
   a Includes Army, Air Force, Navy, and Marine regular service aircraft, as well as Reserve and National Guard Aircraft.
   b Prior years data provided by Office of the Secretary of Defense and limited to aircraft in the continental United States.
   c Includes 34 gliders.
   d Includes 11 gliders.
   f Includes 32 gliders.

ACTIVE U.S. CIVIL AIRCRAFT[a]
As of December 31, 1967–2001
(Thousands)

Year	TOTAL	Air Carrier[b]	General Aviation Aircraft					
			Fixed-Wing Aircraft				Rotor-craft[c]	Other[d]
			TOTAL	Multi-Engine	Single-Engine			
					4-place & over	3-place & less		
1967	116.6	2.452	114.2	14.7	56.9	39.7	1.9	1.1
1968	126.8	2.586	124.2	16.8	61.0	42.8	2.4	1.3
1969	133.5	2.690	130.8	18.1	63.7	45.0	2.6	1.4
1970	134.4	2.679	131.7	18.3	64.8	44.9	2.3	1.6
1971	133.8	2.642	131.1	17.9	64.5	44.8	2.4	1.7
1972	147.6	2.583	145.0	19.8	71.0	49.4	2.8	1.9
1973	156.1	2.599	153.5	21.9	74.8	51.4	3.1	2.3
1974	164.0	2.472	161.5	23.4	78.9	53.0	3.6	2.5
1975	171.0	2.495	168.5	24.6	82.6	54.4	4.1	2.8
1976	180.8	2.492	178.3	25.7	88.2	56.7	4.5	3.2
1977	186.8	2.473	184.3	26.7	92.0	57.3	4.7	3.6
1978	201.3	2.545	198.8	28.8	101.5	59.2	5.3	4.0
1979	213.9	3.609	210.3	31.3	106.0	62.4	5.9	4.8
1980	214.9	3.808	211.0	31.7	107.9	60.5	6.0	4.9
1981	217.2	3.973	213.2	33.3	108.0	59.9	7.0	5.0
1982	213.9	4.027	209.8	34.2	106.5	57.7	6.2	6.2
1983	217.5	4.203	213.3	34.6	107.1	59.1	6.5	5.9
1984	225.3	4.370	220.9	35.6	109.9	62.0	7.1	6.3
1985	201.2	4.678	196.5	31.3	98.5	54.9	6.0	5.8
1986	210.2	4.909	205.3	32.0	102.0	58.3	6.5	6.5
1987	208.0	5.253	202.7	30.8	100.4	59.3	5.9	6.3
1988	201.9	5.660	196.2	30.1	98.1	55.6	6.0	6.4
1989	210.8	5.778	205.0	31.9	100.5	58.4	7.0	7.2
1990	204.1	6.083	198.0	30.6	97.6	56.4	6.9	6.6
1991	202.9	6.054	196.9	29.7	97.8	55.1	6.2	8.1
1992	193.0	7.320	185.7	26.8	91.6	53.2	6.0	8.0
1993	184.4	7.297	177.1	22.8	91.6	42.5	4.7	15.5
1994	180.3	7.370	172.9	22.3	87.3	40.5	4.7	18.1
1995	190.0	7.411	188.1	24.6	93.6	44.1	5.8	19.9
1996	194.8	7.478	191.1	25.6	93.8	44.3	6.6	20.9
1997	200.0	7.616	192.4	26.2	95.0	45.7	6.8	18.8
1998	212.8	8.111	204.7	29.9[r]	103.6[r]	41.8	7.4	22.1
1999	227.7	8.228	219.5	32.8	109.3	42.6	7.4	27.3
2000	225.6	8.055	217.5	33.2	108.0	42.1	7.2	27.1
2001	219.9	8.497	211.4	31.7	106.3	39.7	6.8	27.0

Source: Federal Aviation Administration.
 a "Active aircraft" must have a current U.S. registration and have flown during the calendar year. Prior to 1971, only a current U.S. registration was necessary.
 b Includes certificated route air carriers, supplemental air carriers (charters), multi-engine aircraft in commuter passenger service, and all aircraft over 12,500 pounds operated by air taxis, commercial operators, and travel clubs.
 c Includes autogiros; excludes air carrier helicopters.
 d Includes gliders, dirigibles, balloons, and experimental aircraft.

U.S. GENERAL AVIATION[a]
TYPE OF AIRCRAFT AND HOURS FLOWN
Calendar Years 1997–2001

	1997	1998	1999	2000	2001
NUMBER OF ACTIVE AIRCRAFT BY TYPE (Thousands)					
All Aircraft—TOTAL	192.4	204.7	219.5	217.5	211.4
Fixed-Wing:	166.9	175.2	184.7	183.3	177.7
Piston:	156.1	163.0	171.9	170.5	163.3
Single-Engine	140.0	144.2	150.9	149.4	145.0
Twin-Engine	15.9	18.7	20.9	21.0	18.2
Other............................	0.1	0.1	0.1	0.1	0.1
Turboprop:	5.6	6.2	5.7	5.8	6.6
Twin-Engine	4.9	5.1	4.6	5.0	5.6
Other............................	0.7	1.1	1.0	0.7	1.0
Turbojet:	5.2	6.1	7.1	7.0	7.8
Twin-Engine	4.6	5.5	6.4	6.2	5.6
Other............................	0.5	0.6	0.7	0.8	0.8
Rotorcraft:	6.8	7.4	7.4	7.2	6.8
Piston	2.3	2.5	2.6	2.7	2.3
Turbine...............................	4.5	4.9	4.9	4.5	4.5
Balloons, Dirigibles, and Gliders...	4.1	5.6	6.8	6.7	6.5
Experimental	14.7	16.5	20.5	20.4	20.4
HOURS FLOWN BY TYPE OF AIRCRAFT (Thousands)					
All Aircraft—TOTAL	27,713	28,100	31,756	30,972[r]	29,134
Fixed-Wing: Piston	20,743	20,402	22,895	22,199	20,883
Turboprop	1,655	1,765	1,811	2,031	1,913
Turbojet	1,713	2,226	2,738	2,755	2,658
Rotorcraft: Piston	343	430	556	531	583
Turbine..................	1,739	1,912	2,188	1,777	1,559
Balloons, Dirigibles, and Gliders...	192	295	318	374	324
Experimental	1,327	1,071	1,247	1,307	1,214
AVERAGE HOURS FLOWN ANNUALLY BY TYPE					
All Aircraft—TOTAL	144.0	137.3	144.7	142.4	137.8
Fixed-Wing: Piston	132.9	125.2	133.2	130.2	127.9
Turboprop	294.5	285.8	319.0	352.5	290.0
Turbojet	330.7	367.0	384.6	393.5	341.3
Rotorcraft: Piston	152.2	169.0	217.0	198.1	254.2
Turbine..................	384.3	391.8	448.0	397.6	347.0
Balloons, Dirigibles, and Gliders...	46.8	52.8	47.1	55.8	49.6
Experimental	90.4	64.9	60.8	64.0	59.4

Source: Federal Aviation Administration.
a Excludes commuters.

U.S. GENERAL AVIATION
ACTIVE AIRCRAFT AND HOURS FLOWN BY PRIMARY USE[a]
Calendar Years 1997–2001

Primary Use	1997	1998	1999	2000[r]	2001
ACTIVE AIRCRAFT AS OF DECEMBER 31 (Thousands)					
TOTAL	192.4	204.7	219.5	217.5	211.4
Executive	10.4	11.3	10.8	11.0	10.5
Business	27.7	32.6	24.5	25.2	25.5
Air Taxi[b]	4.8	4.9	4.3	3.7	3.6
Instructional	14.7	11.4	16.1	14.9	14.3
Personal	115.6	124.3	147.1	148.2	144.0
Aerial Application	4.9	4.6	4.3	4.3	3.8
Aerial Observation	3.3	3.2	3.2	5.1	5.0
Aerial Other	NA	NA	0.4	1.0	0.6
Sight Seeing	0.7	0.7	0.8	0.9	0.9
Public Use	4.1	4.0	4.1	NA	NA
Air Tours	0.2	0.3	0.3	0.3	0.4
External Load	0.2	0.3	0.2	0.2	0.2
Medical	NA	NA	0.8	0.9	0.9
Other Work	0.7	1.1	2.4	1.8	1.5
Other	5.3	6.0	NA	NA	NA
HOURS FLOWN (Thousands)					
TOTAL	27,713	28,100	31,756	30,972	29,134
Executive	2,878	3,213	3,616	3,765	3,411
Business	3,006	3,523	3,598	3,604	3,583
Air Taxi[b]	2,008	2,400	1,897	1,694	1,491
Instructional	4,956	3,961	5,893	5,375	5,075
Personal	9,644	9,781	11,294	11,711	11,314
Aerial Application	1,562	1,306	1,415	1,401	1,093
Aerial Observation	1,261	812	1,243	1,621	1,596
Aerial Other	NA	NA	120	244	189
Sight Seeing	127	169	220	198	201
Air Tours	114	183	146	224	190
Public Use	1,096	1,373	1,111	NA	NA
Medical	NA	NA	461	442	456
External Load	112	153	128	171	177
Other Work	139	286	613	522	359
Other	819	940	NA	NA	NA

Source: Federal Aviation Administration, "General Aviation and Air Taxi Activity Survey" (Annually).
   a   Definitions of "primary use" categories available in Glossary of "FAA Statistical Handbook."
   b   Air taxis under 12,500 pounds.

ACTIVE U.S. CIVIL AIRCRAFT
BY PRIMARY USE AND TYPE OF AIRCRAFT
As of December 31, 2001

Primary Use	TOTAL	Fixed-Wing			Rotor-craft[a]	Other[b]
		Turbojet	Turboprop	Piston		
TOTAL................................	219,943	14,083	8,090	163,894	6,910	26,966
Air Carrier—TOTAL	8,497	6,296	1,494	580	127	—
Large	7,556	6,260	1,253	43	—	—
Small	941	36	241	537	127	—
General Aviation—TOTAL	211,446	7,787	6,596	163,314	6,783	26,966
Executive...........................	10,554	5,167	2,564	2,274	381	157
Business	25,525	1,042	1,634	22,486	444	420
Air Taxi[c]	3,598	716	720	1,329	648	185
Instructional	14,254	17	34	13,011	645	547
Personal	144,031	702	1,001	117,104	1,155	24,069
Aerial Application	3,779	208	371	2,583	562	56
Aerial Observation.............	5,039	17	85	3,047	1,687	203
Aerial Other	633	28	38	330	206	30
Sight Seeing	918	15	—	188	190	526
Air Tours	408	—	20	95	171	120
External Load	202	—	—	34	161	8
Medical	940	34	138	217	525	26
Other Work	1,528	42	91	718	107	570

Source: Federal Aviation Administration.
NOTE: Detail may not add to totals because of estimating procedures.
    a Includes helicopters and autogiros.
    b Includes gliders, dirigibles, balloons, and experimental aircraft.
    c Limited to Air taxis under 12,500 pounds. Otherwise, aircraft included in "Air Carrier."

U.S. CIVIL AND JOINT-USE AIRCRAFT FACILITIES[a]
BY STATE AND BY TYPE
As of December 31, 2002

State	Total[a]	Public[b]	Paved	Lighted	State	Total[a]	Public[b]	Paved	Lighted
Alabama	266	95	174	104	Nevada	127	53	67	39
Alaska	640	405	74	175	New Hampshire	114	26	55	23
Arizona	305	81	173	88	New Jersey	376	53	159	58
Arkansas	304	101	180	113	New Mexico	174	62	80	55
California	941	264	668	283	New York	578	163	224	151
Colorado	420	79	182	85	North Carolina	376	115	161	123
Connecticut	154	25	93	31	North Dakota	440	92	90	90
Delaware	48	11	17	15	Ohio	722	176	289	179
Dist. of Col.	16	3	15	4	Oklahoma	437	149	217	132
Florida	816	132	356	183	Oregon	445	98	173	84
Georgia	434	109	195	122	Pennsylvania	789	138	326	147
Hawaii	47	13	38	15	Rhode Island	27	8	19	8
Idaho	250	121	87	54	South Carolina	184	67	88	75
Illinois	876	119	306	188	South Dakota	183	75	79	78
Indiana	625	113	173	118	Tennessee	288	82	161	93
Iowa	317	122	179	138	Texas	1,845	383	873	459
Kansas	410	144	142	129	Utah	140	47	89	49
Kentucky	201	63	117	67	Vermont	79	17	19	11
Louisiana	484	82	260	89	Virginia	418	68	170	94
Maine	138	65	47	33	Washington	488	137	232	138
Maryland	230	38	86	51	West Virginia	117	37	70	36
Massachusetts	227	44	120	42	Wisconsin	554	132	195	151
Michigan	476	232	201	179	Wyoming	119	41	57	41
Minnesota	512	156	162	147	50 States—TOTAL	19,507	5,269	8,526	5,185
Mississippi	239	83	122	87	Puerto Rico	45	11	37	13
Missouri	539	131	238	147	Virgin Islands	8	2	3	2
Montana	263	122	109	92	S. Pacific[c]	18	10	12	7
Nebraska	303	91	119	92	TOTAL	19,578	5,292	8,578	5,207

FACILITIES BY CLASS

Class	TOTAL[a]	Public[b]	Private
Airports	13,791	5,013	8,778
Heliports	5,226	79	5,147
Seaplane Bases	473	197	276
Stolports	88	3	85
TOTAL	19,578	5,292	14,286

Source: Federal Aviation Administration.
  a Included in these data are facilities having joint civil-military use.
  b "Public" refers to use, whether publicly or privately owned.
  c American Samoa, Guam, and Trust Territories.

HELIPORTS/HELIPADS[a] IN THE UNITED STATES BY STATE
As of 2002

State	TOTAL Helipads in State	Private Use		Public Use	
		Heliports & Helistops	Helipads at Airports	Heliports & Helistops	Helipads at Airports
Alabama	95	94	—	—	1
Alaska	39	29	2	7	1
Arizona	118	109	1	1	7
Arkansas	83	80	—	—	3
California	416	393	2	—	21
Colorado	174	169	—	—	5
Connecticut	95	89	—	3	3
Delaware	15	14	—	1	—
District of Columbia	18	17	—	1	—
Florida	286	278	2	4	2
Georgia	108	106	—	—	2
Hawaii	19	17	—	—	2
Idaho	42	40	1	—	1
Illinois	266	257	4	4	1
Indiana	123	116	4	2	1
Iowa	89	88	—	—	1
Kansas	41	36	1	—	4
Kentucky	58	58	—	—	—
Louisiana	248	240	2	4	2
Maine	12	11	—	—	1
Maryland	72	69	1	—	2
Massachusetts	133	132	—	—	1
Michigan	88	85	1	2	—
Minnesota	54	53	—	—	1
Mississippi	50	49	—	1	—
Missouri	133	130	1	1	1
Montana	31	28	—	2	1
Nebraska	38	36	1	—	1
Nevada	33	30	—	—	3
New Hampshire	57	56	—	—	1

(Continued on next page)

HELIPORTS/HELIPADS[a] IN THE UNITED STATES BY STATE
As of 2002, continued

State	TOTAL Helipads in State	Private Use		Public Use	
		Heliports & Helistops	Helipads at Airports	Heliports & Helistops	Helipads at Airports
New Jersey	254	247	—	4	3
New Mexico	27	25	2	—	—
New York	171	156	3	7	5
North Carolina	71	67	—	4	—
North Dakota	21	20	—	—	1
Ohio	204	192	1	10	1
Oklahoma	93	88	—	5	—
Oregon	104	100	3	1	—
Pennsylvania	319	308	1	8	2
Rhode Island	17	16	—	1	—
South Carolina	33	30	—	—	3
South Dakota	29	29	—	—	—
Tennessee	96	93	1	1	1
Texas	459	445	3	5	6
Utah	46	44	—	—	2
Vermont	19	19	—	—	—
Virginia	138	134	—	—	4
Washington	144	136	3	1	4
West Virginia	36	34	—	—	2
Wisconsin	90	89	—	—	1
Wyoming	27	25	—	—	2
TOTAL	5,432	5,206	40	80	106

Source: Helicopter Association International, "2003 Helicopter Annual" (Annually).
NOTE: 96.6 percent of all U.S. helicopter landing areas are private, while 3.4 percent are public.
a Excludes temporary heliports, offshore heliports, and infrequently used helicopter landing sites.

RESEARCH & DEVELOPMENT

The National Science Foundation (NSF) estimates that the United States funded a total of $292 billion of R&D in 2002—the latest figures available. Industry is shouldering the largest, but declining share of R&D spending. In 2000, industry's share of total R&D spending was 69%. That figure has fallen down a percentage point or so each year; and in 2002, the $193 billion spent by industry on R&D accounted for some 66% of the total. At the same time, the federal government's spending is rising in absolute terms and as a percentage of the total. In 2000, the federal government supplied a little more than 25% of the R&D dollars in the United States. By 2002, the federal government's $81 billion accounted for 27.8%. At $213 billion, industry also performed the majority of R&D, according to the NSF's Annual Survey of Industrial R&D. Colleges and universities combined were the next-largest R&D performer in 2002, accounting for $37 billion of the year's R&D dollars. The federal government accounted for $22 billion.

Funding for aerospace industry-performed R&D declined $2.5 billion, or 24%, in 2001—again using the latest figures available from the NSF. Federal funding of aerospace industry R&D totaled $3.8 billion—down from $6.4 billion and company funding grew $0.2 billion to $4.1 billion. This marks the lowest level in two decades before adjustment for inflation and even longer after. Coincident with this decline in funding, the number of R&D-performing scientists and engineers (R&D S&Es) employed by the aerospace industry has dropped from 144,800 in 1986 to just 19,100 in 2002. Similarly, the percentage of R&D S&Es employed in the aerospace industry has fallen from 21.6% to 1.8%.

AIA has been at the forefront of this crisis and the U.S. government has responded. In FY 2002, federal outlays for R&D (total, not just aerospace) increased $7.8 billion—the second year of real growth—after languishing for six years at the same real spending level. DoD outlays increased $3.7 billion to $45 billion while NASA R&D spending increased 4.6% to $6.8 billion and Energy R&D rose 3.4%. The DoD continued to be the government's largest single spender on R&D, accounting for half of all federal funding. Other agencies, such as the NSF, the National Institutes of Health, and the Transportation and Agriculture Departments saw their collective R&D outlays rise 14% to $29 billion. Further, in FY 2003, federally-funded R&D is scheduled to increase $14 billion to $102 billion. DoD R&D is due to increase $8.5 billion and Energy R&D will grow 11% or $0.8 billion. Likewise, NASA's R&D funding will grow 11% or $0.8 billion.

Ballistic Missile Defense continues to dominate DoD's RDT&E account. BMD funding totaled $6.9 billion in FY 2002 and is scheduled to increase to $7.7 billion in FY 2004. Other DoD aerospace programs receiving the greatest levels of RDT&E funding in FY 2002 included: Joint Strike Fighter, $1.4 billion; F-22 Raptor, $877 million; RAH-66 Comanche, $754 million; V-22 Osprey, $653 million; and SBIRS-High, $525 million.

101

TOTAL U.S. FUNDS FOR RESEARCH AND DEVELOPMENT
BY SOURCE AND PERFORMER[a]
Calendar Years 1999–2002
(Millions of Dollars)

Source of Funds	TOTAL, All Performers	Performer				
		Federal Government	Industry	Colleges & Universities	Federally-Funded Research & Development Centers	Non-Profit Institutions
1999[r]						
All Sources—TOTAL	$243,562	$17,851	$182,711	$28,156	$5,660	$ 9,184
Federal Government	67,014	17,851	22,535	16,215	5,660	4,754
Gov't, Non-Federal	2,101	—	—	2,101	—	—
Industry	163,245	—	160,176	2,094	—	975
Colleges & Universities	5,628	—	—	5,628	—	—
Nonprofit Institutions	5,573	—	—	2,118	—	3,455
2000						
All Sources—TOTAL	$264,616	$17,469	$199,539	$30,974	$5,801	$10,834
Federal Government	66,208	17,469	19,118	17,975	5,801	5,845
Gov't, Non-Federal	2,257	—	—	2,257	—	—
Industry	183,724	—	180,421	2,201	—	1,103
Colleges & Universities	6,210	—	—	6,210	—	—
Nonprofit Institutions	6,217	—	—	2,331	—	3,886
2001[p]						
All Sources—TOTAL	$281,767	$19,130	$209,955	$34,176	$5,940	$12,576
Federal Government	72,920	19,130	20,513	20,179	5,940	7,158
Gov't, Non-Federal	2,387	—	—	2,387	—	—
Industry	192,873	—	189,442	2,272	—	1,160
Colleges & Universities	6,830	—	—	6,830	—	—
Nonprofit Institutions	6,757	—	—	2,508	—	4,249
2002[E]						
All Sources—TOTAL	$291,663	$21,566	$213,116	$37,491	$6,059	$13,431
Federal Government	81,004	21,566	23,201	22,531	6,059	7,646
Gov't, Non-Federal	2,473	—	—	2,473	—	—
Industry	193,420	—	189,915	2,342	—	1,163
Colleges & Universities	7,459	—	—	7,459	—	—
Nonprofit Institutions	7,308	—	—	2,686	—	4,622

Source: National Science Foundation, "Annual Survey of Industrial Research and Development" (Annually).
   a   Source/performer detail not available by industry.

FEDERAL OUTLAYS FOR CONDUCT OF RESEARCH AND DEVELOPMENT
Fiscal Years 1990–2004
(Millions of Dollars)

Year	TOTAL	DoD	NASA	Energy[a]	Other[b]
CURRENT DOLLARS					
1990	$ 63,810	$38,247	$6,325	$5,957	$13,281
1991	62,183	35,330	7,072	5,892	13,889
1992	64,728	35,504	7,617	6,043	15,564
1993	68,378	37,666	8,088	6,036	16,588
1994	68,453	35,474	7,878	5,904	19,197
1995	68,432	35,356	8,992	6,195	17,889
1996	68,439	36,936	8,083	6,135	17,285
1997	71,073	37,702	9,374	5,819	18,178
1998	72,803	37,558	9,881	5,971	19,393
1999	74,136	37,571	9,433	6,077	21,055
2000	73,947	38,279	6,369	6,282	23,017
2001[r]	80,089	41,157	6,473	6,613	25,846
2002	87,911	44,903	6,772	6,835	29,401
2003[E]	101,761	53,396	7,499	7,607	33,259
2004[E]	112,108	58,680	8,325	8,318	36,785
CONSTANT DOLLARS[c]					
1990	$ 74,198	$44,473	$7,355	$6,927	$15,443
1991	69,556	39,519	7,911	6,591	15,536
1992	70,587	38,718	8,306	6,590	16,973
1993	72,820	40,113	8,613	6,428	17,666
1994	71,305	36,952	8,206	6,150	19,997
1995	69,829	36,078	9,176	6,321	18,254
1996	68,439	36,936	8,083	6,135	17,285
1997[r]	69,679	36,963	9,190	5,705	17,822
1998	70,409	36,323	9,556	5,775	18,755
1999[r]	70,740	35,850	9,001	5,799	20,091
2000[r]	69,239	35,842	5,963	5,882	21,551
2001[r]	73,207	37,621	5,917	6,045	23,625
2002	79,342	40,526	6,112	6,169	26,535
2003[E]	90,696	47,590	6,684	6,780	29,643
2004[E]	98,427	51,519	7,309	7,303	32,296

Source: Office of Management and Budget, "The Budget of the United States Government" (Annually).
    a Includes defense and nondefense-related atomic energy R&D with nondefense energy R&D.
    b Includes but not limited to NSF, National Institutes of Health, DoT, & Agriculture.
    c Based on Fiscal Year GDP deflator, 1996=100.

FUNDS FOR INDUSTRIAL RESEARCH AND DEVELOPMENT
IN ALL INDUSTRIES AND THE AEROSPACE INDUSTRY
BY FUNDING SOURCE
Calendar Years 1987–2001
(Millions of Dollars)

Year	All Industries[a]			Aerospace Industry[b]		
	TOTAL	Federal Funds	Company Funds[c]	TOTAL	Federal Funds	Company Funds[c]
CURRENT DOLLARS						
1987	$ 92,155	$30,752	$ 61,403	$24,458	$18,519	$5,939
1988	97,015	30,343	66,672	24,168	18,402	5,766
1989	102,055	28,554	73,501	22,331	16,828	5,503
1990	109,727	28,125	81,602	20,635	15,248	5,387
1991	116,952	26,372	90,580	16,629	11,096	5,533
1992	119,110	24,722	94,388	17,158	10,287	6,871
1993	117,400	22,809	94,591	15,056	9,372	5,684
1994	119,595	22,463	97,131	14,260	8,794	5,466
1995	132,103	23,451	108,652	16,951	11,462	5,489
1996	144,667	23,653	121,015	16,224	10,515	5,710
1997	157,539	23,928	133,611	17,865	10,904	6,961
1998	169,180	24,164	145,016	16,359	9,838	6,521
1999	182,823	22,535	160,288	14,425	9,117	5,309
2000	199,539	19,118	180,421	10,319	6,424	3,895
2001	198,505	16,899	181,606	7,868	3,785	4,083
CONSTANT DOLLARS[d]						
1987	$118,756	$39,629	$ 79,128	$31,518	$23,865	$7,653
1988	120,966	37,834	83,132	30,135	22,945	7,190
1989	122,515	34,279	88,236	26,808	20,202	6,606
1990	126,852	32,514	94,338	23,855	17,628	6,228
1991	130,381	29,400	100,981	18,538	12,370	6,168
1992	129,749	26,930	102,819	18,691	11,206	7,485
1993	124,761	24,239	100,522	16,000	9,960	6,040
1994	124,578	23,399	101,178	14,854	9,160	5,694
1995	134,662	23,905	110,756	17,279	11,684	5,595
1996	144,667	23,653	121,015	16,224	10,515	5,710
1997	154,602	23,482	131,120	17,532	10,701	6,831
1998	163,934	23,415	140,519	15,852	9,533	6,319
1999	174,616	21,523	153,093	13,777	8,708	5,071
2000	186,485	17,867	168,618	9,644	6,004	3,640
2001	181,449	15,447	166,002	7,192	3,460	3,732

Source: National Science Foundation, "Annual Survey of Industrial Research and Development" (Annually).
  a Includes all manufacturing industries, plus those non-manufacturing industries known to conduct or finance research and development.
  b Companies classified in NAICS code 3364, having as their principal activity the manufacture of aerospace products and parts. Prior to 1999, data categorized using SIC system and reported combining codes 372 and 376.
  c Company funds include all funds for industrial R&D work performed within company facilities except funds provided by the Federal Government. Excluded are company-financed research and development contracted to outside organizations such as research institutions, universities and colleges, or other non-profit organizations.
  d Based on GDP deflator, 1996=100.

FUNDS FOR INDUSTRIAL RESEARCH AND DEVELOPMENT IN THE AEROSPACE INDUSTRY BY TYPE OF RESEARCH AND FUNDING SOURCE

Calendar Years 1964–2001
(Millions of Dollars)

Year	TOTAL	Basic Research			Applied Research			Development		
		TOTAL	Federal Funds	Company Funds	TOTAL	Federal Funds	Company Funds	TOTAL	Federal Funds	Company Funds
1964	$ 5,078	$ 67	$ 34	$ 28	$ 766	$ 607	$ 159	$ 4,244	$ 3,948	$ 296
1965	5,148	71	41	30	735	563	172	4,342	3,921	421
1966	5,526	69	36	33	773	563	210	4,685	4,162	523
1967	5,669	71	33	38	726	490	236	4,871	4,071	800
1968	5,765	68	26	42	677	426	251	5,021	4,145	876
1969	5,882	65	24	41	597	347	250	5,220	4,216	1,004
1970	5,219	63	20	43	565	352	213	4,591	3,718	873
1971	4,881	54	37	17	461	279	182	4,365	3,583	782
1972	4,950	60	44	16	451	267	184	4,438	3,722	716
1973	5,052	50	21	29	512	308	204	4,491	3,633	858
1974	5,278	51	19	32	609	360	249	4,617	3,735	882
1975	5,713	54	17	37	614	381	233	5,044	4,119	925
1976	6,339	54	21	33	666	365	301	5,619	4,521	1,098
1977	7,033	56	25	31	753	419	334	6,223	5,017	1,206
1979[a]	8,041	86	44	42	880	499	381	7,076	5,314	1,762
1981[a]	11,968	131	60	71	1,484	897	587	10,353	7,738	2,615
1983	13,853	146	NA	NA	3,466	NA	NA	10,241	7,668	2,573
1984	16,033	247	NA	NA	3,067	NA	NA	12,718	9,870	2,848
1985	17,619	304	162	142	3,785	2,776	1,009	13,530	10,483	3,047
1986	21,050	311	208	103	3,198	1,571	1,627	17,541	13,205	4,336
1987	24,488	425	335	90	2,949	1,709	1,239	21,115	16,475	4,640
1988	25,900	366	263	104	2,997	1,915	1,082	22,537	17,700	4,838
1989	25,638	668	553	116	3,081	2,113	968	21,889	16,967	4,921
1990	25,356	658	519	139	3,340	1,931	1,409	21,358	16,766	4,592
1991	16,983	364	302	62	2,091	1,105	986	14,528	10,043[b]	4,485
1992	17,158	270	235	35	1,739	976	763	15,148	9,076	6,072
1993	15,056	NA	NA	NA	1,453	825	628	NA	NA	NA
1994	14,260	NA	NA	NA	<1,473	<816	<657	12,787	7,978	4,809
1995	16,951	252	250	2	1,987	564	1,423	14,712	10,648	4,064
1996	16,224	NA	NA	108	<2,858	<1,251	<1,607	13,259	9,264	3,995
1997	17,865[c]	NA	NA	10	NA	NA	1,508	13,275	9,115	4,159
1998	16,359[c]	NA	NA	172	NA	NA	272	12,800	8,136	4,664
1999	14,425	NA	NA	173	<2,712	<2,057	655	11,541	7,060	4,480
2000	10,319	NA	NA	NA	<3,553	<2,493	<1,060	6,766	3,931	2,835
2001	7,868	<530	<229	301	1,639	735	904	>5,693	>2,821	2,877

Source: National Science Foundation, "Annual Survey of Industrial Research and Development" (Annually).
  a Break-outs by Research Type and Funding Source available only for odd-numbered years between 1977 and 1983.
  b Computed by AIA as difference between total and company funds. Figure withheld by NSF because of imputation of more than 50 percent.
  c Funding by type of research not revised nor published despite revised totals.

105

RESEARCH AND DEVELOPMENT FUNDS AS PERCENT OF NET SALES
ALL MANUFACTURING INDUSTRIES AND THE AEROSPACE INDUSTRY
Calendar Years 1978–2001

Year	All Manufacturing Industries[a]		Aerospace Industry[b]	
	Total Funds	Company Funds	Total Funds	Company Funds
1978	2.9%	2.0%	13.3%	3.2%
1979	2.6	1.9	12.9	3.5
1980	3.0	2.1	13.7	3.8
1981	3.1	2.2	16.0	4.6
1982	3.8	2.6	17.1	5.1
1983	3.9	2.6	15.2	4.1
1984	3.9	2.6	15.4	4.0
1985	4.4	3.0	14.9	3.9
1986	4.7	3.2	13.4	4.0
1987	4.6	3.1	14.7	3.6
1988	4.5	3.1	16.3	3.9
1989	4.3	3.1	13.5	3.3
1990	4.2	3.1	11.8	3.1
1991	4.2	3.2	12.1	4.0
1992	4.2	3.3	11.8	4.7
1993	3.8	3.1	12.5	4.7
1994	3.6	2.9	13.8	5.3
1995	3.6	2.9	12.9	4.2
1996	4.0	3.3	12.9	4.5
1997	3.9	3.3	8.4	3.3
1998	3.7	3.2	7.2	2.9
1999	3.7	3.2	8.8	3.2
2000	3.6	3.3	7.3	2.8
2001	4.0	3.6	5.7	3.0

Source: National Science Foundation, "Annual Survey of Industrial Research and Development" (Annually).
   a   Includes all manufacturing industries known to conduct or finance research and development.
   b   Companies classified in NAICS code 3364, having as their principal activity the manufacture of aerospace products and parts. Prior to 1999, data categorized using SIC system and reported combining codes 372 and 376.

FEDERAL AERONAUTICS RESEARCH AND DEVELOPMENT
Fiscal Years 1986–2002
(Millions of Dollars)

Year	TOTAL	NASA[a]	DoD[b]	DoT[c]
BUDGET AUTHORITY				
1986	$ 6,660	$ 601	$4,927	$1,132
1987	5,824	698	4,179	946
1988	6,974	723	4,989	1,262
1989	10,656	872	8,240	1,544
1990	10,690	932	7,867	1,891
1991	9,417	968	6,149	2,300
1992	11,110	1,117	7,366	2,627
1993	11,359	1,245	7,582	2,532
1994	10,703	1,546	6,848	2,309
1995	10,718	1,310	7,196	2,212
1996	10,159	1,315	6,792	2,052
1997	9,721	1,252	6,323	2,146
1998	9,682	1,327	6,256	2,099
1999	8,997	1,194	5,532	2,271
2000	9,848	1,060	6,587	2,201
2001	9,867	926	6,149	2,792
2002	10,941	997	6,995	2,949
OUTLAYS				
1986	$ 6,073	$ 648	$4,373	$1,052
1987	5,867	622	4,182	1,063
1988	6,340	679	4,448	1,213
1989	8,491	855	6,420	1,216
1990	10,009	889	7,649	1,471
1991	9,501	1,017	6,793	1,691
1992	10,011	1,122	6,790	2,099
1993	11,162	1,212	7,572	2,378
1994	11,137	1,330	7,203	2,604
1995	11,155	1,153	7,132	2,870
1996	10,837	1,187	6,974	2,676
1997	10,430	1,302	6,600	2,528
1998	10,122	1,339	6,354	2,429
1999	9,499	1,217	5,913	2,369
2000	9,577	1,014	6,320	2,243
2001	9,735	867	6,297	2,571
2002	10,410	956	6,655	2,799

Source: NASA, "Aeronautics and Space Report of the President" (Annually).
a Research and Development, Construction of Facilities, Research and Program Management.
b Research, Development, Test, and Evaluation of aircraft and related equipment.
c Federal Aviation Administration: Research, Engineering, and Development; and Facilities, Engineering, and Development.

DEPARTMENT OF DEFENSE OUTLAYS
FOR RESEARCH, DEVELOPMENT, TEST, AND EVALUATION
Fiscal Years 1972–2004
(Millions of Dollars)

Year	TOTAL	Air Force	Army	Navy	Other
1972	$ 7,881	$ 3,205	$1,779	$ 2,427	$ 470
1973	8,157	3,362	1,912	2,404	479
1974	8,582	3,240	2,190	2,623	529
1975	8,866	3,308	1,964	3,021	573
1976	8,923	3,338	1,842	3,215	528
Tr.Qtr.	2,203	830	437	778	161
1977	9,795	3,618	2,069	3,481	627
1978	10,508	3,626	2,342	3,825	715
1979	11,152	4,080	2,409	3,826	837
1980	13,127	5,017	2,707	4,381	1,021
1981	15,278	6,341	2,958	4,783	1,196
1982	17,729	7,794	3,230	5,240	1,465
1983	20,554	9,182	3,658	5,854	1,861
1984	23,117	10,353	3,812	6,662	2,289
1985	27,103	11,573	3,950	8,054	3,527
1986	32,283	13,417	3,984	9,667	5,215
1987	33,596	13,347	4,721	9,176	6,352
1988	34,792	14,302	4,624	8,828	7,038
1989	37,002	14,912	4,966	9,291	7,833
1990	37,458	14,443	5,513	9,160	8,342
1991	34,589	13,050	5,559	7,586	8,371
1992	34,632	11,998	5,978	7,826	8,830
1993	36,968	12,338	6,218	8,944	9,467
1994	34,786	12,513	5,746	7,990	8,537
1995	34,710	12,052	5,081	9,230	8,347
1996	36,561	13,056	4,925	9,404	9,175
1997	37,027	14,040	4,859	8,220	9,908
1998	37,420	14,499	4,881	7,836	10,204
1999	37,363	14,172	5,027	8,052	10,112
2000	37,606	13,839	4,777	8,857	10,133
2001	40,599	14,310	5,837	9,465	10,987
2002	44,389	14,228	6,569	10,360	13,232
2003 [E]	52,838	17,476	7,022	12,232	16,108
2004 [E]	58,194	19,039	8,210	13,547	17,398

Source: Office of Management and Budget, "The Budget of the United States Government" (Annually).

DEPARTMENT OF DEFENSE APPROPRIATIONS FOR RESEARCH, DEVELOPMENT, TEST, AND EVALUATION
Fiscal Years 2002–2004
(Millions of Dollars)

	2002	2003^E	2004^E
TOTAL	$48,623	$57,025	$61,827
BY APPROPRIATION			
Army	$ 7,018	$ 7,535	$ 9,123
Navy	11,379	13,631	14,107
Air Force	14,479	18,561	20,336
Defense Agencies	15,518	17,061	17,974
Operational Test & Evaluation	229	238	287
RECAP OF BUDGET ACTIVITIES			
Basic Research	$ 1,350	$ 1,417	$ 1,309
Applied Research	4,094	4,289	3,670
Advanced Technology Development	4,430	5,067	5,253
Advanced Component Development & Prototypes	10,125	10,754	13,197
System Development & Demonstration	10,676	13,737	15,913
RDT&E Management Support	3,646	3,106	3,028
Operational Systems Development	14,303	18,656	19,458
RECAP OF FYDP PROGRAMS			
Strategic Forces	$ 195	$ 243	$ 333
General Purpose Forces	3,191	3,945	4,202
Intelligence and Communications	9,334	12,602	13,390
Mobility Forces	545	673	781
Guard and Reserve Forces	11	13	5
Research and Development (FYDP Program 6)	34,475	38,637	42,183
Central Supply and Maintenance	374	327	286
Training Medical and Other	—	0	3
Administration and Associated Activities	115	91	197
Support of Other Nations	4	4	29
Special Operations Forces	380	490	416

Source: Department of Defense Budget, "RDT&E Programs (R-1)" (Annually).

DEPARTMENT OF DEFENSE PRIME CONTRACT AWARDS
FOR RESEARCH, DEVELOPMENT, TEST, AND EVALUATION
Fiscal Years 1998–2002
(Millions of Dollars)

Program Categories	1998	1999	2000	2001	2002
TOTAL	$20,103	$19,437	$19,246	$21,444	$26,908
Research	1,646	1,785	1,756	2,213	3,164
Exploratory Development	2,053	2,255	2,509	2,835	3,111
Other Development / Support	16,404	15,397	14,981	16,396	20,633
Aircraft—TOTAL	$ 4,609	$ 4,108	$ 4,037	$ 4,361	$ 5,526
Research	207	156	261	276	393
Exploratory Development	106	110	305	319	250
Other Development / Support	4,297	3,842	3,471	3,766	4,883
Missile and Space Systems—TOTAL	5,268	4,793	4,556	5,361	6,268
Research	252	188	55	81	324
Exploratory Development	416	536	580	881	1,052
Other Development / Support	4,600	4,069	3,921	4,399	4,891
Electronics & Communications Equipment—TOTAL	2,955	3,173	2,645	3,192	3,688
Research	170	212	162	252	376
Exploratory Development	312	320	352	424	422
Other Development / Support	2,472	2,640	2,132	2,516	2,890
All Other—TOTAL[a]	7,271	7,364	8,008	8,530	11,426
Research	1,017	1,230	1,278	1,604	2,071
Exploratory Development	1,219	1,289	1,272	1,211	1,387
Other Development / Support	5,035	4,846	5,457	5,715	7,969

Source: Department of Defense, "Prime Contract Awards by Service Category and Federal Supply Classification" (Annually).
a "All Other" includes ships, tank-automotive, weapons, ammunition, services, and other.

DEPARTMENT OF DEFENSE PRIME CONTRACT AWARDS OVER $25,000 FOR RESEARCH, DEVELOPMENT, TEST, AND EVALUATION BY REGION AND TYPE OF CONTRACTOR

Fiscal Year 2002

Region	TOTAL	Type of Contractor		
		Educational Institutions	Other Non-Profit Institutions[a]	Business Firms
TOTAL (Millions of Dollars)	$26,510	$836	$1,814	$23,860
New England	$ 2,611	$340	$ 300	$ 1,971
Middle Atlantic	2,254	83	149	2,022
East North Central	1,120	51	142	927
West North Central	1,720	18	4	1,698
South Atlantic	6,105	131	619	5,355
East South Central	3,314	36	5	3,273
West South Central	1,696	32	55	1,609
Mountain	1,902	41	5	1,855
Pacific[b]	5,788	103	536	5,149
PERCENT OF TOTAL	100.0%	100.0%	100.0%	100.0%
New England	9.8%	40.7%	16.5%	8.3%
Middle Atlantic	8.5	9.9	8.2	8.5
East North Central	4.2	6.1	7.8	3.9
West North Central	6.5	2.1	0.2	7.1
South Atlantic	23.0	15.7	34.1	22.4
East South Central	12.5	4.3	0.3	13.7
West South Central	6.4	3.8	3.0	6.7
Mountain	7.2	5.0	0.3	7.8
Pacific[b]	21.8	12.3	29.5	21.6

Source: Department of Defense, Washington Headquarters Services, Directorate for Information Operations and Reports.
   a Includes contracts with other government agencies.
   b Includes Alaska and Hawaii.

MILITARY AIRCRAFT PROGRAMS
RESEARCH, DEVELOPMENT, TEST, AND EVALUATION[a]
BY AGENCY AND MODEL

Fiscal Years 2002, 2003, and 2004
(Millions of Dollars)

Agency and Model	2002	2003[E]	2004[E]
AIR FORCE			
B-1B	$ 95.9	$ 157.2	$ 88.7
B-2 Spirit	163.5	259.7	176.8
B-52	65.0	54.7	28.6
C-5 Galaxy	157.5	284.7	356.6
C-17 Globemaster III	106.0	153.8	184.1
C-130J Hercules	—	9.8	13.6
E-3 AWACS	36.7	169.6	270.4
E-8C JSTARS[b]	147.7	60.3	58.4
F-15E Eagle	100.0	60.4	112.1
F-16 Falcon	107.0	81.6	87.5
F-22 Raptor	877.3	905.9	936.5
ARMY			
AH-64D Longbow Apache	$ 39.6	$ 44.1	$ —
*RAH-66 Comanche	754.4	874.0	1,079.3
UH-60 Black Hawk	69.5	110.0	70.2
DEFENSE AIRBORNE RECONNAISSANCE OFFICE			
UAVs[c]	$ 406.0	$ 805.0	$ 870.0
NAVY			
AV-8B Harrier	$ 34.3	$ 18.2	$ 10.5
E-2C Hawkeye	7.0	7.8	9.1
EA-6B Prowler	85.4	52.6	36.6
F/A-18 Hornet	252.9	210.5	179.0
H-1	167.7	236.0	90.6
*JSF[b]	1,445.0	3,406.7	4,365.8
MH-60R	141.4	92.8	77.0
MH-60S	39.4	22.7	59.1
V-22 Osprey	652.9[d]	484.8	543.9

Source: Department of Defense Budget, "Program Acquisition Costs by Weapon System" (Annually) and "RDT&E Programs (R-1)" (Annually).

NOTE: See Aircraft Production Chapter for aircraft program procurement authorization data.

a   Total Obligational Authority.
b   Air Force and Navy funding.
c   Air Force, Navy, and Army funding.
d   Includes 2 test aircraft.
*   Programs in R&D only.

EMPLOYMENT AND COST OF R&D SCIENTISTS AND ENGINEERS
ALL INDUSTRIES AND AEROSPACE INDUSTRY
Calendar Years 1979–2002

Year	Employment[a]			Cost Per R&D Scientist and Engineer[d]	
	All Industries[b] (Thousands)	Aerospace[c] (Thousands)	Aerospace as a Percent of All Industries	All Industries[b]	Aerospace[c]
1979	423.9	86.5	20.4%	$ 87,400	$ 93,300
1980	450.6	85.9	19.1	94,900	101,600
1981	487.8	95.2	19.5	103,900	128,400
1982	509.8	91.1	17.9	111,600	148,800
1983	540.9	103.1	19.1	116,000	143,600
1984	584.1	111.5	19.1	124,000	156,000
1985	622.5	130.2	20.9	130,200	161,700
1986	671.0	144.8	21.6	128,500	149,800
1987	695.8	136.3	19.6	128,800	180,400
1988	708.6	136.4	19.2	132,300	193,300
1989	722.5	134.8	18.7	134,500	207,300
1990	743.6	115.3	15.5	141,300	213,700
1991	773.4	100.2	13.0	148,600	177,000
1992	779.3	92.9	11.9	157,912	180,552
1993	764.7	97.9	12.8	153,336	176,450
1994	768.5	72.8	9.5	157,459	186,898
1995	746.1	63.5	8.5	167,339	213,328
1996	832.8	95.5	11.5	168,362	170,733
1997	885.7	94.6	10.7	171,499	208,217
1998	951.5	77.0	8.1	173,589	228,159
1999	997.7	66.4	6.7	179,997	237,058
2000	1,033.7	55.3	5.3	192,327	256,692
2001	1,041.3	25.1	2.4	188,917	356,018
2002	1,060.2	19.1	1.8	NA	NA

Source: National Science Foundation.
  a Employment as of January. Scientists and engineers working less than full time have been included in terms of their full time equivalent number.
  b All manufacturing industries and those non-manufacturing industries known to conduct or finance research and development.
  c Companies classified in NAICS code 3364, having as their principal activity the manufacture of aerospace products and parts. Prior to 1999, data categorized using SIC system and reported combining codes 372 and 376.
  d The arithmetic mean of the numbers of R&D scientists and engineers reported for January in two consecutive years, divided into the total R&D expenditures of each industry during the earlier year.

FOREIGN TRADE

Even as the manufacturing sector saw total exports and trade balance fall, the aerospace industry enjoyed a growing trade surplus in 2002. Rising $3.5 billion in 2002 to $30 billion, the aerospace trade surplus reversed a three-year slide.

Aerospace exports, at $57 billion, constituted 8.2% of the total value of U.S.-exported merchandise. Two years ago, when aerospace exports recently bottomed at $46 billion, aerospace accounted for 7.0%; and four years ago that percentage recently peaked at 9.4% of merchandise exports.

Civil products comprised 83% of the total value of aerospace exports. Reduced by declining commercial transport production, civil exports decreased $2.0 billion to $47 billion. Declines in complete aircraft engine exports and aircraft and engine parts exports compounded the $0.5 billion fewer jetliner exports.

Military products, which constituted 17% of aerospace exports, increased to $9.4 billion. While parts exports increased $0.6 billion, complete aircraft declined by a roughly equal amount. In particular, transport exports dropped to nothing after rebounding 58% in 2001, while helicopter exports increased greatly.

Aerospace imports fell $5.2 billion to $27 billion—ending six consecutive years of record imports. Imports of commercial transport aircraft declined in 2002 from 167 to 136. In 2002, the value of imported jetliners fell to $4.6 billion. This follows a doubling in the previous two years.

Imports of general aviation aircraft continued to rise. Up 15 aircraft in 2002, general aviation imports grew to $6.4 billion. General aviation aircraft imports, in dollars, have more than doubled since 1997.

The France was the largest importer of U.S. aerospace exports—$5.6 billion in 2002. The next five largest in order were: Japan, $5.1 billion; United Kingdom, $4.3 billion; China, $3.5 billion; Singapore, $3.5 billion; and Canada, $3.3 billion. Four of these six countries, which imported a total of $18 billion of U.S. aerospace exports, are also leading aerospace producers. The U.S. imported from France, $7.6 billion; Canada, $7.0 billion; United Kingdom, $3.6 billion; and Japan, $1.5 billion. Their combined aerospace exports to the United States totaled $20 billion indicat-

ing a somewhat balanced trade between aerospace-producing countries.

The Export-Import Bank of the United States (Eximbank) promotes U.S. exports by offering foreign customers loans and loan guarantees competitive with

the official export credit organizations of our foreign competitors. In FY 2002, Eximbank loans and guarantees enabled the purchase of 72 jet aircraft worth $4.4 billion.

U.S. TOTAL AND AEROSPACE FOREIGN TRADE[a]
Calendar Years 1968–2002
(Millions of Dollars)

Year	Total U.S. Merchandise Trade			Aerospace		
	Trade Balance	Exports	Imports	Trade Balance	Exports	Imports
1968	$ 837	$ 34,063	$ 33,226	$ 2,661	$ 2,994	$ 333
1969	1,289	37,332	36,043	2,831	3,138	307
1970	3,225	43,176	39,952	3,097	3,405	308
1971	(1,476)[b]	44,087	45,563	3,830	4,203	373
1972	(5,729)	49,854	55,583	3,230	3,795	565
1973	2,390	71,865	69,476	4,360	5,142	782
1974	(3,884)	99,437	103,321	6,350	7,095	745
1975	9,551	108,856	99,305	7,045	7,792	747
1976	(7,820)	116,794	124,614	7,267	7,843	576
1977	(28,353)	123,182	151,534	6,850	7,581	731
1978	(30,205)	145,847	176,052	9,058	10,001	943
1979	(23,922)	186,363	210,285	10,123	11,747	1,624
1980	(19,696)	225,566	245,262	11,952	15,506	3,554
1981	(22,267)	238,715	260,982	13,134	17,634	4,500
1982	(27,510)	216,442	243,952	11,035	15,603	4,568
1983	(52,409)	205,639	258,048	12,619	16,065	3,446
1984	(106,703)	223,976	330,678	10,082	15,008	4,926
1985	(117,712)	218,815	336,526	12,593	18,725	6,132
1986	(138,279)	227,159	365,438	11,826	19,728	7,902
1987	(152,119)	254,122	406,241	14,575	22,480	7,905
1988	(118,526)	322,426	440,952	17,860	26,947	9,087
1989	(109,399)	363,812	473,211	22,083	32,111	10,028
1990	(101,718)	393,592	495,311	27,282	39,083	11,801
1991	(66,723)	421,730	488,453	30,785	43,788	13,003
1992	(84,501)	448,164	532,665	31,356	45,018	13,662
1993	(115,568)	465,091	580,659	27,235	39,418	12,183
1994	(150,630)	512,626	663,256	25,010	37,373	12,363
1995	(158,801)	584,742	743,543	21,561	33,071	11,509
1996	(170,214)	625,075	795,289	26,602	40,270	13,668
1997	(180,522)	689,182	869,704	32,239	50,374	18,134
1998	(229,758)	682,138	911,896	40,960	64,071	23,110
1999	(328,821)	695,797	1,024,618	37,381	62,444	25,063
2000	(436,104)	781,918	1,218,022	26,734	54,679	27,944
2001	(411,899)	729,100	1,140,999	26,035	58,508	32,473
2002	(470,260)	693,302	1,163,561	29,533	56,775	27,242

Source: Bureau of the Census, Foreign Trade Division and Aerospace Industries Association, based on data from International Trade Administration.

NOTE: The Commerce Department began reporting international trade using the Harmonized Tariff Schedules of the United States in 1989. Previous years based on the Tariff Schedules of the United States Annotated.

a Total U.S. and aerospace foreign trade are reported as (1) exports of domestic merchandise, including Department of Defense shipments and undocumented exports to Canada, free alongside-ship basis, (2) imports for consumption, customs value basis.

b First U.S. trade deficit since 1888.

TOTAL U.S. EXPORTS AND EXPORTS OF AEROSPACE PRODUCTS
Calendar Years 1968–2002
(Millions of Dollars)

Year	Total Exports of U.S. Merchandise[a]	Exports of Aerospace Products				
		TOTAL	Percent of Total U.S. Exports	Civil		Military
				Total	Trans-ports	
1968	$ 34,063	$ 2,994	8.8%	$ 2,289	$ 1,200	$ 705
1969	37,332	3,138	8.4	2,027	947	1,111
1970	43,176	3,405	7.9	2,516	1,283	889
1971	44,087	4,203	9.5	3,080	1,567	1,123
1972	49,854	3,795	7.6	2,954	1,119	841
1973	71,865	5,142	7.2	3,788	1,664	1,354
1974	99,437	7,095	7.1	5,273	2,655	1,822
1975	108,856	7,792	7.2	5,324	2,397	2,468
1976	116,794	7,843	6.7	5,677	2,468	2,166
1977	123,182	7,581	6.2	5,049	1,936	2,532
1978	145,847	10,001	6.9	6,018	2,558	3,983
1979	186,363	11,747	6.3	9,772	4,998	1,975
1980	225,566	15,506	6.9	13,248	6,727	2,258
1981	238,715	17,634	7.4	13,312	7,180	4,322
1982	216,442	15,603	7.2	9,608	3,834	5,995
1983	205,639	16,065	7.8	10,595	4,683	5,470
1984	223,976	15,008	6.7	9,659	3,195	5,350
1985	218,815	18,725	8.6	12,942	5,518	5,783
1986	227,159	19,728	8.7	14,851	6,276	4,875
1987	254,122	22,480	8.8	15,768	6,377	6,714
1988	322,426	26,947	8.4	20,298	8,766	6,651
1989	363,812	32,111	8.8	25,619	12,313	6,492
1990	393,592	39,083	9.9	31,517	16,691	7,566
1991	421,730	43,788	10.4	35,548	20,881	8,239
1992	448,164	45,018	10.0	36,906	22,379	8,111
1993	465,091	39,418	8.5	31,823	18,146	7,596
1994	512,626	37,373	7.3	30,050	15,931	7,322
1995	584,742	33,071	5.7	25,079	10,606	7,991
1996	625,075	40,270	6.4	29,477	13,624	10,792
1997	689,182	50,374	7.3	40,075	21,028	10,299
1998	682,138	64,071	9.4	51,999	29,168	12,072
1999	695,797	62,444	9.0	50,624	25,694	11,820
2000	781,918	54,679	7.0	45,566	19,615	9,113
2001	729,100 [r]	58,508	8.0	49,371	22,151	9,137
2002	693,302	56,775	8.2	47,348	21,661	9,427

Source: Bureau of the Census, Foreign Trade Division and Aerospace Industries Association, based on data from International Trade Administration.

NOTE: International trade reported using Harmonized Tariff Schedules after 1988.

a Includes DoD shipments and undocumented exports to Canada, free alongside-ship basis.

117

U.S. EXPORTS OF AEROSPACE PRODUCTS[a]
BY MAJOR COUNTRIES OF DESTINATION
Calendar Years 1998–2002
(Millions of Dollars)

Country of Destination	1998	1999	2000	2001	2002
Australia	$1,050	$1,426	$1,284	$1,112	$3,182
Brazil	1,461	1,575	1,636	2,473	1,867
Canada	3,107	3,438	3,747	4,071	3,321
China	3,731	2,491	1,794	2,591	3,526
France	4,286	5,322	4,691	5,248	5,566
Germany	4,214	4,325	4,581	4,417	2,991
Israel	1,595	1,789	877	1,275	954
Italy	587	1,426	873	823	1,854
Japan	6,057	5,401	4,257	3,795	5,071
Korea, South	1,888	1,899	2,157	2,844	2,742
Malaysia	1,382	539	353	696	964
Mexico	865	571	518	778	609
Netherlands	1,037	1,566	1,796	1,285	1,438
Saudi Arabia	5,008	3,299	1,960	1,432	315
Singapore	2,296	2,069	1,387	4,160	3,500
Spain	281	1,305	1,381	720	663
Sweden	792	1,295	1,347	608	494
Taiwan	2,915	2,237	1,622	1,609	1,114
Turkey	883	957	1,307	842	1,033
United Kingdom	7,569	7,845	6,478	6,536	4,319

Source: Aerospace Industries Association, based on data from the International Trade Administration.

a   Includes all civil products, free alongside-ship basis; excludes military products whose country of destination are not reported.

U.S. IMPORTS OF AEROSPACE PRODUCTS[a]
BY MAJOR COUNTRIES OF ORIGIN
Calendar Years 1998–2002
(Millions of Dollars)

Country of Origin	1998	1999	2000	2001	2002
Australia	$ 160	$ 144	$ 109	$ 137	$ 125
Brazil	917	1,285	1,494	1,973	1,868
Canada	4,867	5,087	6,253	7,985	7,003
France	5,814	6,313	8,071	8,721	7,591
Germany	2,044	2,707	3,364	3,775	2,488
Israel	493	428	515	576	589
Italy	643	736	506	527	711
Japan	2,148	1,710	1,614	1,986	1,507
Korea, South	196	186	195	302	214
Mexico	144	158	149	162	399
Netherlands	225	161	173	173	167
Singapore	325	87	96	122	126
Sweden	306	147	132	159	127
Switzerland	139	164	164	174	170
United Kingdom	5,173	4,968	4,197	4,818	3,600

Source: Aerospace Industries Association, based on data from the International Trade Administration.
a   Includes civil and military products, c.i.f. (Cost, Insurance, and Freight) basis.

U.S. EXPORTS OF AEROSPACE PRODUCTS
Calendar Years 1999–2002
(Millions of Dollars)

Use and Type	1999	2000	2001	2002
TOTAL..................................	$62,444	$54,679	$58,508	$56,775
CIVIL—TOTAL.............................	$50,624	$45,566	$49,371	$47,348
Complete Aircraft—TOTAL.........	$28,450	$22,156	$24,787	$25,617
Transports	25,694	19,615	22,151	21,661
General Aviation[a]......................	1,309	1,136	1,357	1,180
Helicopters	137	170	170	116
Used Aircraft...........................	1,286	1,208	1,078	2,640
Other, incl. Spacecraft[b]	435	167	188	351
Aircraft Engines—TOTAL	3,714	4,610	5,258	4,347
Turbine Engines	3,602	4,510	5,142	4,226
Piston Engines	112	101	116	121
Aircraft and Engine Parts incl. Spares—TOTAL..................	18,051	18,660	19,169	17,054
Aircraft Parts & Accessories......	11,943	12,289	12,606	10,815
Aircraft Engine Parts	6,108	6,371	6,563	6,239
MILITARY—TOTAL	$11,820	$ 9,113	$ 9,137	$ 9,427
Complete Aircraft—TOTAL[c].......	$ 4,221	$ 2,556	$ 2,096	$ 1,574
Fighters & Fighter Bombers	2,543	1,287	339	366
Transports	878	408	645	—
Helicopters	358	594	572	957
Used Aircraft...........................	303	85	247	205
Other, incl. Spacecraft[b]	509	303	432	348
Aircraft Engines—TOTAL	581	333	281	310
Turbine Engines	500	248	147	230
Piston Engines	81	85	134	80
Aircraft and Engine Parts incl. Spares—TOTAL..................	5,557	5,049	5,503	6,063
Aircraft Parts & Accessories......	4,558	4,151	4,602	4,657
Aircraft Engine Parts	999	898	901	1,405
Guided Missiles, Rockets, & Parts—TOTAL..................	1,091	1,053	1,119	1,178
Guided Missiles & Rockets.........	576	402	223	244
Missile & Rocket Parts	505	643	893	919
Missile & Rocket Engines..........	10	9	3	15
Missile & Rocket Engine Parts ...	—	—	—	—

Source: Aerospace Industries Association, based on data from International Trade Administration.
  a All fixed-wing aircraft under 33,000 pounds.
  b Products within this category are not designated civil or military by the Harmonized Tariff Schedules. Historically, aircraft herein have been predominantly civil. Also, spacecraft not included in "Complete Aircraft—Total."
  c Includes aircraft exported under Military Assistance Programs and Foreign Military Sales.

U.S. IMPORTS OF AEROSPACE PRODUCTS
Calendar Years 1999–2002
(Millions of Dollars)

Use and Type	1999	2000	2001	2002
TOTAL.................................	$25,063	$27,944	$32,473	$27,242
CIVIL—TOTAL.................................	$18,709	$21,994	$25,670	$21,334
Complete Aircraft—TOTAL	$ 8,773	$12,388	$14,709	$12,647
Transports	3,397	5,560	6,686	4,576
General Aviation............................	4,279	5,005	6,283	6,384
Helicopters	432	489	419	332
Other, including Used Aircraft, & Gliders, Balloons, & Airships[a]........	665	1,334	1,321	1,355
Aircraft Engines—TOTAL	2,257	1,864	2,418	1,887
Turbine Engines[b]...........................	2,233	1,846	2,394	1,845
Piston Engines	23	17	23	42
Aircraft & Engine Parts—TOTAL ...	7,680	7,742	8,543	6,800
Aircraft Parts and Accessories[b]......	4,848	4,679	5,250	3,948
Turbine Engine Parts[b]	2,327	2,554	2,880	2,440
Piston Engine Parts.......................	110	121	147	136
Spacecraft, Other Parts & Accessories[bc]	396	389	266	276
MILITARY—TOTAL	$ 6,354	$ 5,951	$ 6,804	$ 5,908
Complete Aircraft—TOTAL.............	$ 7	$ 11	$ 2	$ 33
Aircraft Engines—TOTAL	2,257	1,884	2,432	1,915
Turbine Engines[b]...........................	2,233	1,846	2,394	1,845
Piston Engines including Parts.......	24	38	37	70
Aircraft & Engine Parts—TOTAL....	4,091	4,056	4,370	3,960
Aircraft Parts[b]	1,311	1,129	1,216	1,202
Turbine Engine Parts[b]	2,361	2,543	2,856	2,430
Spacecraft, Missiles, Rockets, Other Parts, & Accessories[bc]	418	384	298	329

Source: Aerospace Industries Association, based on data from International Trade Administration.
  a Products within this category are not designated civil or military by the Harmonized Tariff Schedules. Historically, these products have been predominantly civil.
  b Category contains products whose use (civil or military) is unspecified by the Harmonized Tariff Schedules. Figures for those products distributed equally between civil and military.
  c Includes satellites, propulsion engines, and parts.

U.S. EXPORTS OF MILITARY AIRCRAFT[a]
Calendar Years 1998–2002

Type of Aircraft	1998	1999	2000	2001	2002
NUMBER OF AIRCRAFT	364	309	344	260	264
Fighters and Fighter Bombers..........	65	68	36	13	14
Transports	12	17	8	3	—
Helicopters	29	75	63	37	64
New Aircraft, NEC	163	66	88	96	52
Used or Rebuilt Aircraft	95	83	149	111	134
VALUE (Millions of Dollars).............	$3,821	$4,221	$2,556	$2,096	$1,574
Fighters and Fighter Bombers..........	$2,514	$2,543	$1,287	$ 339	$ 366
Transports	618	878	408	645	—
Helicopters	360	358	594	572	957
New Aircraft, NEC	119	140	181	293	47
Used or Rebuilt Aircraft	213	303	85	247	205

Source: Aerospace Industries Association, based on data from the International Trade Administration.
   a Includes aircraft exported under Military Assistance Programs and Foreign Military Sales.
 NEC Not elsewhere classified.

U.S. EXPORTS OF CIVIL AIRCRAFT
Calendar Years 1998–2002

Type and Size	1998	1999	2000	2001	2002
NUMBER OF AIRCRAFT[a]	1,518	1,451	1,472	1,480[r]	1,341
Helicopters—TOTAL	238	181	304	309	294
Under 2,200 lbs	196	147	259	277	259
Over 2,200 lbs	42	34	45	32	35
General Aviation—TOTAL	399	503	411	446	321
Single-Engine	208	253	186	194	110
Multi-Engine, under 4,400 lbs	64	66	61	70	55
Multi-Engine, 4,400-10,000 lbs	48	113	60	52	41
Multi-Engine, 10,000-33,000 lbs	79	71	104	130	115
Transports—TOTAL	375	341	268	253	262
Passenger Aircraft, over 33,000 lbs	362	326	255	238	247
Cargo Aircraft, over 33,000 lbs	13	13	12	15	15
Other, over 33,000 lbs, incl. Pass./Cargo Combi	—	2	1	—	—
Other Aircraft—TOTAL[a]	506	426	489	472	464
Used or Rebuilt Aircraft	506	426	489	472	464
Other Aircraft, including Balloons, Gliders, & Kites	526	563	535	567	562
VALUE (Millions of Dollars)	$31,427	$28,450	$22,156	$24,787	$25,617
Helicopters—TOTAL	$ 148	$ 137	$ 170	$ 170	$ 116
Under 2,200 lbs	47	24	70	54	38
Over 2,200 lbs	101	113	120	116	78
General Aviation—TOTAL	813	1,309	1,136	1,357	1,180
Single-Engine	100	140	80	102	75
Multi-Engine, under 4,400 lbs	21	24	21	39	21
Multi-Engine, 4,400-10,000 lbs	206	519	227	199	139
Multi-Engine, 10,000-33,000 lbs	486	627	809	1,016	945
Transports—TOTAL	29,168	25,694	19,615	22,151	21,661
Passenger Aircraft, over 33,000 lbs	27,700	23,733	17,472	19,487	18,785
Cargo Aircraft, over 33,000 lbs	1,468	1,621	1,963	2,664	2,876
Other, over 33,000 lbs, incl. Pass./Cargo Combi	—	340	180	—	—
Other Aircraft—TOTAL[a]	1,298	1,311	1,235	1,109	2,660
Used or Rebuilt Aircraft	1,270	1,286	1,208	1,078	2,640
Other Aircraft, including Balloons, Gliders, & Kites	28	25	27	31	21

Source: Aerospace Industries Association, based on data from International Trade Administration.
a Numbers of gliders, balloons, & kites excluded from civil aircraft totals.

U.S. IMPORTS OF COMPLETE AIRCRAFT
Calendar Years 1999–2002

Use and Type	1999	2000	2001	2002
NUMBER OF AIRCRAFT	1,928	2,159	2,140	2,441
Civil Aircraft—TOTAL........................	1,893	2,143	2,129	2,413
New Complete Aircraft:				
Helicopters	217	238	229	169
General Aviation:				
Single-Engine.................................	162	142	144	223
Multi-Engine, under 4,400 lbs	3	4	—	4
Multi-Engine, 4,400-10,000 lbs	1	7	14	25
Multi-Engine, Turbojet/Turbofan,				
10,000-33,000 lbs	239	286	345	343
Multi-Engine, Other, including				
Turboshaft, 10,000-33,000 lbs	27	21	16	2
Transports, Multi-Engine, over				
33,000 lbs....................................	98	147	167	136
Other Civil Aircraft:				
Gliders[a]	92	133	122	158
Balloons & Airships[a]	101	75	80	44
Others including Kites[a]..................	683	849	739	1,041
Used or Rebuilt	270	241	273	268
Military Aircraft—TOTAL....................	35	16	11	28
New Complete Aircraft	9	2	—	4
Used or Rebuilt	26	14	11	24
TOTAL VALUE (Millions of Dollars)	$8,779.6	$12,399.1	$14,711.1	$12,680.2
Civil Aircraft—TOTAL.........................	$8,772.7	$12,388.3	$14,709.0	$12,647.2
New Complete Aircraft:				
Helicopters	431.7	489.3	419.1	331.9
General Aviation:				
Single-Engine.................................	145.5	134.8	161.2	136.5
Multi-Engine, under 4,400 lbs	0.2	2.5	—	1.7
Multi-Engine, 4,400-10,000 lbs	4.5	15.0	35.8	70.0
Multi-Engine, Turbojet/Turbofan,				
10,000-33,000 lbs	3,879.1	4,647.8	5,879.4	6,141.3
Multi-Engine, Other, including				
Turboshaft, 10,000-33,000 lbs	249.7	205.0	206.4	34.1
Transports, Multi-Engine, over				
33,000 lbs....................................	3,396.8	5,559.6	6,685.8	4,576.4
Other Civil Aircraft:				
Gliders[a]	1.6	2.3	2.0	3.1
Balloons & Airships[a]	7.2	8.2	9.9	6.7
Others including Kites[a]..................	7.0	9.5	9.0	7.2
Used or Rebuilt	649.4	1,314.4	1,300.4	1,338.2
Military Aircraft—TOTAL....................	$ 6.9	$ 10.9	$ 2.1	$ 33.0
New Complete Aircraft	2.5	0.2	—	5.6
Used or Rebuilt	4.4	10.7	2.1	27.4

Source: Aerospace Industries Association, based on data from International Trade Administration.

a Products within this category are not designated civil or military by the Harmonized Tariff Schedules. Historically, these products have been predominantly civil.

U.S. EXPORTS OF COMMERCIAL TRANSPORT AIRCRAFT[a]
Calendar Years 1998–2002

Region of Destination	1998	1999	2000	2001	2002
NUMBER OF AIRCRAFT	375	341	268	253	262
Canada & Greenland	—	4	—	9	12
Latin America & Caribbean	23	19	12	17	14
Europe	150	169	142	85	74
Middle East	36	55	38	28	26
Asia	150	81	57	81	87
Oceania	9	9	11	12	35
Africa	7	4	8	21	14
VALUE (Millions of Dollars)	$29,168	$25,694	$19,615	$22,151	$21,661
Canada & Greenland	$ —	$ 237	$ —	$ 510	$ 382
Latin America & Caribbean	1,215	807	607	1,184	660
Europe	9,885	11,852	10,015	6,892	5,981
Middle East	3,871	3,797	2,231	2,570	2,130
Asia	12,894	7,872	5,618	8,818	9,384
Oceania	628	725	710	816	2,329
Africa	674	404	433	1,360	796

Source: Aerospace Industries Association, based on data from the International Trade Administration.
  a Airframe weight exceeding 33,000 pounds.

U.S. EXPORTS OF CIVIL HELICOPTERS[a]
Calendar Years 1998–2002

Region of Destination	1998	1999	2000	2001	2002
NUMBER OF AIRCRAFT	238	181	304	309	294
Canada & Greenland	6	9	14	6	11
Latin America & Caribbean	57	25	55	59	13
Europe	133	100	126	123	124
Middle East	—	1	4	16	53
Asia	26	25	60	46	35
Oceania	14	17	23	49	46
Africa	2	4	22	10	12
VALUE (Millions of Dollars)	$148.1	$136.6	$169.9	$169.7	$116.0
Canada & Greenland	$ 8.4	$ 4.8	$ 6.1	$ 2.0	$ 6.3
Latin America & Caribbean	25.6	15.2	24.7	12.2	6.3
Europe	65.8	56.4	60.8	53.7	35.2
Middle East	—	1.6	13.9	13.9	9.4
Asia	43.4	55.1	56.9	72.5	49.5
Oceania	4.7	1.4	3.1	6.6	7.2
Africa	0.3	0.2	4.4	8.8	2.2

Source: Aerospace Industries Association, based on data from the International Trade Administration.
a Excludes used helicopters.

U.S. IMPORTS OF CIVIL HELICOPTERS[a]
Calendar Years 1998–2002

Country of Origin	1998	1999	2000	2001	2002
NUMBER OF AIRCRAFT	274	217	238	229	169
Canada	189	146	144	113	73
France...	56	47	64	80	71
Germany	12	8	14	11	9
Italy	11	13	12	23	14
Others[b]...	6	3	4	2	2
VALUE (Millions of Dollars)	$535.7	$431.7	$489.3	$419.1	$331.9
Canada	$419.1	$330.0	$355.0	$267.4	$191.5
France...	60.4	50.0	60.1	70.4	88.5
Germany	27.8	20.3	38.0	29.2	22.0
Italy	27.4	31.4	35.3	50.8	26.2
Others[b]...	1.0	0.1	0.9	1.4	3.6

Source: Aerospace Industries Association, based on data from the International Trade Administration.

a Excludes used helicopters.

b Includes 2 from Australia, 2 from Japan, 1 from Papua New Guinea, and 1 from Poland in 1998; 2 from Japan and 1 from New Zealand in 1999; 3 from Japan and 1 from Switzerland in 2000; 2 from Sweden in 2001; and 1 from Japan and 1 from Sweden in 2002.

U.S. EXPORTS OF GENERAL AVIATION AIRCRAFT[a]
Calendar Years 1998–2002

Region of Destination	1998	1999	2000	2001	2002
NUMBER OF AIRCRAFT	399	503	411	446	321
Canada & Greenland	25	22	39	33	32
Latin America & Caribbean	117	181	89	100	58
Europe..	140	189	180	191	134
Middle East	10	19	18	30	18
Asia	35	26	23	41	22
Oceania..	36	32	26	18	33
Africa	36	34	36	33	24
VALUE (Millions of Dollars)...........	$813.0	$1,309.0	$1,136.4	$1,357.0	$1,179.6
Canada & Greenland	$101.4	$ 54.6	$ 195.1	$ 141.4	$ 126.7
Latin America & Caribbean	192.8	324.4	234.6	252.9	236.9
Europe..	256.0	571.3	449.4	612.9	436.5
Middle East	11.9	96.6	67.8	78.0	65.8
Asia	137.8	97.8	103.2	170.2	113.5
Oceania..	52.3	55.7	15.6	30.5	127.3
Africa	60.8	108.5	70.7	71.3	73.0

Source: Aerospace Industries Association, based on data from the International Trade Administration.

a All fixed-wing aircraft under 33,000 pounds.

U.S. IMPORTS OF GENERAL AVIATION AIRCRAFT[a]
Calendar Years 1998–2002

Country of Origin	1998	1999	2000	2001	2002
NUMBER OF AIRCRAFT	340	432	460	519	597
Brazil	58	84	92	117	115
Canada....................................	104	139	134	153	247
France	57	78	84	106	106
Germany	27	26	39	39	41
Israel	9	19	32	33	25
Poland	13	9	2	—	1
Russia	4	3	1	1	—
Sweden	20	1	—	—	—
Switzerland.............................	30	50	56	56	33
United Kingdom.......................	1	—	—	1	3
Other	17	23	20	13	26
VALUE (Millions of Dollars).......	$3,530.4	$4,279.1	$5,005.0	$6,282.7	$6,383.7
Brazil	$ 782.6	$1,162.8	$1,411.5	$1,877.4	$1,828.3
Canada....................................	1,521.9	1,737.5	1,839.8	2,603.3	2,800.2
France	857.3	1,015.8	1,201.4	1,160.3	1,256.2
Germany	39.6	97.6	191.3	209.0	74.0
Israel	81.8	135.1	234.6	283.8	264.6
Poland	1.9	1.3	0.2	—	0.1
Russia	0.4	0.4	0.1	0.1	—
Sweden	176.6	9.0	—	—	—
Switzerland.............................	66.8	112.7	119.6	128.3	89.7
United Kingdom.......................	0.1	—	—	0.0	4.1
Other	1.3	6.9	6.4	20.4	66.5

Source: Aerospace Industries Association, based on data from the International Trade Administration.
a All fixed-wing aircraft under 33,000 pounds.

U.S. EXPORTS OF AIRCRAFT ENGINES
Calendar Years 2000–2002
(Values in Millions of Dollars)

Type of Engine	2000		2001		2002	
	Number	Value	Number	Value	Number	Value
TOTAL..................................	21,501	$4,943	31,495	$5,539	22,140	$4,657
Turbine Engines—TOTAL....	10,424	$4,758	9,962	$5,289	8,711	$4,456
Civil	8,958	4,510	8,717	5,142	7,627	4,226
Military.................................	1,466	248	1,245	147	1,084	230
Piston Engines—TOTAL......	11,077	185	21,533	250	13,429	202
Civil, New, under 500 HP ...	705	14	1,894	20	1,283	20
Civil, New, over 500 HP	531	10	830	18	1,339	22
Civil, Used	3,660	77	8,568	78	3,451	79
Military.................................	6,181	85	10,241	34	7,356	80

Source: Aerospace Industries Association, based on data from the International Trade Administration.

U.S. IMPORTS OF AIRCRAFT ENGINES[a]
Calendar Years 2000–2002
(Values in Millions of Dollars)

Type of Engine	2000		2001		2002	
	Number	Value	Number	Value	Number	Value
TOTAL...............................	10,412	$3,726	7,999	$4,826	7,928	$3,770
Turbine Engines	4,459	$3,692	3,375	$4,789	3,218	$3,690
Piston Engines—TOTAL	5,953	34	4,624	38	4,710	80
Military..................................	2,736	17	1,756	14	2,404	38
Civil, New, Small	892	2	1,342	4	812	5
Civil, New, Large	1,691	4	948	4	475	9
Civil, Used	634	11	578	15	1,019	29

Source: Aerospace Industries Association, based on data from the International Trade Administration.
   a New and used.

EXPORT-IMPORT BANK
TOTAL AUTHORIZATIONS OF LOANS AND GUARANTEES
AND AUTHORIZATIONS IN SUPPORT OF AIRCRAFT EXPORTS
Fiscal Years 1988–2002
(Millions of Dollars)

Year	Total Authorizations	Authorizations in Support of Aircraft Exports			
		TOTAL	Percent of Total Authorizations	Commercial Jet Aircraft[a]	Other Aircraft[b]
LOANS[c]					
1988	$ 685	$ —	—%	$ —	$ —
1989	695	166.4	23.9	158.0	8.4
1990	614	5	0.8	—	5.0
1991	777	—	—	—	—
1992	817	—	—	—	—
1993	1,748	—	—	—	—
1994	3,016	—	—	—	—
1995	1,598	—	—	—	—
1996	1,236	—	—	—	—
1997	1,549	—	—	—	—
1998	103	—	—	—	—
1999	903	590.8	65.4	590.8	—
2000	933	75.7	8.1	75.7	—
2001	871 [r]	—	—	—	—
2002	296	—	—	—	—
GUARANTEES[d]					
1988	$ 601	$ 89.2	14.8%	$ 73.4	$ 15.8
1989	1,292	496.4	38.4	390.4	106.0
1990	3,333	1,666.3	50.0	224.7	1,441.6
1991	6,034	606.0	10.1	566.9	40.0
1992	7,301	1,667.0	22.8	1,597.1	69.9
1993	9,095	3,488.6	38.4	3,488.6	—
1994	7,609	2,959.0	38.9	2,959.0	—
1995	5,712	977.0	17.1	977.0	—
1996	6,412	1,155.0	18.0	1,155.0	—
1997	7,761	1,959.0	25.2	1,959.0	—
1998	6,151	2,542.5	41.3	2,542.5	—
1999	8,299	5,543.8	66.8	5,543.8	—
2000	8,413	3,647.4	43.4	3,437.8	209.6
2001	6,101	2,736.5	44.8	2,540.5	196.0
2002	7,408	3,823.1	51.6	3,800.9	22.2

Source: Export-Import Bank of the United States.
a Includes complete aircraft, engines, parts, and retrofits.
b Includes business aircraft, general aviation aircraft, helicopters, and related goods and services.
c Loans are commitments for direct financing by the Export-Import Bank to foreign buyers of U.S. equipment and services, which are made to commercial banks and may subsequently be guaranteed by the Export-Import Bank, in which case the value of the loans is also included with Guarantees.
d Guarantees by the Export-Import Bank provide assurances of repayment of principal and interest on loans made by private lending institutions, such as commercial banks, for major export transactions. Excludes insurance.

EXPORT-IMPORT BANK
SUMMARY OF COMMERCIAL JET AIRCRAFT AUTHORIZATIONS
FOR LOANS[a] AND GUARANTEES[b]

Fiscal Years 1976–2002
(Values in Millions of Dollars)

Year	No. of Jet Aircraft[c]		Export Value[c]		No. of New Commitments		Gross Authorizations	
	Loans	Guar-antees	Loans	Guar-antees	Loans	Guar-antees	Loans	Guar-antees
New Authorizations:								
1976	77	6	$1,017	$ 139	34	11	$ 398	$ 87
Tr.Qtr.	15	5	219	182	6	3	94	59
1977	31	25	330	902	16	14	138	294
1978	29	5	479	253	18	5	189	77
1979	118	7	2,938	317	35	10	1,399	239
1980	136	21	3,975	901	36	24	1,693	1,088
1981	121	18	4,568	637	26	17	2,550	533
1982	11	6	441	113	5	2	199	78
1983	21	9	779	619	3	4	384	601
1984	37	8	1,023	327	7	4	532	294
1985	—	14	19	481	1	5	13	289
1986	3	13	74	451	1	9	46	277
1987	—	27	22	1,449	1	14	13	808
1988	—	2	—	94	—	2	—	73
1989	3	5	253	459	1	2	158	390
1990	—	6	—	264	—	2	—	225
1991	—	12	—	665	—	3	—	567
1992	—	37	—	1,889	—	12	—	1,597
1993	—	70	—	4,122	—	27	—	3,489
1994	—	59	—	3,507	—	19	—	2,959
1995	—	27	—	1,205	—	12	—	974
1996	—	18	—	1,089	—	8	—	923
1997	—	34	—	2,357	—	14	—	1,959
1998	—	65	—	3,059	—	24	—	2,543
1999	17	106	1,170	6,464	2	32	591	5,544
2000	5	53	150	4,047	2	17	76	3,438
2001	—	60	—	3,052	—	12	—	2,540
2002	—	72	—	4,370	—	17	—	3,801

Source: Export-Import Bank of the United States.

  a Loans are commitments for direct financing by the Export-Import Bank to foreign buyers of U.S. equipment and services, which are made by the Export-Import Bank to commercial banks and which subsequently may be guaranteed by the Export-Import Bank in which case the value of the loans is included with Guarantees.

  b Guarantees by the Export-Import Bank provide assurances of repayment of principal and interest on loans made by private lending institutions, such as commercial banks, for major export transactions. Excludes insurance.

  c For Export-Import Bank commitments including both loan and guarantee authorization, number of aircraft and export value reported under "Loans."

EXPORT-IMPORT BANK
AUTHORIZATIONS OF LOANS AND GUARANTEES
IN SUPPORT OF EXPORTS OF COMMERCIAL JET AIRCRAFT
Fiscal Years 2001–2002
(Values in Millions of Dollars)

Customer (Country/Airline)	Number and Aircraft Model or Related Product	Export Value	Authorizations				
			Loans (Direct Credits)				Guar-antees
			Amount	Percent Cover-age[a]	Interest Rate	Repay-ment Terms[b]	Amount
FY 2002							
TOTAL	72 aircraft	$4,370	$—	—%	—%	—	$3,801
Algeria/Air Algerie	1 x 737	NA	—	—	—	—	$ 10
Australia/Quantas Airways	~12 x 737	NA	—	—	—	—	567
Austria/Austrian Airlines	NA	NA	—	—	—	—	203
Canada/WestJet Airlines	? x 737	NA	—	—	—	—	478
Ireland/Ryanair..................	~7 x 737	NA	—	—	—	—	221
Israel/El Al Isreal Airlines ...	1 x 777	NA	—	—	—	—	102
Korea/Asiana Airlines.........	1 x 747, 1 x 777	NA	—	—	—	—	93
Korea/Korean Airlines	NA	NA	—	—	—	—	411
Luxembourg/Cargolux Airlines International	1 x 747	NA	—	—	—	—	113
Malaysia/Ministry of Finance	NA	NA	—	—	—	—	617
Morocco/Royal Air Maroc...	1 x 737	NA	—	—	—	—	36
Panama/Copa Airlines	3 x 737	NA	—	—	—	—	114
Taiwan/EVA Airways...........	1 x 747	NA	—	—	—	—	131
Thailand/Thai Airways International	2 x 747	NA	—	—	—	—	241
Turkey/Turkish Airlines.......	2 x 737	NA	—	—	—	—	68
Unallocable/GATX Financial Corporation	NA	NA	—	—	—	—	397

(Continued on next page)

EXPORT-IMPORT BANK
AUTHORIZATIONS OF LOANS AND GUARANTEES
IN SUPPORT OF EXPORTS OF COMMERCIAL JET AIRCRAFT
Fiscal Years 2001–2002, continued
(Values in Millions of Dollars)

Customer (Country/Airline)	Number and Aircraft Model or Related Product	Export Value	Authorizations				
			Loans (Direct Credits)				Guarantees
			Amount	Percent Coverage[a]	Interest Rate	Repayment Terms[b]	Amount
FY 2001							
TOTAL	60 aircraft	$3,052	—	—	—	—	$2,540
Algeria/Air Algerie	7 x 737	$ 224	—	—	—	—	$ 191
Austria/Austrian Airlines	2 x 737, 1 x 767	166	—	—	—	—	137
Chile/Lan Chile.................	2 x 767	179	—	—	—	—	153
China/Hainan Airlines........	5 x 737	290	—	—	—	—	247
China/Shanghai Airlines....	1 x 767	80	—	—	—	—	67
India/Jet Airways	10 x 737	405	—	—	—	—	346
Korea/Korean Air Lines	4 x 747, 1 x 777	795	—	—	—	—	655
Romania/Tarom Romanian Air Transport	2 x 737	90	—	—	—	—	70
South Africa/South African Airways	16 x 737	320	—	—	—	—	258
Thailand/Thai Airways International	2 x 777	255	—	—	—	—	208
Turkey/Turk Hava Yollari Tao	2 x 737	82	—	—	—	—	68

Source: Aerospace Industries Association, based on data from the Export-Import Bank of the United States.
NOTE: For definitions of Loans and Guarantees, see Export-Import Bank tables on previous pages.
 a Amount of loan as percent of export value.
 b Number of payments and frequency (S=semi-annual).

135

EMPLOYMENT

The aerospace industry, which employed 4.7% of all manufacturing and 7.5% of durable goods manufacturing workers, reduced its workforce in 2002 by 76,000. On an annual average basis, the aerospace industry employed 714,000 workers with an annual payroll of $28 billion. The aircraft sector employed 410,000, while the missiles and space sector employed 82,000 and avionics and other input industries provided another 222,000 jobs.

Of the jobs lost in 2002, the aircraft and parts manufacturing sector accounted for 50,400 of them. Engine sector employment eased 6,500 while the complete aircraft manufacturing sector dropped 27,100 and the aircraft parts manufacturing cut 16,800. Also declining, missiles and space sector's employment dropped by 2,000 and the avionics and other input industry employment fell by 24,000.

Earnings of production workers increased on average to $21.74 per hour—up from $21.11 in 2001. Production workers doing aircraft final assembly earned the highest hourly wage—$24.52. Final assembly workers in the missiles and space sector were next with $23.42 per hour; followed by aircraft engine workers, $21.31, and aircraft parts, $19.23.

Final assembly workers in the missiles and space sector logged the highest average overtime—7.0 hours per week, down from 10.2 in 2001 and 8.1 in 2000. Similarly, these workers logged the longest average workweek—42.9 hours. This compares with 42.2 in the engine sector, 41.7 for other aircraft parts, and 39.6 for aircraft final assembly.

The Bureau of Labor Statistics (BLS) reported that the hourly labor cost, including benefits, is $45.85 for all workers in the aircraft manufacturing industry. This is composed of $28.71 in wages and salaries and $17.14 in benefits. On average, white-collar workers cost $49.04 per hour and blue-collar workers cost $40.77 per hour.

The aerospace industry suffered three work stoppages in 2002. A total of 7,500 employees and 118,100 work-days went idle, according to statistics published by the BLS. The year before, one work-stoppage idled 5,000 workers and 45,000 work-days were lost.

National employment of R&D-performing scientists and engineers across all industries has steadily grown since 1995, while aerospace employment of R&D-performing scientists has steadily declined. In 1996, 95,500 R&D scientists and engineers found employment in the aerospace industry. By 2002, that number had dropped to 19,100. The aerospace share of national employment has fallen to the lowest level on record—just 1.8%. Despite fewer R&D jobs in aerospace, most experts agree that engineers and technical workers remain in demand. Further, most aerospace companies say they still need mechanical, structural, and aerodynamics engineers, as well as soft-

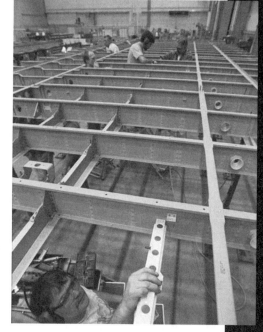

ware engineers and information technology specialists.

ANNUAL AVERAGE EMPLOYMENT IN ALL MANUFACTURING, DURABLE GOODS, AND AEROSPACE INDUSTRIES
Calendar Years 1979–2002
(Thousands)

Year	All Manu-facturing Industries[r]	Durable Goods Industries[r]	Aerospace Industry[a]		
				As Percent of	
			Total	All Manufac-turing[r]	Durable Goods[r]
1979	19,426	12,220	1,007	5.2%	8.2%
1980	18,733	11,679	1,080	5.8	9.2
1981	18,634	11,611	1,087	5.8	9.4
1982	17,363	10,610	1,038	6.0	9.8
1983	17,048	10,326	1,019	6.0	9.9
1984	17,920	11,050	1,058	5.9	9.6
1985	17,819	11,034	1,151	6.5	10.4
1986	17,552	10,795	1,241	7.1	11.5
1987	17,609	10,767	1,282	7.3	11.9
1988	17,906	10,969	1,294	7.2	11.8
1989	17,985	11,004	1,314	7.3	11.9
1990	17,695	10,736	1,302	7.4	12.1
1991	17,068	10,219	1,214	7.1	11.9
1992	16,799	9,945	1,100	6.5	11.1
1993	16,774	9,900	966	5.8	9.8
1994	17,021	10,131	855	5.0	8.4
1995	17,241	10,372	796	4.6	7.7
1996	17,237	10,485	796	4.6	7.6
1997	17,419	10,704	859	4.9	8.0
1998	17,560	10,910	896	5.1	8.2
1999	17,322	10,830	847	4.9	7.8
2000	17,263	10,876	799	4.6	7.3
2001	16,441	10,335	790	4.8	7.6
2002	15,306	9,517	714	4.7	7.5

Source: Bureau of Labor Statistics and Aerospace Industries Association estimates.
   a See Glossary for detailed explanation of "Aerospace Employment."

ANNUAL PAYROLL
OF ALL MANUFACTURING AND AEROSPACE INDUSTRIES
Calendar Years 1979–2002
(Millions of Dollars)

Year	All Manufacturing Industries[a]	Aerospace Industry[b]			Aerospace As Percent of All Manufacturing
		TOTAL	Production Workers	Other Workers	
1979	$335,200	$15,150	$ 6,465	$ 8,685	4.5%
1980	356,200	18,026	7,658	10,368	5.1
1981	387,600	19,906	8,152	11,754	5.1
1982	385,700	20,750	8,043	12,707	5.4
1983	400,700	21,644	8,071	13,573	5.4
1984	445,400	23,773	8,746	15,027	5.3
1985	468,500	26,749	9,837	16,911	5.7
1986	480,700	29,547	11,038	18,509	6.1
1987	496,900	31,101	11,700	19,401	6.3
1988	529,900	32,566	11,744	20,822	6.1
1989	547,900	34,154	12,440	21,714	6.2
1990	561,400	35,590	13,020	22,570	6.3
1991	562,500	34,520	12,536	21,984	6.1
1992	583,500	33,123	11,812	21,311	5.7
1993	592,400	30,391	10,673	19,718	5.1
1994	620,300	28,395	9,901	18,494	4.6
1995	647,500	26,603	9,272	17,331	4.1
1996	673,700	27,987	10,105	17,882	4.2
1997	718,400	31,575	12,092	19,483	4.4
1998	756,600	32,981	12,769	20,213	4.4
1999	782,000	31,143	11,661	19,481	4.0
2000	829,400	31,160	11,153	20,007	3.8
2001	789,400[r]	31,258	11,155	20,103	4.0[r]
2002	758,700	28,252	9,579	18,673	3.7

Source: Bureau of Economic Analysis, "Survey of Current Business" (Monthly) and Aerospace Industries Association estimates based on data from the Bureau of Labor Statistics.
  a See Glossary for explanation of "Payroll, All Manufacturing."
  b Based on combined annual average employment and average weekly earnings for SICs 372 and 376.

EMPLOYMENT IN THE AEROSPACE INDUSTRY[a]
Calendar Years 1988–2002
(Thousands)

Year	TOTAL	Aircraft, Engines, & Parts (SIC 372)	Missiles & Space Vehicles (SIC 376)	Other[b]
TOTAL EMPLOYMENT				
1988	1,294	684	208	402
1989	1,314	711	194	408
1990	1,302	712	185	405
1991	1,214	669	168	378
1992	1,100	612	146	342
1993	966	542	124	300
1994	855	482	108	266
1995	796	451	98	248
1996	796	458	90	248
1997	859	501	91	267
1998	896	525	92	279
1999	847	496	87	263
2000	799	464	86	248
2001	790	461	84	246
2002	714	410	82	222
PRODUCTION WORKERS				
1988	422	331	63	28
1989	432	344	60	29
1990	430	345	57	29
1991	399	324	48	27
1992	355	291	40	24
1993	308	253	35	20
1994	271	222	31	18
1995	252	208	28	17
1996	260	218	25	17
1997	295	251	25	20
1998	311	266	25	21
1999	285	244	23	19
2000	259	220	22	17
2001	255	219	20	17
2002	221	187	19	15

Source: Bureau of Labor Statistics and Aerospace Industries Association estimates.
a   Annual average. See Glossary for detailed explanation of "Aerospace Employment."
b   Communications, navigation, flight control, and displays (aerospace-related portions of SICs 366, 381, & 382).

EMPLOYMENT IN THE AIRCRAFT, ENGINES, AND PARTS INDUSTRY[a]
Calendar Years 1988–2002
(Thousands)

Year	TOTAL (SIC 372)	Aircraft (SIC 3721)	Engines and Parts (SIC 3724)	Other Parts & Equipment (SIC 3728)
TOTAL EMPLOYMENT				
1988	683.5	368.5	155.8	159.3
1989	711.0	382.2	153.5	175.2
1990	712.3	381.0	151.7	179.5
1991	669.2	355.6	143.2	170.3
1992	611.7	332.1	126.6	153.0
1993	542.0	301.4	109.2	131.4
1994	481.5	271.3	95.1	115.1
1995	450.5	243.6	93.0	113.9
1996	458.1	243.1	94.7	120.4
1997	500.6	262.4	99.8	138.4
1998	525.1	271.6	103.3	150.2
1999	496.3	253.9	101.2	141.2
2000	464.1	233.9	100.6	129.6
2001	460.6	232.6	98.9	129.1
2002	410.2	205.5	92.4	112.3
PRODUCTION WORKERS				
1988	331.3	162.1	77.1	92.1
1989	343.7	167.4	76.8	99.5
1990	344.6	164.1	77.2	103.2
1991	323.6	151.6	73.1	98.8
1992	291.4	137.8	64.3	89.2
1993	252.5	122.7	53.6	76.2
1994	222.0	108.1	46.9	67.0
1995	207.5	93.6	46.2	67.7
1996	217.7	95.6	48.8	73.3
1997	251.1	110.1	53.6	87.4
1998	265.5	114.9	54.0	96.5
1999	243.8	105.2	49.3	89.3
2000	220.1	91.3	48.1	80.7
2001	218.5	88.8	48.4	81.3
2002	187.1	72.2	45.0	69.9

Source: Bureau of Labor Statistics.
  a Annual average. See Glossary for detailed explanation of "Aerospace Employment."

AVERAGE WEEKLY EARNINGS IN THE AEROSPACE INDUSTRY
Production Workers Only
Calendar Years 1979–2002

| Year | TOTAL[a] | Aircraft and Parts (SIC 372) | | | | Guided Missiles, Space Vehicles & Parts (SIC 376) | Complete Guided Missiles, & Space Vehicles (SIC 3761) |
		TOTAL[a]	Aircraft (SIC 3721)	Engines & Parts (SIC 3724)	Other Parts & Equipment (SIC 3728)		
AVERAGE WEEKLY EARNINGS[b]							
1979	$351	$351	$360	$361	$322	$347	$ 348
1980	389	390	404	394	358	378	383
1981	424	426	444	422	396	410	420
1982	460	462	485	454	426	447	461
1983	486	487	513	476	453	480	494
1984	513	516	532	523	486	496	508
1985	531	534	547	542	506	515	527
1986	545	550	568	561	520	517	533
1987	556	558	578	567	523	541	556
1988	573	575	596	582	529	567	585
1989	593	594	616	616	542	589	611
1990	624	626	656	637	570	612	634
1991	648	651	694	654	583	632	649
1992	685	689	736	689	615	652	666
1993	714	717	756	715	657	696	727
1994	754	756	800	753	688	738	779
1995	758	757	809	770	677	765	812
1996	801	802	859	813	721	790	837
1997	844	844	918	838	756	842	896
1998	847	847	932	840	751	840	892
1999	842	841	923	859	731	852	896
2000	888	892	993	898	774	847	875
2001	900	900	994	908	793	901	951
2002	895	891	971	899	802	935	1,005

Source: Bureau of Labor Statistics and Aerospace Industries Association estimates.
   a TOTAL columns are employment-based weighted averages.
   b Includes overtime premiums.

AVERAGE HOURLY EARNINGS IN THE AEROSPACE INDUSTRY
Production Workers Only
Calendar Years 1979–2002

| Year | TOTAL[a] | Aircraft and Parts (SIC 372) | | | | Guided Missiles, Space Vehicles & Parts (SIC 376) | Complete Guided Missiles, & Space Vehicles (SIC 3761) |
		TOTAL[a]	Aircraft (SIC 3721)	Engines & Parts (SIC 3724)	Other Parts & Equipment (SIC 3728)		
AVERAGE HOURLY EARNINGS[b]							
1979	$ 8.26	$ 8.26	$ 8.50	$ 8.53	$ 7.48	$ 8.25	$ 8.38
1980	9.27	9.28	9.66	9.42	8.40	9.22	9.33
1981	10.29	10.31	10.74	10.41	9.35	10.06	10.34
1982	11.20	11.23	11.85	11.16	10.17	10.95	11.21
1983	11.79	11.82	12.58	11.61	10.73	11.59	11.84
1984	12.24	12.32	12.91	12.40	11.37	11.82	12.01
1985	12.54	12.62	13.18	12.85	11.66	12.14	12.36
1986	12.75	12.86	13.48	13.08	11.90	12.20	12.48
1987	13.10	13.17	13.74	13.33	12.23	12.73	13.09
1988	13.48	13.55	14.18	13.80	12.28	13.13	13.53
1989	14.10	14.17	14.89	14.42	12.81	13.70	14.20
1990	14.73	14.79	15.66	14.84	13.37	14.39	14.82
1991	15.51	15.60	16.72	15.38	14.05	14.90	15.21
1992	16.46	16.53	17.70	16.28	14.89	15.99	16.45
1993	17.18	17.23	18.43	16.70	15.72	16.80	17.43
1994	17.89	17.95	19.50	17.31	16.01	17.48	18.29
1995	17.99	18.02	19.97	17.34	15.93	17.74	18.58
1996	18.56	18.57	20.49	18.22	16.42	18.51	19.34
1997	18.94	18.88	20.76	18.58	16.76	19.53	20.75
1998	19.24	19.17	21.08	18.93	17.02	19.96	21.38
1999	19.67	19.60	21.83	19.47	17.08	20.39	21.96
2000	20.52	20.50	23.14	20.17	17.76	20.76	21.98
2001	21.11	21.08	23.83	20.64	18.44	21.40	22.60
2002	21.74	21.72	24.52	21.31	19.23	21.96	23.42

Source: Bureau of Labor Statistics and Aerospace Industries Association estimates.
   a TOTAL columns are employment-based weighted averages.
   b Includes overtime premiums.

AVERAGE HOURS IN THE AEROSPACE INDUSTRY
Production Workers Only
Calendar Years 1988–2002

| Year | TOTAL[a] | Aircraft and Parts (SIC 372) | | | | Guided Missiles, Space Vehicles & Parts (SIC 376) | Complete Guided Missiles, & Space Vehicles (SIC 3761) |
		TOTAL[a]	Aircraft (SIC 3721)	Engines & Parts (SIC 3724)	Other Parts & Equipment (SIC 3728)		
AVERAGE WEEKLY HOURS							
1988	42.5	42.4	42.0	42.2	43.1	43.2	43.2
1989	42.1	41.9	41.4	42.7	42.3	43.0	43.0
1990	42.3	42.3	41.9	42.9	42.6	42.5	42.8
1991	41.8	41.7	41.5	42.5	41.5	42.4	42.7
1992	41.6	41.7	41.6	42.3	41.3	40.8	40.5
1993	41.6	41.6	41.0	42.8	41.8	41.4	41.7
1994	42.1	42.1	41.0	43.5	43.0	42.2	42.6
1995	42.1	42.0	40.5	44.4	42.5	43.1	43.7
1996	43.1	43.2	41.9	44.6	43.9	42.7	43.3
1997	44.6	44.7	44.2	45.1	45.1	43.1	43.2
1998	44.0	44.2	44.2	44.4	44.1	42.1	41.7
1999	42.8	42.9	42.3	44.1	42.8	41.8	40.8
2000	43.3	43.5	42.9	44.5	43.6	40.8	39.8
2001	42.7	42.7	41.7	44.0	43.0	42.1	42.1
2002	41.1	41.0	39.6	42.2	41.7	42.6	42.9
AVERAGE WEEKLY OVERTIME HOURS							
1988	4.6	4.6	4.3	4.6	5.1	4.5	4.6
1989	5.0	5.1	5.0	5.4	5.0	4.4	4.5
1990	4.5	4.6	4.3	5.3	4.5	3.8	4.1
1991	4.0	4.0	4.1	4.5	3.5	3.9	4.5
1992	3.6	3.7	3.6	4.4	3.3	2.8	3.1
1993	3.8	3.9	3.7	4.6	3.7	2.9	3.2
1994	4.5	4.6	4.1	5.3	4.8	3.7	3.8
1995	4.8	4.9	4.2	5.9	5.2	4.2	4.6
1996	5.7	5.9	5.3	6.5	6.3	3.9	4.2
1997	6.9	7.2	7.2	6.8	7.3	4.3	4.3
1998	5.9	6.1	5.9	6.0	6.3	3.8	3.6
1999	4.4	4.5	4.3	5.4	4.3	3.5	3.1
2000	4.9	4.8	4.6	6.0	4.4	5.7	8.1
2001	4.8	4.6	4.1	6.0	4.4	6.5	10.2
2002	3.9	3.8	3.4	5.1	3.3	4.6	7.0

Source: Bureau of Labor Statistics and Aerospace Industries Association estimates.
a TOTAL columns are employment-based weighted averages.

EMPLOYER COSTS FOR EMPLOYEE COMPENSATION IN THE AIRCRAFT MANUFACTURING INDUSTRY

March[a] 1998–2003

	1998	1999	2000	2001	2002	2003
ALL OCCUPATIONS						
TOTAL.................................	$34.27	$35.33	$37.87	$40.09	$41.75	$45.85
Wages and Salaries..............	23.32	24.28	25.47	26.79	27.80	28.71
Benefits—TOTAL..................	10.95	11.05	12.39	13.30	13.95	17.14
Paid Leave.........................	3.23	3.34	3.51	3.69	3.82	4.02
Supplemental Pay.............	1.08	1.19	1.67	1.79	1.78	2.81
Insurance..........................	2.48	2.60	2.67	3.13	3.51	4.18
Retirement & Savings.......	1.42	0.97	1.20	1.36	1.41	2.40
Legally Required...............	2.69	2.77	2.92	3.12	3.20	3.50
Other.................................	0.04	0.18	0.42	0.21	0.22	0.23
WHITE-COLLAR OCCUPATIONS						
TOTAL.................................	$36.97	$38.12	$40.76	$43.63	$44.98	$49.04
Wages and Salaries..............	25.68	26.88	28.31	29.68	30.64	31.59
Benefits—TOTAL..................	11.30	11.24	12.44	13.95	14.34	17.45
Paid Leave.........................	3.52	3.71	4.04	4.22	4.36	4.60
Supplemental Pay.............	0.77	0.71	0.81	1.56	1.28	2.24
Insurance..........................	2.48	2.60	2.69	3.19	3.60	4.19
Retirement & Savings.......	1.61	1.12	1.32	1.50	1.56	2.55
Legally Required...............	2.88	2.87	2.99	3.23	3.30	3.63
Other.................................	0.04	0.24	0.59	0.26	0.23	0.24
BLUE-COLLAR OCCUPATIONS						
TOTAL.................................	$29.56	$30.56	$33.33	$34.18	$36.56	$40.77
Wages and Salaries..............	19.24	19.84	20.94	22.00	23.26	24.11
Benefits—TOTAL..................	10.32	10.72	12.39	12.18	13.30	16.67
Paid Leave.........................	2.72	2.70	2.66	2.81	2.95	3.08
Supplemental Pay.............	1.63	2.02	3.13	2.18	2.59	3.77
Insurance..........................	2.49	2.60	2.61	3.02	3.35	4.14
Retirement & Savings.......	1.08	0.73	1.02	1.10	1.15	2.13
Legally Required...............	2.35	2.58	2.83	2.94	3.06	3.32
Other.................................	0.05	0.09	0.13	0.13	0.21	0.22

Source: Bureau of Labor Statistics, "Employer Costs for Employee Compensation" (Annually).
   a Based on the pay period including March 12th.

WORK STOPPAGES IN THE AEROSPACE INDUSTRY
Calendar Years 1979–2002

Year	Number of Strikes[a]	Number of Workers Involved	Work-Days Idle in Year
1979	12	6,600	103,400
1980	17	4,400	92,900
1981	12	6,100	188,900
1982[b]	4	11,900	45,200
1983	2	8,700	404,100
1984	4	14,600	188,200
1985	4	19,700	289,800
1986	—	—	—
1987	—	—	—
1988	3	10,600	415,800
1989	2	58,500	1,848,000
1990	1	2,300	56,700
1991	1	1,500	—
1992	1	3,800	11,400
1993	2	27,800	34,600
1994	—	—	—
1995	1	33,000	1,551,000
1996	2	7,800	90,100
1997	—	—	—
1998	—	—	—
1999	—	—	—
2000	3	22,400	566,400
2001	1	5,000	45,000
2002	3	7,500	118,100

Source: Bureau of Labor Statistics, "Compensation and Working Conditions" (Quarterly).
a Strikes beginning during calendar year.
b Effective 1982, data not available for work stoppages involving fewer than 1,000 employees.

OCCUPATIONAL INJURY AND ILLNESS INCIDENCE RATES[a]
ALL MANUFACTURING AND AEROSPACE INDUSTRIES
Calendar Years 1997–2001

Manufacturing Sector	1997	1998	1999	2000	2001
All Manufacturing:					
Total Cases	10.3	9.7	9.2	9.0	8.1
Lost Workday Cases	4.8	4.7	4.6	4.5	4.1
Nonfatal Cases Without Lost Workdays	5.4	5.0	4.6	4.5	4.0
Aircraft and Parts (SIC 372):					
Total Cases	8.7	8.7	8.2	7.1	7.7
Lost Workday Cases	3.8	4.2	4.1	3.4	3.7
Nonfatal Cases Without Lost Workdays	4.9	4.5	4.1	3.7	4.0
Aircraft (SIC 3721):					
Total Cases	8.5	8.9	8.9	7.5	7.4
Lost Workday Cases	3.7	4.3	4.4	3.7	3.8
Nonfatal Cases Without Lost Workdays	4.8	4.6	4.5	3.7	3.7
Aircraft Engines and Parts (SIC 3724):					
Total Cases	7.7	6.2	5.8	5.5	6.4
Lost Workday Cases	3.3	2.8	2.9	2.2	2.8
Nonfatal Cases Without Lost Workdays	4.5	3.4	2.9	3.3	3.6
Aircraft Parts (SIC 3728):					
Total Cases	9.9	10.0	8.7	7.6	9.1
Lost Workday Cases	4.5	5.0	4.4	3.7	4.2
Nonfatal Cases Without Lost Workdays	5.4	5.0	4.3	3.9	4.9
Guided Missiles, Space Vehicles & Parts (SIC 376):					
Total Cases	3.2	3.3	2.8	2.2	2.9
Lost Workday Cases	1.5	1.5	1.3	1.1	1.6
Nonfatal Cases Without Lost Workdays	1.7	1.8	1.5	1.1	1.3
Guided Missiles & Space Vehicles (SIC 3761):					
Total Cases	2.9	3.0	2.7	2.0	2.4
Lost Workday Cases	1.3	1.3	1.3	1.0	1.3
Nonfatal Cases Without Lost Workdays	1.6	1.8	1.4	1.0	1.1
Space Propulsion Units & Parts (SIC 3764):					
Total Cases	NA	3.2	NA	3.0	4.2
Lost Workday Cases	NA	1.6	NA	1.5	2.5
Nonfatal Cases Without Lost Workdays	NA	1.7	NA	1.6	1.7
Other Space Vehicle Equipment (SIC 3769):					
Total Cases	NA	4.3	3.5	2.2	NA
Lost Workday Cases	NA	2.6	1.6	1.1	NA
Nonfatal Cases Without Lost Workdays	NA	1.8	2.0	1.1	NA

Source: Bureau of Labor Statistics, "Survey of Occupational Injuries and Illnesses" (Annually).
   a   Defined as the number of injuries and illnesses per 100 full-time workers. Separate incidence rates also available for occupational injuries only.

EMPLOYMENT IN NATIONAL AERONAUTICS
AND SPACE ADMINISTRATION PROGRAMS
End of Fiscal Years 1965–2004

Year	TOTAL	NASA Employees	Contractor Employees[a]
1965	409,900	33,200	376,700
1966	393,924	33,924	360,000
1967	306,926	33,726	273,200
1968	267,871	32,471	235,400
1969	218,345	31,745	186,600
1970	160,850	31,350	129,500
1971	143,578	29,478	114,100
1972	138,800	27,500	111,300
1973	134,850	26,850	108,000
1974	125,220	25,020	100,200
1975	127,733	24,333	103,400
1976	130,739	24,039	108,000
1977	124,136	23,636	100,500
1978	124,637	23,237	101,400
1979	131,931	22,831	109,100
1980	135,613	22,613	113,000
1981	133,473	21,873	111,600
1982	128,730	22,430	106,300
1983	129,246	22,246	107,000
1984	162,080	22,080	140,000
1985	131,991	21,991	110,000
1986	154,660	21,660	133,000
1987	165,001	22,001	143,000
1988	172,326	22,326	150,000
1989	213,054	23,054	190,000
1990	221,829	23,829	198,000
1991	223,149	24,149	199,000
1992	230,513	24,513	206,000
1993	228,674	24,174	204,500
1994	217,910	23,873	194,037
1995	209,355	22,355	187,000
1996	198,113	21,113	177,000
1997	189,070	20,070	169,000
1998	183,109	19,109	164,000
1999	181,469	18,469	163,000
2000	173,375	18,375	155,000
2001[r]	171,678	18,678	153,000
2002	179,596	18,596	161,000
2003[E]	181,050	19,050	162,000
2004[E]	178,906	18,906	160,000

Source: Office of Management and Budget, "Budget of the United States Government" (Annually) and NASA Headquarters.
  a Includes estimates of manpower for hardware and related contracts, as well as actual work-years for support service contracts. Increase in FY 1984 caused by change in estimating methodology to reflect more accurately the mix of support and development contractors.

FEDERAL CIVILIAN EMPLOYMENT[a] IN THE DEPARTMENT OF DEFENSE
Fiscal Years 1968–2004

Year	TOTAL	Civil Functions[b]	Military Functions[c]
1968	1,288,130	32,062	1,256,068
1969	1,257,091	31,214	1,225,877
1970	1,159,935	30,293	1,129,642
1971	1,092,804	30,063	1,062,741
1972	1,040,147	30,585	1,009,562
1973	987,281	29,971	957,310
1974	1,002,850	29,072	973,778
1975	983,790	29,069	954,721
1976	951,034	28,648	922,386
1977	940,549	28,912	911,637
1978	933,071	28,962	904,109
1979	914,582	28,592	885,990
1980	907,700	27,700	880,000
1981	981,400	34,400	947,000
1982	1,009,192	31,111	978,081
1983	1,015,622	30,816	984,806
1984	1,040,213	28,681	1,011,532
1985	1,065,624	28,754	1,036,870
1986	1,069,863	28,511	1,041,352
1987	1,059,669	28,352	1,031,317
1988	1,053,000	28,419	1,024,581
1989	1,051,166	28,081	1,023,085
1990	1,048,814	27,651	1,021,163
1991	1,001,183	27,385	973,798
1992	1,000,453	27,584	972,869
1993	958,855	27,055	931,800
1994	896,293	28,001	868,292
1995	849,529	27,790	821,739
1996	806,122	27,180	778,942
1997	771,914	26,164	745,750
1998	732,097	24,855	707,242
1999	705,826	24,830	680,996
2000	685,085[r]	24,800[r]	660,285
2001	674,591[r]	24,700[r]	649,891
2002	674,875	25,000	649,875
2003[E]	667,600	24,800	642,800
2004[E]	660,600	24,800	635,800

Source: Office of Management and Budget, "The Budget of the United States Government" (Annually).

a Full-time equivalent civilian employment.

b Data are estimated for portions of Civil Functions.

c The Department of Defense is exempt from full-time equivalent controls. Data shown are estimated civilian employment for military functions and military assistance.

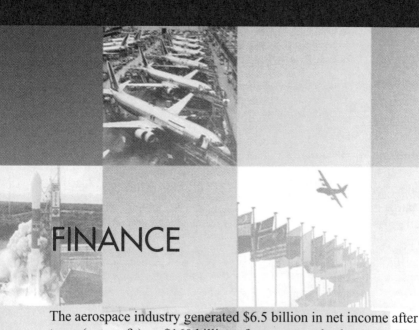

FINANCE

The aerospace industry generated $6.5 billion in net income after taxes (net profit) on $160 billion of corporate sales last year. Net profit as a percentage of sales rose to 4.1%—the second lowest level since 1995. The corresponding profit margin for all manufacturing corporations was 3.3%—up sharply from 2001's 0.8%, but the second worst showing since 1993. Similarly, the aerospace industry's net profit as a percentage of assets and shareholders' equity rose marginally to 3.7% and 11.7%, respectively. For comparison, prior year aerospace returns were 3.6% and 11.6%; and the averages for all manufacturing corporations in 2002 were 2.9% and 7.7%, respectively. Industry-wide working capital improved significantly in 2002.

The aerospace industry's capital equipment expenditures increased slightly to $2.4 billion in 2001, the latest data available. Missile/space sector investment fell to $390 million after sharply declining the prior year. Meanwhile, the aircraft sector's capital equipment investment rebounded slightly—up $165 million to $2.1 billion.

DoD awarded $35 billion in aircraft procurement contracts in FY 2002. The West South Central and Pacific regions received $1.5 billion and $1.2 billion more aircraft procurement contracts than they had in the previous year, respectively. South Atlantic, however, did much worse—booking $1.0 billion fewer orders than last year. Awards for missile and space systems jumped

$3.7 billion to $13.1 billion; and electronics and communications equipment procurement increased $1.9 billion to $15.8 billion. Companies in the Pacific region received the most missile and space systems contracts, $4.4 billion, while companies in the South Atlantic region garnered the most electronics and communications equipment contracts, $5.5 billion.

Lockheed Martin retained its position as the DoD's largest contractor in FY 2002, winning $17.0 billion in prime contract awards, or about 10% of all the available DoD prime contract dollars that year. The company's contract wins were 16% higher than in 2001, and it was the sixth year in a row that Lockheed Martin topped the DoD list. Boeing made the second spot for the sixth straight year, winning $16.6 billion worth of prime contracts. Rounding out the top ten DoD contractors were: Northrop Grumman, $8.7 billion; Raytheon, $7.0 billion; General Dynamics, $7.0 billion; United Technologies, $3.6 billion; Science Applications International, $2.1 billion; TRW, $2.0 billion; Health Net, $1.7 billion; and L-3 Communications, $1.7 billion. Together the top

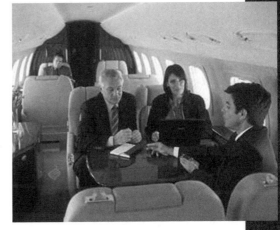

ten contractors accounted for 39% of the 2002 total prime contract dollars awarded, or more than $67 billion.

United Space Alliance topped NASA's contractor list in FY 2002 with awards totaling $1.8 billion. The Boeing Company ranked second with $988 million. At $611 million, Lockheed Martin captured third. Other subsidiaries and affiliates of Lockheed Martin and The Boeing Company won additional contracts.

INCOME STATEMENT AND OPERATING RATIOS
FOR AEROSPACE COMPANIES[a]
Calendar Years 1999–2002
(Millions of Dollars)

INCOME STATEMENT	1999	2000	2001	2002
Net Sales, Receipts, Operating Revenues......	$157,087	$154,877	$168,756	$159,581
Less: Depreciation, Depletion, & Amortization of Property, Plant, and Equipment	4,212	4,330	3,895	3,581
Less: All Other Operating Costs & Expenses, including Selling Costs & General & Administrative Expenses...........................	140,228	137,714	152,182	143,066
Income (or Loss) from Operations	$ 12,648	$ 12,833	$ 12,679	$ 12,934
Net Non-Operating Income (Expense)...........	1,775	(1,886)	(4,059)	(153)
Income (or Loss) before Income Taxes (= Total Income)	$ 14,423	$ 10,947	$ 8,618	$ 7,874
Less: Provision for Current & Deferred Domestic Income Taxes	4,208	3,686	2,054	1,326
Income (or Loss) after Income Taxes (= Net Profit).............................	$ 10,214	$ 7,260	$ 6,565	$ 6,547
Cash Dividends Charged to Retained Earnings...	2,501	2,684	2,561	2,861
Net Income Retained in Business	$ 7,713	$ 4,576	$ 4,003	$ 3,686
Retained Earnings at Beginning of Year[b]	34,832	44,949	52,966	49,771
Adjustments to Retained Earnings[c]	(607)	(633)	(1,597)	(3,304)
Retained Earnings at End of Year[d]	$ 41,938	$ 48,892	$ 55,373	$ 50,153

OPERATING RATIOS				
Income before Taxes as Percent of Net Sales	9.2%	7.1%	5.1%	4.9%
Provision for Current & Deferred Domestic Income Taxes as Percent of Income before Taxes (Total Income)........................	29.2	33.7	23.8	16.8
Income after Taxes (Net Profit) as Percent of Net Sales...	6.5	4.7	3.9	4.1
Income after Taxes (Net Profit) as Percent of Stockholders' Equity[f].............................	21.8	14.2	11.6	11.7
Income after Taxes (Net Profit) as Percent of Total Assets[f]	6.2	4.3	3.6	3.7

Source: Bureau of the Census, "Quarterly Financial Report for Manufacturing, Mining, and Trade Corporations" (Quarterly).

a Based on sample of corporate entities classified in NAICS code 3364, having as their principal activity the manufacture of aerospace products and parts. Prior to 2001, data categorized using SIC system and reported combining codes 372 and 376.

b Beginning-of-year retained earnings for any particular year do not equal end-of-year retained earnings for the previous year because of rotation of small companies in survey sample.

c Other direct credits (or charges) to retained earnings (net), including stock and other non-cash dividends, etc.

d Retained Earnings at End of Year CALCULATED AS Retained Earnings at Beginning of Year PLUS Income (Loss) after Income Taxes MINUS Cash Dividends Charged to Retained Earnings PLUS Adjustments to Retained Earnings.

f Average of four quarters.

BALANCE SHEET FOR AEROSPACE COMPANIES[a]
As of December 31, 1999–2002
(Millions of Dollars)

	1999	2000	2001	2002
Assets:				
Current Assets:				
Cash	$ 2,898	$ 2,969	$ 3,004	$ 8,083
Securities, Commercial Paper, & Other				
Short-term Financial Investments	3,165	1,353	638	1,112
Total Cash and U.S. Government				
and Other Securities	$ 6,063	$ 4,322	$ 3,642	$ 9,195
Receivables (Total)	18,082	20,283	19,438	17,644
Inventories (Gross)	41,216	41,683	42,343	40,288
Other Current Assets	8,320	8,987	10,450	9,353
Current Assets—TOTAL	$ 73,681	$ 75,275	$ 75,872	$ 76,481
Net Plant, Property, & Equipment	28,613	28,274	28,722	27,567
Other Non-Current Assets	67,701	70,908	79,410	79,684
Assets—TOTAL	$169,995	$174,457	$184,004	$183,732
Liabilities:				
Current Liabilities:				
Short Term Loans	$ 4,009	$ 3,901	$ 2,084	$ 1,637
Trade Accounts & Notes Payable	11,001	11,758	10,458	9,184
Income Taxes Accrued	1,987	3,609	1,778	2,726
Installments Due on Long Term Debts	1,793	2,772	2,534	2,722
Other Current Liabilities	43,204	43,668	49,708	45,802
Current Liabilities—TOTAL	$ 61,994	$ 65,709	$ 66,562	$ 62,071
Long Term Debt	33,485	32,418	33,882	32,554
Other Non-Current Liabilities	24,173	23,840	27,054	40,330
Liabilities—TOTAL	$119,652	$121,967	$127,497	$134,954
Stockholders' Equity:				
Capital Stock	$ 5,682	$ 3,276	$ 4,190	($ 1,838)
Retained Earnings	44,661	49,214	52,318	50,615
Stockholders' Equity—TOTAL	$ 50,343	$ 52,490	$ 56,508	$ 48,777
Liabilities & Stockholders' Equity—TOTAL	$169,995	$174,457	$184,004	$183,732
Net Working Capital	$ 11,688	$ 9,566	$ 9,311	$ 14,410

Source: Bureau of the Census, "Quarterly Financial Report for Manufacturing, Mining, and Trade Corporations" (Quarterly).
a Based on sample of corporate entities classified in NAICS code 3364, having as their principal activity the manufacture of aerospace products and parts. Prior to 2001, data categorized using SIC system and reported combining codes 372 and 376.

NET PROFIT AFTER TAXES
AS A PERCENT OF SALES, ASSETS, AND EQUITY
FOR ALL MANUFACTURING CORPORATIONS
AND THE AEROSPACE INDUSTRY
Calendar Years 1988–2002

PERCENT OF SALES

Year	All Manufacturing Corporations	Non-Durable Goods	Durable Goods	Aerospace[a] Industry
1988	6.0%	6.7%	5.2%	4.3%
1989	5.0	5.8	4.1	3.3
1990	4.0	4.9	3.0	3.4
1991	2.5	4.2	0.6	1.8[b]
1992	1.0	3.2	(1.4)	(1.4)[b]
1993	2.8	3.7	1.9	3.6
1994	5.4	5.5	5.2	4.7
1995	5.7	6.1	5.3	3.8
1996	6.0	6.6	5.5	5.6
1997	6.2	6.6	5.8	5.2
1998	6.0	6.1	5.9	5.0
1999	6.2	6.2	6.2	6.5
2000	6.1	6.9	5.4	4.7
2001	0.8	5.7	(3.3)	3.9
2002	3.3	6.0	1.1	4.1

Year	Percent of Assets[c]		Percent of Equity[c]	
	All Manufacturing	Aerospace[a] Industry	All Manufacturing	Aerospace[a] Industry
1988	6.9%	4.4%	16.2%	14.9%
1989	5.6	3.3	13.7	10.7
1990	4.3	3.4	10.7	11.5
1991	2.6	1.9[b]	6.4	6.1[b]
1992	1.0	(1.2)[b]	2.6	(5.2)[b]
1993	2.9	3.5	8.1	13.2
1994	5.8	4.3	15.6	14.8
1995	6.2	3.5	16.2	11.1
1996	6.5	5.1	16.8	17.1
1997	6.6	4.8	16.6	17.3
1998	6.1	4.8	15.7	18.0
1999	6.1	6.2	16.5	21.8
2000	5.9	4.3	15.2	14.2
2001	0.8	3.6	1.9	11.6
2002	2.9	3.7	7.7	11.7

Source: Bureau of the Census, "Quarterly Financial Report for Manufacturing, Mining, and Trade Corporations" (Quarterly).
  a Based on a sample of corporate entities classified in NAICS code 3364, having as their principal activity the manufacture of aerospace products and parts. Prior to 2001, data categorized using SIC system and reported combining codes 372 and 376.
  b Reflects unusually large non-operating expenses totalling $3.4 and $8.7 billion in 1991 and 1992, respectively, due to restructuring changes and the implementation of a change in accounting for future retirement benefit costs.
  c Average of four quarters
  ( ) Net loss after taxes.

CAPITAL EXPENDITURES
Calendar Years 1967–2001
(Millions of Dollars)

Year	All Manufacturing Industries	Aerospace Industry[a]	Aircraft, Engines, & Parts	Missiles, Space Vehicles, & Parts
1967	$ 21,503	$ 520	$ 408	$ 111
1968	20,613	399	282	117
1969	22,291	429	340	89
1970	22,164	244	181	62
1971	20,941	115	59	56
1972	24,073	261	169	92
1973	26,979	362	258	104
1974	35,696	407	283	124
1975	37,262	478	369	109
1976	40,545	557	431	126
1977	47,459	673	508	164
1978	55,209	948	775	174
1979	61,533	1,551	1,301	250
1980	70,113	1,923	1,618	306
1981	78,632	2,006	1,637	369
1982	74,562	2,142	1,680	462
1983	61,931	2,159	1,530	629
1984	75,186	3,050	2,091	960
1985	83,058	3,784	2,429	1,356
1986	76,355	4,145	2,818	1,327
1987	78,650	3,612	2,536	1,075
1988	81,593	3,388	2,362	1,026
1989	98,738	3,921	2,800	1,121
1990	105,018	3,490	2,621	869
1991	103,003	3,407	2,823	584
1992	103,188	3,860	3,384	476
1993	103,133	2,725	2,307	418
1994	112,784	2,363	1,969	395
1995	128,473	2,114	1,734	380
1996	139,323	2,513	2,023	490
1997[b]	151,511	3,132	2,380	752
1998	152,708	3,477	2,613	864
1999	150,325	3,422	2,338	1,084
2000[r]	154,479	2,326	1,894	432
2001	143,651	2,449	2,059	390

Source: Bureau of the Census, "Annual Survey of Manufactures" (Annually).
  a Combined total for establishments in Aircraft, Missiles, Space Vehicles, and Parts Manufacturing.
  b Prior to 1997, figures included only new capital expenditures.

KEY OPERATING COSTS FOR SELECTED AEROSPACE MANUFACTURING CENTERS
As of 2003

State	Location	Total Annual Operating Cost[a] (in Millions)	Hourly Labor Cost		
			Manufacturing	Technical	Clerical
AZ	Phoenix/Tempe	$34.03	$20.34	$33.43	$14.19
AZ	Tucson	32.86	19.40	31.87	13.52
CA	Chula Vista	37.20	21.71	35.68	14.47
CA	El Segundo/Long Beach/ Redondo Beach/Seal Beach/ Torrance	39.00	23.14	38.03	16.14
CA	Sunnyvale	42.88	23.99	39.42	16.72
CO	Denver	35.32	21.36	35.10	14.89
CT	Hartford/Stratford/Windsor Locks	37.56	22.46	36.90	15.66
FL	Melbourne	32.12	19.32	31.73	13.46
GA	Marietta	34.44	20.60	33.84	14.35
GA	Savannah	32.53	19.71	32.38	13.74
IA	Cedar Rapids	33.72	20.32	33.40	14.17
IL	Rockford	34.87	21.01	34.52	14.65
IN	Indianapolis	34.17	20.35	33.87	14.37
KS	Wichita	33.87	20.49	33.67	14.28
MA	Lexington/Marlborough	35.89	21.34	35.07	14.88
MN	Hopkins/Minneapolis	35.71	21.69	35.65	15.12
MO	St. Louis	35.22	21.24	34.90	14.81
NC	Charlotte	34.18	20.34	33.43	14.19
NH	Nashua	36.04	21.34	35.07	14.88
OH	Cleveland	35.30	21.03	34.56	14.66
OH	Cincinnatti/Evandale	34.44	20.77	34.12	14.48
PA	King of Prussia	36.45	21.95	36.06	15.30
SC	Greenville	32.05	19.38	31.84	13.50
TX	Dallas/Ft. Worth/Grand Prairie/ Irving	33.96	20.41	33.54	14.23
UT	Magna	33.44	20.18	33.16	14.07
WA	Auburn/Everett/Renton	36.36	21.77	35.78	15.18

(Continued on next page)

KEY OPERATING COSTS FOR SELECTED AEROSPACE MANUFACTURING CENTERS
As of 2003, continued

Power (¢/kwh)	Lease Rates ($/sq ft) Industrial	Lease Rates ($/sq ft) Office	Construction ($/sq ft)	State	Location
5.49¢	$ 4.20	$22.00	$49.46	AZ	Phoenix/Tempe
7.44	5.40	20.70	48.56	AZ	Tucson
10.66	7.20	31.20	59.18	CA	Chula Vista
12.89	4.60	16.55	60.27	CA	El Segundo/Long Beach/ Redondo Beach/Seal Beach/ Torrance
12.48	15.15	44.55	66.38	CA	Sunnyvale
4.81	3.00	20.00	49.14	CO	Denver
6.45	4.35	23.85	59.89	CT	Hartford/Stratford/Windsor Locks
5.22	3.51	16.00	51.56	FL	Melbourne
4.73	4.60	22.55	46.76	GA	Marietta
4.73	3.15	13.05	43.22	GA	Savannah
4.44	3.80	16.75	50.18	IA	Cedar Rapids
5.96	3.70	13.75	60.34	IL	Rockford
3.79	5.00	16.85	52.82	IN	Indianapolis
4.04	3.00	20.00	46.76	KS	Wichita
7.26	4.45	24.55	59.56	MA	Lexington/Marlborough
4.40	2.90	14.00	64.07	MN	Hopkins/Minneapolis
4.19	3.00	24.00	59.37	MO	St. Louis
4.81	6.00	18.75	43.29	NC	Charlotte
8.08	6.40	15.50	53.26	NH	Nashua
9.25	3.50	21.50	56.93	OH	Cleveland
4.48	3.50	19.50	51.84	OH	Cincinnatti/Evandale
5.29	3.00	24.30	64.33	PA	King of Prussia
4.48	3.05	16.40	43.87	SC	Greenville
6.76	3.13	19.04	46.38	TX	Dallas/Ft. Worth/Grand Prairie/ Irving
4.08	3.36	19.23	49.54	UT	Magna
5.62	4.60	20.00	59.09	WA	Auburn/Everett/Renton

Source: The Boyd Company (Princeton, NJ), BizCosts ® data bank.
a   Includes all major geographically-variable operating costs for a representative 200,000 sq. ft. aerospace manufacturing facility. Costs reflect a 500-worker plant site having 250 production employees, 150 engineers, and 100 administrative support workers. Annual costs for electric power, real estate, and construction are scaled accordingly.

DEPARTMENT OF DEFENSE MAJOR CONTRACTORS
Fiscal Years 1998–2002
Listed by rank according to net value of
prime contracts awarded during last fiscal year
(Millions of Dollars)

Company	1998	1999	2000	2001	2002
TOTAL CONTRACT AWARDS........	$118,139	$125,037	$133,232	$144,635	$170,783
Lockheed Martin Corp.	$ 12,341	$ 12,675	$ 15,126	$ 14,687	$ 16,997
The Boeing Co.	10,866[b]	11,568[b]	12,041	13,341	16,552
Northrop Grumman Corp.[c]	4,335	5,290	5,817	5,153	8,733
Raytheon Co.	5,661	6,401	6,331	5,576	6,995
General Dynamics Corp.	3,680	4,564	4,196	4,907	6,962
United Technologies Corp.	1,983	2,368	2,072	3,373	3,607
Science Applications Int'l Corp.	1,224	1,358	1,522	1,748	2,075
TRW Inc.	1,346	1,431	2,005	1,903	2,027
Health Net Inc.	(a)	(a)	551	939	1,691
L-3 Communications Holding, Inc. ...	225	316	378	495	1,660
General Electric Co.	1,161	1,714	1,609	1,747	1,560
United Defense Industries Inc.	1,329	1,336	1,195	1,232[d]	1,514
Dyncorp.......................................	537	566	771	909	1,359
Humana, Inc.	867	620	129	394	1,305
Honeywell International Inc.	655[f]	746[f]	951	902	1,278
BAE Systems PLC	732[g]	729[g]	997	865	1,116
Bechtel Corp.	201	600	695	621	1,030
ITT Industries Inc.	781	659	554	808	994
Textron Inc.	1,838	1,423	1,164	572	909
Triwest Healthcare Alliance Co.	420	414	336	554	824
Computer Sciences Corp.	647	744	1,165	819	808
URS Corp.	(a)	171	145	165	801
Booz Allen & Hamilton	312	370	420	435	688
GM GDLS Defense Group	(a)	(a)	(a)	840	678
Alliant Techsystems Inc.	317	422	470	494	674
Boeing Sikorsky Comanche Team ...	197	296	385	528	662
Cardinal Health, Inc.	(a)	(a)	(a)	416	650
North American Airlines	(a)	(a)	(a)	(a)	622
Oshkosh Truck Corp.	137	253	373	558	602
Exxon Mobil Corp.	381[h]	208[h]	325	705	571

Source: Department of Defense, "100 Companies Receiving the Largest Dollar Volume of Prime Contract Awards" (Annually).
  a Not in top 100 companies for indicated year(s).
  b Includes awards previously reported separately as Rockwell International Corp.
  c Includes awards previously reported separately as Litton Industries Inc.
  d Listed previously as Carlyle Group and FMC Corp.
  f Includes awards previously reported as Allied Signal Inc.
  g Includes awards previously reported as General Electric Co. PLC.
  h Includes awards previously reported as Mobil Corp. and Exxon Corp.

NATIONAL AERONAUTICS AND SPACE ADMINISTRATION
MAJOR CONTRACTORS
Fiscal Years 1999–2002
Listed by rank according to net value of prime
contracts awarded during last fiscal year
(Millions of Dollars)

Company	1999	2000	2001	2002
TOTAL PROCUREMENTS	$12,675	$12,504	$12,748	$13,303
Awards to Business Firms	9,386	9,273	9,210	9,569
% of TOTAL PROCUREMENTS	74%	74%	72%	72%
United Space Alliance LLC...................	$ 1,465	$ 1,609	$ 1,659	$ 1,798
The Boeing Co.	1,205	1,236	952	988
Lockheed Martin Corp.	906	710	608	611
Lockheed Martin Space Operations Co.	296	485	494	504
Thiokol Corp.	395	368	378	390
Boeing North America	272	258	304	348
Space Gateway Support	221	218	261	310
McDonnell Douglas Corp.	416	320	282	222
Lockheed Martin Engrg. & Science.......	231	287	228	212
QSS Group Inc.	22	83	126	158
Science Applications Int'l Corp.	91	107	138	152
Computer Sciences Corp.	174	143	126	149
Raytheon Information Systems Co.	123[b]	130	128	132
Swales & Associates Inc.	57	63	116	113
TRW Inc.	184	124	83	97
Delta Launch Services	(a)	(a)	62	92
Boeing Satellite Systems	174	88	104	89[c]
United Technologies Corp.	104	107	89	88
OAO Corp.	55	76	37	81
Raytheon Technical Services Co.	49	62	86	74
Ball Aerospace & Tech. Corp.	63	67	81	71
Sverdrup Technology Inc.	58	74	70	68
Honeywell Technology Solutions	85	67	60[d]	62
Science Systems Applications	19	20	57	61
Orbital Sciences Corp.	73	82	74	60
Wyle Laboratories	46	55	53	55
ACS Government Solutions Group	(a)	(a)	(a)	54
Mississippi Space Services..................	16	57	59	53
Northrop Grumman Systems Corp.	(a)	(a)	(a)	51
Hamilton Sundstrand Space Systems...	58	55	55	50

Source: National Aeronautics and Space Administration, "Annual Procurement Report" (Annually).
  a Not in list of major contractors for indicated year(s).
  b Previously reported as Hughes Information Technology Corp.
  c Previously reported as Hughes Aircraft Co.
  d Previously reported as Allied Signal Technical Services.

DEPARTMENT OF DEFENSE PRIME CONTRACT AWARDS OVER $25,000
FOR SELECTED MAJOR MILITARY HARD GOODS
BY GEOGRAPHIC REGION
Fiscal Years 2000, 2001, and 2002

Program and Region	Millions of Dollars			Percent of Program Total		
	2000	2001	2002	2000	2001	2002
AIRCRAFT—TOTAL.......	$33,285	$33,491	$34,707	100.0%	100.0%	100.0%
New England...................	$ 2,094	$ 3,319	$ 4,072	6.3%	9.9%	11.7%
Middle Atlantic................	2,663	2,258	2,485	8.0	6.7	7.2
East North Central..........	2,936	3,163	1,935	8.8	9.4	5.6
West North Central..........	4,373	4,560	4,210	13.1	13.6	12.1
South Atlantic	5,525	7,423	6,375	16.6	22.2	18.4
East South Central	814	734	406	2.4	2.2	1.2
West South Central	7,001	4,257	5,795	21.0	12.7	16.7
Mountain	1,792	1,888	2,360	5.4	5.6	6.8
Pacific[a]	6,087	5,889	7,070	18.3	17.6	20.4
MISSILE & SPACE SYSTEMS—TOTAL........	$ 9,444	$ 9,347	$13,050	100.0%	100.0%	100.0%
New England...................	$ 611	$ 355	$ 609	6.5%	3.8%	4.7%
Middle Atlantic................	390	494	411	4.1	5.3	3.1
East North Central..........	146	61	140	1.5	0.7	1.1
West North Central..........	139	149	172	1.5	1.6	1.3
South Atlantic	1,149	596	1,320	12.2	6.4	10.1
East South Central	446	594	693	4.7	6.4	5.3
West South Central	512	416	1,464	5.4	4.4	11.2
Mountain	2,309	2,773	3,797	24.5	29.7	29.1
Pacific[a]	3,742	3,911	4,444	39.6	41.8	34.1
ELECTRONICS & COMMUNICATIONS EQUIPMENT—TOTAL ...	$11,916	$13,875	$15,763	100.0%	100.0%	100.0%
New England...................	$ 1,329	$ 1,860	$ 1,527	11.2%	13.4%	9.7%
Middle Atlantic................	1,677	1,808	2,298	14.2	13.0	14.6
East North Central..........	696	887	1,061	5.8	6.4	6.7
West North Central..........	710	741	868	6.0	5.3	5.5
South Atlantic	4,104	4,433	5,481	34.4	31.9	34.8
East South Central	202	204	197	1.7	1.5	1.3
West South Central	819	857	977	6.9	6.2	6.2
Mountain	622	845	770	5.2	6.1	4.9
Pacific[a]	1,758	2,240	2,584	14.8	16.1	16.4

Source: Department of Defense, Washington Headquarters Services, Directorate for Information Operations and Reports.
   a   Includes Alaska and Hawaii.

GLOSSARY

Aeronautics: the science and art of designing and constructing aircraft, also, the art or science of operating aircraft.

Aerospace Employment: annual average calculated as one-twelfth of sum of monthly estimates of total number of persons employed during a designated pay period by the aircraft, missile, and space industries (SICs 372 and 376) plus estimated aerospace-related employment in the communications equipment (SIC 3662), instruments (SICs 381 and 382), and in certain other industries (SICs 28, 35, 73, 89, etc.)

Aerospace Industry: the industry engaged in research, development, and manufacture of aerospace systems including: manned and unmanned aircraft; missiles; spacecraft; space launch vehicles; propulsion, guidance, and control units for all of the foregoing; and a variety of airborne and ground-based equipment essential to the test, operation, and maintenance of flight vehicles.

Aerospace Payroll: estimated on the basis of average weekly *earnings* for a given calendar year for *production workers* plus an estimated annual salary for other employees.

Aerospace Sales: the *AIA* estimate of *aerospace industry sales*, developed by summing: *DoD* expenditures for *aircraft*, *missiles*, and space-related *procurement* and *RDT&E*; *NASA* expenditures for *research and development* and space flight control and data communications; *outlays* for space activities by other U.S. government departments and agencies; commercial sales of space-related products; net domestic and export

sales of civil aircraft, engines, and parts; *Foreign Military Sales* and commercial exports of military aircraft, missiles, propulsion, and related parts; sales of *related products and services* including: electronics, software, and ground support equipment; and sales of *non-aerospace products* which are produced in aerospace-manufacturing *establishments* and which use technology, processes, and materials derived from the aerospace industry.

AIA: Aerospace Industries Association of America, Inc., formerly Aircraft Industries Association.

Air Carriers: the commercial system of air transportation, consisting of domestic and international scheduled and charter service.

Aircraft: all airborne vehicles supported either by buoyancy or by dynamic action. Used in this volume in a restricted sense to mean an airplane—any winged aircraft including helicopters, but excluding gliders and guided missiles.

Aircraft Agreement (Agreement on Trade in Civil Aircraft): negotiated in the Tokyo Round of the *Multilateral Trade Negotiations* and implemented January 1, 1980, providing for elimination of tariff and non-tariff trade barriers in the civil aircraft sector.

Aircraft Industry: the industry primarily engaged in the manufacture of aircraft, aircraft engines, and parts including propellers and auxiliary equipment. A sector of the *Aerospace Industry*.

161

Airframe: the structural components of an airplane, such as: fuselage, empennage, wings, landing gear, and engine mounts, but excluding such items as: engines, accessories, electronics, and other parts that may be replaced from time to time.

Airlines: see *Air Carriers*.

Appropriation (Federal Budget): an act of Congress authorizing an agency to incur *obligations* and make payments out of funds held by the Department of the Treasury.

Assets, Net: the sum of all recorded assets after reducing such amount by allowance of reserve for bad debts, *depreciation*, and amortization, but before deducting any liabilities, mortgages, or other indebtedness.

Astronautics: the art and science of designing, building, and operating manned or unmanned space objects.

Average Weekly Hours: average hours for which pay was received; different from standard or scheduled hours.

Avionics: communications, navigation, flight controls, and displays.

Backlog: the *sales* value of *orders* accepted (supported by legal documents) that have not yet passed through the sales account.

BMDO: Ballistic Missile Defense Organization, an agency of the Department of Defense.

Budget Authority: authority provided by the Congress; mainly in the form of *Appropriations*, which allows Federal agencies to incur *obligations* to spend or lend money.

Bureau of Economic Analysis (BEA): an agency of the Department of Commerce.

Bureau of Labor Statistics (BLS): an agency of the Department of Labor.

Bureau of the Census: an agency of the Department of Commerce.

Constant Dollars: calculated by dividing current ("then-year") dollars by appropriate price *deflator* and multiplying the result by 100.

Deflator: index used to convert a price level to one comparable with the price level at a different time, offsetting the effect of inflation. The base period, which equals 100, is usually specified as either a given fiscal or calendar year.

Depreciation: the general conversion of the depreciable cost of a fixed asset into expense, spread over its remaining life. There are a number of methods, all based on a periodic charge to an expense account and a corresponding credit to a reserve account.

Development: the process or activity of working out a basic design, idea, or piece of equipment. See also *Research and Development*.

DoD: Department of Defense.

DoE: Department of Energy.

DoT: Department of Transportation.

Durable Goods Industry: comprised of major manufacturing industry groups with SIC Codes 24, 25, and 32-39. All major manufacturing industry groups in SIC Codes 20-23 and 26-31 are considered nondurable goods manufacturing industry groups.

Earnings: the actual return to the worker for a stated period of time. Irregular bonuses, retroactive items, payments of various welfare benefits, and payroll taxes paid by employers are excluded.

162

Average Hourly Earnings: on a "gross" basis, reflecting not only changes in basic hourly and incentive wage rates, but also such variable factors as: premium pay for overtime, late shift work, and changes in output of workers paid for an incentive plan.

Average Weekly Earnings: derived by multiplying *average weekly hours* by *average hourly earnings*.

Establishment: the basis for reporting to the Census of Manufacturers; an operating facility in a single location.

Evaluation (Department of Defense): determination of technical suitability of material, equipment, or a system. See *RDT&E*.

Expenditures (Federal Budget): see *Outlays*.

Export-Import Bank of the United States (Eximbank): created in 1934 and established as an independent U.S. government agency in 1945, Eximbank is designed "... to aid in financing and to facilitate *exports*..." Eximbank receives no *appropriations* from the U.S. Congress. It is directed by statute to: (1) offer financing that is competitive with that offered exporters of other countries by their official export credit institutions, (2) determine that the transactions supported provide for a reasonable assurance of repayment, (3) supplement, but not compete with private sources of export financing, and (4) take into account the effect of its activities on small business, the domestic economy, and U.S. employment.

Exports: domestic merchandise including commodities which are grown, produced, or manufactured in the United States and commodities of foreign origin which have been changed in the United States from the form in which they were imported or which have been enhanced in value by further manufacture in the United States and which are traded or sold to other nations.

FAA: Federal Aviation Administration (formerly the Federal Aviation Agency), an agency of the Department of Transportation.

Facility: a physical plant or installation including: real property, building, structures, improvements, and plant equipment.

Fiscal Year (Federal Budget): beginning October 1, 1976, the fiscal years run from October 1 through September 30 and are designated by the year in which they end.

Flyaway Value: includes the cost of the *airframe*, engines, electronics, communications, armament, and other installed equipment.

Footnotes: common to many tables throughout this edition are the following:

E	Estimate.
NA	Not available/ Not applicable.
p	Preliminary.
r	Revised.
Tr.Qtr.	*Transition Quarter*.
NOTE:	Detail may not add to totals because of rounding.

Foreign Military Sales (FMS): export *sales* to foreign governments arranged through the Department of Defense, whereby *DoD* recovers full purchase price and administrative costs; often mistakenly used to include foreign military aid and foreign commercial sales as well.

FY: see *Fiscal Year*.

GDP (Gross Domestic Product): the market value of goods and services produced by labor and property located in the United States.

General Agreement on Tariffs and Trade (GATT): a multilateral treaty among more than 100 governments whose primary mission is the reduction of trade barriers. The World Trade Organization was established January 1, 1995 to implement the agreement and provide a forum to discuss trade issues.

General Aviation: all civil flying except that of *air carriers*.

Helicopter: a rotary-wing *aircraft* which depends principally for its support and motion in the air upon the lift generated by one or more power-driven rotors, rotating on substantially vertical axes. A helicopter is a *V/STOL*.

Heliport: an area, either at ground level or elevated on a structure, that is used for the landing and take-off of helicopters and includes some or all of the various facilities useful to *helicopter* operations such as: helicopter parking, hangar, waiting room, fueling, and maintenance equipment.

Helistop: a minimum facility *heliport*, either at ground level or elevated on a structure for the landing and takeoff of helicopters, but without such auxiliary facilities as: waiting room, hangar parking, etc.

ICBM: InterContinental Ballistic Missile, with a range of more than 5,000 miles.

Imports: classified as "general imports" or "imports for consumption." This volume refers generally to "imports for consumption," which are entries for immediate consumption plus merchandise withdrawn from bonded storage warehouses for consumption. Data are compiled from Import Entries filed with U.S. Customs officials and are in general based on the market value or price in the foreign country at the time of exportation of such merchandise, including the cost of containers and coverings, as well as other charges and expenses incidental to placing the merchandise in condition, packed and ready for shipment to the United States, but excluding import duties, insurance, freight, and other charges incidental to arrival of the goods in the United States. The foreign values of imported merchandise are converted into U.S. currency at the rate of exchange prevailing on the day the merchandise is shipped to the United States.

Income:

> **Net Operating Income:** total *sales* less total operating costs.
>
> **Other Income and Expenses:** includes interest income, royalty income, capital gains and losses, interest expense, cash discounts, etc.
>
> **Net Income (Before Income Taxes):** *Net Operating Income* plus or minus *Other Income and Expenses*.
>
> **Net Income (After Income Taxes):** *Net Income (Before Income Taxes)* less federal income taxes.

Lump-Sum Wage Payment: a one-time payment given in lieu of general wage increases and/or cost of living adjustments in labor settlements.

Manufacturing Industries: those *establishments* engaged in the mechanical or chemical transformation of inorganic or organic substances into new products, and usually described as plants, factories, or mills, which characteristically use power-driven machines and materials-handling equipment; also establishments engaged in assembling component parts of manufactured products if the new product is neither a structure nor other fixed improvement.

Merchandise Trade Balance: the difference between the value of U.S. goods exported to other countries and foreign goods imported into this country. The trade balance is generally regarded as "favorable" when *exports* exceed *imports*—a trade surplus—and "unfavorable" when imports exceed exports—a trade deficit.

Missile: sometimes applied to space launch vehicles, but more properly connotes automated weapons of warfare, that is, a weapon which has an integral system of guidance, as opposed to the unguided rocket.

Multilateral Trade Negotiations (MTN): a forum within the *GATT* in which countries negotiate to overcome their trade problems. Awaiting ratification by each of the 112 nations involved in the MTN, the "Uruguay Round" seeks to strengthen the GATT and expand its disciplines to new areas such as: services, agriculture, and trade-related intellectual property rights.

NAICS (North American Industry Classification System): a system developed by Canada, Mexico, and the U.S. government that groups *establishments* into industries based on a production-oriented concept in order to provide uniformity and comparability of statistical data and facilitate economic analyses between industries and the three North American countries.

NASA: National Aeronautics and Space Administration.

NATO: North Atlantic Treaty Organization.

New Obligational Authority (Federal Budget): see *Budget Authority.*

Non-Aerospace Products and Services: products and services other than *aircraft, missiles, space vehicles,* and related

propulsion and parts, produced or performed by *establishments* whose principal business is the development and/or manufacture of aerospace products.

OASD: Office of the Assistant Secretary of Defense.

Obligations (Federal Budget): commitments made by Federal agencies to pay out money for products, services, or other purposes—as distinct from the actual payments. Obligations incurred may not be larger than *budget authority.*

Orders, Net New: the *sales* value of new orders (supported by legal documents) minus cancellations during the period.

Other Aerospace Products and Services: all conversions, modifications, site activation, other aerospace products (including drones), services, plus *research and development* under contract, defined as: *basic* and *applied research* in the sciences and in engineering and design and *development* of prototype products and processes.

Other Customers: all customers other than the U.S. government to include but not limited to: *air carriers*, private citizens and corporations, and state, local, and foreign governments.

Outlays: checks issued, interest accrued on the public debt, or other payments made, net of refunds and reimbursements.

Overtime Hours: that portion of the gross *average weekly hours* which was in excess of regular hours and for which premium payments were made.

Passenger-Mile: one passenger moved one mile.

Payroll, All Manufacturing: includes the gross *earnings* paid in the calendar year to all employees on the payroll of operating manufacturing *establishments*. Includes all forms of compensation paid directly to workers such as: salaries, wages, commissions, dismissal pay, all bonuses, vacation and sick leave pay, and compensation in kind; prior to such deductions as: employees' Social Security contributions, withholding taxes, group insurance, union dues, and savings bonds. Does not include employers' Social Security contributions or other non-payroll labor costs such as: employees' pension plans, group insurance premiums, and workmen's compensation.

Procurement: the process whereby the executive agencies of the Federal Government acquire goods and services from enterprises other than the Federal Government.

Production Workers: includes working foremen and all non-supervisory workers (including lead-men and trainees) engaged in fabricating, processing, assembling, inspection, receiving, storage, handling, janitorial services, product development, auxiliary production for plant's own use, and recordkeeping and services closely associated with the above production operations.

RDT&E (Department of Defense): Research, Development, Test, and Evaluation.

Related Products and Services: sales of electronics, software, and ground equipment in support of aerospace products, plus sales by aerospace manufacturing *establishments* of systems and equipment which are generally derived from the industry's aerospace technological expertise in design, materials, and processes, but which are intended for applications other than flight.

Research: see *Research and Development*.

Research and Development:

Research: systematic study directed toward fuller scientific knowledge or understanding of the subject studied. Research is classified as either basic or applied according to the objectives of the sponsoring agency.

Applied Research: with the objective of gaining knowledge or understanding necessary for determining the means by which a recognized and specific need may be met.

Basic Research: with the objective of gaining fuller knowledge or understanding of the fundamental aspects of phenomena and of observable facts without specific applications toward processes or products in mind.

Development: the systematic use of scientific knowledge directed toward the production of useful materials, devices, systems, or methods including design and development of prototypes and processes.

Independent Research and Development (IR&D): a term devised by the Department of Defense and used by Federal agencies to differentiate between a contractor's research and development technical effort performed under a contract, grant, or other arrangement (R&D) and that which is self-initiated and self-funded (IR&D).

Industrial Research and Development: research and development work performed within company facilities, funded by company or Federal funds, and excluding company-financed research and development contracted to outside organizations such as: research institutions, universities and colleges, or other non-profit organizations.

166

Rotorcraft: an *aircraft* which, in all its usual flight attitudes, is supported in the air wholly or in part by a rotor or rotors (i.e., airfoils rotating or revolving about an axis). See *Helicopter.*

Sales: net of returns, allowances, and discounts, the dollar value of shipments, including dealer's commissions, if any, which have passed through the sales account.

Satellite: a body that revolves around a larger body, such as the Moon revolving around the Earth, or a man-made object revolving about any body such as the Sun, Earth, or Moon.

SIC (Standard Industrial Classification): a system developed by the U.S. government to define the industrial composition of the economy, facilitating comparability of statistics. See *Aerospace Industry* for explanation of SIC codes applicable to the aerospace industry.

Space Vehicle: an artificial body operating in outer space (beyond the Earth's atmosphere).

Stockholder's Equity: *assets* minus all obligations of the corporation, except those to stockholders. Annual data are average equity for the year (using four end-of-quarter figures). For details, see "Quarterly Financial Report for Manufacturing, Mining and Trade Corporations," compiled by the *Bureau of the Census.*

STOL: short take-off and landing *aircraft.*

Test (Department of Defense): an experiment designed to assess progress in attainment or accomplishment of *development* objectives (see *RDT&E*).

Thrust: the driving force exerted by an engine, particularly an *aircraft* or *missile* engine, in propelling the vehicle to which it is attached.

Ton-Mile: one ton moved one mile.

Total Obligational Authority: the sum of *budget authority* granted or requested from the Congress in a given year, plus unused budget authority from prior years.

Trade Balance: see *Merchandise Trade Balance.*

Transition Quarter (Tr. Qtr.): the three-month interval from July 1, 1976 to September 30, 1976 belonging to neither Fiscal Year 1976 nor Fiscal Year 1977. See *Fiscal Year.*

Turbine, Turbo: a mechanical device or engine that spins in reaction to a fluid flow that passes through or over it. Frequently used in "turboprop" or "turbojet."

UK: United Kingdom.

US: United States of America.

USA: United States Army, an agency of the U.S. Department of Defense.

USAF: United States Air Force, an agency of the U.S. Department of Defense.

USN: United States Navy, an agency of the U.S. Department of Defense.

USSR: Union of Soviet Socialist Republics. Statistics continue to exclude this region until official data from the now independent republics become available.

Utility Aircraft: an aircraft designed for general purpose flying.

V/STOL: vertical short take-off and/or landing *aircraft.*

INDEX

169

172